The Couch and
the Stage

The Couch and the Stage

Integrating Words and Action in Psychotherapy

Robert J. Landy

Forewords by Zerka T. Moreno and
Arthur Robbins

JASON ARONSON
Lanham • Boulder • New York • Toronto • Plymouth, UK

Published in the United States of America
by Jason Aronson
An imprint of Rowman & Littlefield Publishers, Inc.

A wholly owned subsidiary of
The Rowman & Littlefield Publishing Group, Inc.
4501 Forbes Boulevard, Suite 200, Lanham, Maryland 20706
www.rowmanlittlefield.com

Estover Road
Plymouth PL6 7PY
United Kingdom

British Library Cataloguing in Publication Information Available

Library of Congress Cataloging-in-Publication Data
Landy, Robert J.
  The couch and the stage : integrating words and action in psychotherapy /
Robert J. Landy.
    p. ; cm.
  Includes bibliographical references.
  ISBN-13: 978-0-7657-0449-8 (cloth : alk. paper)
  ISBN-10: 0-7657-0449-8 (cloth : alk. paper)
  1. Drama—Therapeutic use. 2. Psychotherapy. 3. Psychoanalysis. I. Title.
[DNLM: 1. Drama. 2. Psychodrama. 3. Psychotherapy—methods.
WM 430.5.P8 L264c 2008]
RC489.P7L327 2007
616.89'1523—dc22   2007011818

Printed in the United States of America

∞™ The paper used in this publication meets the minimum requirements of
American National Standard for Information Sciences—Permanence of Paper
for Printed Library Materials, ANSI/NISO Z39.48-1992.

In the beginning was the Word.

—John 1:1, The New Testament

In the beginning was the act.

—J. L. Moreno, *Psychodrama*, Vol. 1 (1946)

The end of man is an action, and not a thought.

—T. Carlyle, *Sartor Resartus* (1833–1834)

I have always thought the Actions of Men the
best Interpreters of their thoughts.

—J. Locke, *Human Understanding* (1695)

"Actions speak louder than words" is the maxim.

—A. Lincoln, *Collected Works* (1856)

Suit the Action to the Word, the Word to the Action.

—W. Shakespeare, *Hamlet* (1602)

Contents

Foreword: The World of Multiple Stages   ix
  Zerka T. Moreno

Foreword   xv
  Arthur Robbins, Ed.D.

Acknowledgments   xix

Introduction   1

1 Shamans and Psychoanalysts   5

2 Pioneers of Action Psychotherapy   45

3 An Overview of the Dramatic Therapies   75

4 Role Theory and the Role Method of Drama Therapy   97

5 Psychodrama   131

6 Developmental Transformations in Drama Therapy   165

7 A Comparison of the Action Psychotherapies:
    Toward a Model of Theory and Practice   195

8 Applications of Action Psychotherapies to Clinical Disorders   217

9 An Integration   245

References   251

Subject Index   265

Name Index   273

About the Author   277

The World of Multiple Stages

Zerka T. Moreno

All forms of psychotherapy, no matter what their philosophical framework, theory, or practical application, should respond to one universal criterion: to touch the autonomous healing center of the client(s) involved.

As Robert Landy points out in this important and comprehensive book, drama as a healing factor is very old and has roots in a multitude of cultures. The Western tradition of drama derives from a fairly recent one in Greece, where it evolved in a number of stages, from a fertility rite involving the god Dionysus in which all citizens took part, to written comedy and tragedy which separated the actors from the citizens, turning the latter away from action and into observing witnesses. In its turn, that created a new group of beings, the actors.

What distinguishes the drama therapies from the ritual/spiritual approaches, in which the equivalent of a medicine man or woman performs as a major agent or locus of healing from outside the condition or person to be treated, at least at the start, is that in drama therapies the agent or locus of healing is the sufferer him/herself as actor, having been changed from passive and objective involvement as a witness to subjective involvement in bodily action and interaction with others, aided by a guide.

In a step away from shamanic healing, which became verbal therapy as it is known today, Sigmund Freud focused upon the client as the object of healing via the spoken word. However, that process did not call upon the dimension of action on the part of the recipient; it still kept the client uninvolved with the body, whose inner world had to be interpreted by the specialist, an agent of therapy from the outside, who had to extract meaning from verbal communication by the client through analysis of its contents.

In the classic form the client has to establish a projective relationship to the therapist. The therapist is expected to remain a blank screen.

In this book Robert Landy has well formulated how the locus of healing is returned to the client in the form of drama as a therapeutic tool. Here the client is the focus of therapeutic intervention aided by a therapist, but it is also a format in which the therapist has to establish a relationship to the client. This mutual dynamic is essential in the drama therapies and establishes a context for healing to take place which is different from analysis, even if immediate interpretation takes place and directs the course of the interaction.

J. L. Moreno, the originator of a number of action-oriented approaches in Vienna in the 1920s, only one of which is psychodrama, did not believe in verbal therapy or that the word can be relied upon to absorb, embrace, and reproduce the entire human psyche, stating that language is not a sponge. Indeed, he postulated that there were language-resistant portions of the psyche. He reminded us that there is no universal language, which may at least experientially have come alive in him as an immigrant due to the effort of learning to speak English. He once remarked that the best way to learn a new language is to fall in love with a native speaker: in interaction.

Neurolinguists have reported that preverbal children, no matter where they are born, which language they first hear or eventually speak, produce identical sounds. (I have suggested that maybe the Tower of Babel should be called The Tower of Babble.) Arts such as painting, dancing, miming, music, sculpting, do not depend upon language to convey their message, though some are sometimes combined.

Not depending solely upon speech in therapy, Moreno looked for a more primeval, encompassing level of human communication and interaction, more basic than speech. He observed while working with young children that speech, both ontogenetically and phylogenetically, is a fairly late development in humans. What then underlies speech? It is assumed that well before speech, action, interaction, and miming were the tools for communicating, possibly accompanied by sounds, as it is for the child. Moreno found in the drama a more complete model of life, but looked for a form in which all those involved were, at least potentially, actors. These spectator-actors were to embody scenes from their own life without a script, inspired on the spur of the moment, making the actors responsible for their own action. Thus therapy became not merely the function of an outside agent, but rested upon the mutual interaction between the therapist and client(s) and client(s) with others. His ideal design for such a theater in 1924 specified: No Space for Spectators.

The particular human capacity he relied upon was a twin principle: spontaneity/creativity, each of which denotes something not previously extant. Spontaneity comes from the Latin *sua sponte*, from within the self, not imposed from without; creativity means bringing to birth something that did not exist before, something new. Gradually psychodrama developed out of a number of action-based improvisational experiments. Though often dealing with traumas of the past, it is also concerned with problems in the present and expectations of the future, as a rehearsal for living, helping to make alterations as indicated. Role playing can be done as animals, spirits, delusions or hallucinations, voices, body parts, ideas, visions, the departed, intermediary objects as embodied by people, masks, puppets, dolls, stones, or any other form of concretization.

Some writers interpreting Moreno's work have stated that he based psychodrama on Aristotle's observation concerning the effect of tragedy arousing pity and terror in the spectators, which Aristotle described as a catharsis or purging of these emotions. Unfortunately, they have not grasped Moreno's complete intent, because he was not satisfied by Aristotle's exposition. He asked himself: "What kind of a catharsis is this when the spectators know the actors are not the real persons they represent? Is this not more an aesthetic than an emotional catharsis? What if the actors presented themselves with real emotions, real anxiety, real fears? Would not that bring about a primary emotional catharsis on the part of the spectators instead of a secondary one? And would not the actors themselves have a primary catharsis of action?" Shakespeare wrote that we are all actors on the stage of life. However, Moreno pointed out that none of us have been handed a complete script at birth; we have to improvise. We stumble, learn painfully as we go along. All the drama therapies help to make that learning less painful and often even joyous.

Another basis for Moreno's work was his conviction of the significance of the human encounter in life, not limited to the drama, as well as the significance of the present moment in which that encounter takes place. That is why every enactment in psychodrama reflects life and is embodied in the here and now, no matter when the original event occurred or even if it only existed in the client's mind. When the protagonist is fully warmed up, the magic "as if" changes during the drama into the "as," the "if" falling away, making the undertaking completely real. Some protagonists actually "see" the absent other as played by an auxiliary ego, as that real other. The noumenon becomes the phenomenon.

Drama therapies as practiced by Landy and others presented in this book are related in terms of using role playing, although in a variety of ways, but all concerned with bringing about change. There is a rather regrettable notion extant in some quarters that catharsis or purging in the form of abreaction such as crying, laughing, hitting, is the goal of psychotherapy, regrettable because it is only a step along the way. The ultimate goal is the catharsis of integration, intrapersonally as well as interpersonally. A catharsis of abreaction is a momentary here-and-now event even if brought about by a memory, while a catharsis of integration is a process, taking place in time.

There are two concepts described by the Greeks that are shared by all forms of drama, including the therapeutic, which are meaningful to the actor/client. One is *peripeteia*, the other *anagnorisis*. *Peripeteia* refers to a change in the direction of the drama, a change of circumstances for the protagonist; *anagnorisis* means becoming aware of something inherent in the process that was originally overlooked. Either of these may occur within the drama or may lead to new learning upon its completion, sometimes long after the therapy session, as part of a catharsis of integration enabling change. But let us not translate too lightly either of these into intellectually conceived insights. Cognitively based insight is commonly overrated as a form of learning and healing, because it demands transposing thinking into action, which is quite difficult. It is easier to have the experience first and then to extract learning. One may have all the awareness in the world without being able to change. What we are actually dealing with in drama therapies is how children learn; it is action-learning, which may or may not be cognitively conceived and still leads to personal change and development.

Drama therapies uncover and reformulate those aspects of events as perceived by the protagonist, not their totality. Perception is never total. No human being has total perception of themselves or of another human being nor of their interaction. What drama therapies do is to change and enlarge our perceptions. That engenders hope because our perception is subject to change. Facts do not change, but the way we perceive and handle them can change. Change would not be possible if we grasped every aspect of life completely and in its totality. Thus our human failing in that regard may well be a blessing since we can alter how we perceive ourselves and others. This is true also for the therapist.

A striking finding, at least in psychodrama, is that many clients cannot recall what they have dramatically produced, either fully or in part, yet change takes place. We can account for that phenomenon by realizing that total action involvement, which Moreno called "the act-hunger syndrome," removes portions of the personality that form two other parts: the internal observer and the critic. When this hunger for action is fully engaged and allowed to function, it takes over; the actor is in control, burning away the observer and critic in its path, without leaving memory traces. It does not equate repression, since one can only repress that which has been recorded. It simply was not recorded, yet the action took place.

Although not exactly on the same level of intensity, how many times have you driven your car for miles without realizing the distance covered? Where was cognition? Where were you? On automatic pilot, in another space, or was it a different state of unawareness? In any case that image is a fine metaphor for what the human being is capable of: action without memory, the body doing one thing, the recording part of the mind being absent.

But there are also other states of being. In 1943, in a paper titled "Sociometry and the Cultural Order," Moreno postulated that perhaps the psyche is not inside the body, that the body may be enveloped by the psyche. If that is true, it is easier to understand how humans communicate, often without words: their psyches meeting, touching, and interweaving. Such encounters may take place in co-conscious and co-unconscious states. That may be another reason why sometimes memory is incomplete or even lacking.

Drama therapies are in a special, privileged category: They deal with the interweaving of psyches. I believe this facilitates the autonomous healing center. Those of us who work in drama therapies find ourselves astounded and challenged when faced with the complexity of our client's mind, but we also have much for which to be grateful in having such a dynamic tool that helps us all to become more complete beings.

Zerka T. Moreno
Charlottesville, Virginia

Foreword

Arthur Robbins, Ed.D.

Robert Landy's newest book, *The Couch and the Stage: Integrating Words and Action in Psychotherapy*, vividly describes the emergence of a new style of therapeutic interaction, a variety of body-oriented and dramatic role-playing therapies that come under the broad title of action therapies. Landy's background as a drama therapist and his work as a teacher and author have made him a leader in his field. With the publication of this book, he has brought the action therapies into a historical perspective and placed drama therapy within the broad framework of therapeutic practice.

Landy takes us back to the early pioneering efforts of psychoanalysis. He draws us into the drama of the early pioneers and their tumultuous meetings in Freud's living room. Initially, Freud attempts to link up mental operations with neuropsychology. However, there was not enough interest in the medical community to support further investigation. He turns to hypnosis, but the results appear superficial and not long lasting. In this ferment of ideas and egos, the early pioneers struggle with a paternal authority that demands little deviation from his theoretical framework. Some cannot adhere to Freud's closed-in system and map out their own professional identities with new innovations. They are viewed as disloyal dissenters to the movement and are excommunicated from the fold. Others barely exist on the fringe for they have not the passion and loyalty to Freudian theory. Landy cites two pioneers who are rarely referred to in modern psychoanalytic literature but whose work will later play an important role in the establishment of action therapies as a distinct field. Sandor Ferenczi experiments with the acting out of transference and countertransference in the patient-therapist dialogue. Otto Rank emphasizes the impact of creativity as a positive force for change.

A bold offshoot of these early efforts arises with Jacob L. Moreno's development of psychodrama. Moreno moves the patient out of the office and into the theater of the mind. A variety of role-playing exercises are actively engaged in this theater. Even the audience participates in the dramatic exploration. I recall participating in the late 1960s with my introductory class in psychology during a field visit to Moreno's theater. One of the students volunteered to go on stage for a demonstration of this method. The dramatic impact lasted well after the exercise was completed. The variety of roles representing the complex mental structure of the participant was now articulated by options and living words. Today, even psychoanalysis has become exposed to action words that make the drama of reflection more alive and penetrating.

Landy discusses the inevitable divisions that take place within the drama therapy movement. These divisions are described in depth, both in their similarities and differences. As in psychoanalysis, territorial fights and identity splits take place. I am all too familiar with these splits for they are part of my own personal and professional history. I can also see how these divisions parallel those of our present-day culture and society with its splits and polarities. As I review my own personal and professional history I can observe the interplay between personal conflicts, developmental issues, and the emerging identity formation that impacts upon our manner and style of work. Let me offer a very brief review of some of these issues.

By the early 1970s I was already a trained analyst with a very active practice. Nevertheless, coming out of the tail end of the exciting 1960s, I was restless and sought diversity, which eventually pushed me to become a part-time faculty member at Pratt Institute, a premiere art school in New York City. I discovered that teaching psychology to art students was both enlightening and challenging. The class did not just sit back and intellectualize; they were active and virtually unable to contain their passion for the subject. Yet, they were skeptical of psychoanalytic assumptions and had their own creative, perceptive approach to understanding the human condition. These classes were a significant step in my attempt to heal my own internal splits.

I turn now to my family of origin, who were overloaded with values of beauty and aesthetics. However, the rigid order and control of their aesthetic values stifled me. My mother and sister were deeply involved with interior decorating. My father, a manufacturer of artificial flowers, would bring home his latest creations for appraisal by the women. I retreated to the safe atmosphere of my sandbox and became lost in its chaos and dirt. I made my own creations, but they had nothing to do with beauty. My parents became worried about my future—I did not fit into the family mode. In fact, everything about me was a nonconformist mess. Interestingly, in my father's family were four lay analysts, uncles and aunts, who were practicing professionals. This will later become significant for me, but growing up I barely knew them. My mother kept them at arm's length, for they were viewed as disreputable. "What kind of therapists are they," she queries, "who don't have an MD or PhD after their names?" On a deeper level, her attitude is a reflection of her very deep fear of men, and I became the recipient of her projections and identifications.

Psychology and psychoanalysis were my solutions for making some sense out of my life. I became acquainted with my psychoanalyst aunts and uncles, and in fact one of my uncles became my supervisor. I was already a fully trained psychoanalyst in my early forties when I became deeply involved in sculpting, an outgrowth of my internal exploration of my conflicts and fears. I also discovered that beauty is not simply about making things pretty. Now, the father and mother inside of me attempted to make peace with one another. "Wouldn't it be great," I mused, "if art and psychology could come together as a unit?" Just then, the time was ripe for the emergence of a new profession: art therapy. I submitted a proposal to Pratt Institute to create a department of art therapy and the dean's committee approved it along with a grant to support the endeavor. I had emphasized the role of creativity development, and I also added that it might help artists acquire jobs.

Before I knew it, I became part of a split that still exists in the field: Are we practicing art as therapy, or psychotherapeutic art therapy? In the meantime, psychoanalysis has become torn between different formulations. There are now very distinct divisions between self-psychology, object relations, and drive theory.

This brings me to the later developments in the field that are so important in understanding Robert Landy's thesis. Freud's initial dream of creating a neurological basis for understanding the relationship of mental expression to brain function slowly develops through brain research. Mirroring becomes a central form of learning, and we soon see that different forms of psychotherapeutic endeavors utilizing different languages often end up with similar notions. These ideas are supported by greater understanding of mirror neurons that are so basic to our comprehension of empathy. Trauma research and brain functioning now have a much closer relationship to one another. Motor expression and body cues are supported through brain research as channels of empathic connections. Infant and child research supports our understanding of the interconnection of verbal and nonverbal development. These new areas of discovery promise to hold all the therapies together under one large framework. Of course this theoretical organization is still in its early development, but it obviously points to the future of an interdisciplinary theory.

From this perspective, all treatment is both action oriented and reflective. It includes verbal and nonverbal expression. Behavioral, Gestalt, and analytic treatment are no longer polarized, for they are fast becoming part of a bigger picture. Holistic therapy does not rule out analytic or experiential therapies. A few practitioners now combine principles of advanced physics, Buddhism and therapeutic engagement, all taking place at different levels of consciousness. These developments potentially open the professional range of therapeutic intervention. Here, old professional roles break down. Practitioners with different disciplines are exposed to a much broader vision. Each of us creates our own synthesis that integrates our personal style of interaction. We are only limited by our personal and professional identity quests, and by our temperament and personal background.

A theoretical orientation evolves out of our temperamental differences, intellectual inclinations, and our emotional predispositions to work with any given patient. Some of us refuse to be imprisoned by a professional role. For me, therapeutic intervention becomes a process of discovering new forms that fit each patient-therapist dyad. I suspect this view originates from a very nonconforming temperament and a creative interest in moving through chaos to create new forms. From this perspective all therapists are artists, for they are preoccupied with the art of communication. Scientific thinking, then, becomes an important background for creating a center and a ground as well as a discipline.

The integration of a multidiscipline approach may well point to the future growth of the field of therapy. Yet there is a counterforce that inevitably promotes splits and divisions. Landy describes the differences and similarities in the divisions inherent in the profession of drama therapy. However, most important, he holds out the transformative hope that we can grow past our old roles and not be bound by a particular technique or expertise. We are limited by our inability to separate from the past. I am aware that I cannot be all things to all people. We also need our discipline to function as an anchor that permits us to take risks. But I am excited by the fact that the ability to discover and rediscover a particular theory or technique can potentially occur with each therapeutic endeavor. If we are to take this path, change demands a letting go of what we know, separating from the familiar, becoming enmeshed in chaos, and creating new forms out of disorder. Upon reading this book, all of us will be exposed to the potential that dramatic techniques can be integrated into a larger framework of therapy.

Robert Landy's dream of bringing drama therapy into the future development of therapeutic expertise created the foundation for his book. I firmly believe that all therapies can be action oriented as well as reflective. We have the option of confining ourselves to one modality of expression, or of integrating different modalities of interaction. I support therapeutic practitioners who wish to expand their integration of therapeutic practice. This text makes a contribution that promotes a new synthesis for our work with patients.

Arthur Robbins
New York, New York

Acknowledgments

All books exist because they are championed by someone who believes in them and is willing to see them through the birthing process. My champion is Arthur Pomponio, who had the courage and foresight to cross over the conventional borders separating words and action in psychotherapy and the belief that the creative arts therapies add a significant dimension to psychoanalysis. I am very fortunate to have found Art as my editor and guide.

The idea for the book grew out of my work at New York University on the research film, *Three Approaches to Drama Therapy*. I am deeply grateful to all those involved on the film, especially my cotherapists, Nina Garcia and David Read Johnson. My very special gratitude goes to "Derek," the subject of the film, who trusted the process and the people involved enough to offer up his life story in dramatic form. Throughout the process of making the film and writing the book I held him close.

As a teacher, I am fortunate to have such vibrant and bright students with whom I can indulge in the pleasures of dialogue. I want to single out those who participated in the making of the film and whose voices stayed with me throughout the writing of the book: Darien Acevedo, Melissa Bulman, Brooke Campbell, Donna Gabriel Ellaby, Andrew Gaines, Sara Miller Gordon, Melissa Erin Monahan, Tamar Peled, Russell G. Roten, Kate Schettler, and Krista M. Verrastro.

A number of people read and commented upon an early version of the manuscript. I am very appreciative of Adam Blatner, Nina Garcia, and David Read Johnson, all of whom challenged me to discover a better way to understand the meaning of action in psychotherapy. I am deeply grateful to Arthur Robbins, a pioneer in developing expressive forms of psychoanalysis and art therapy, for reading the manuscript, writing a very moving foreword, and engaging with me in dialogue that felt clarifying in the intellectual exchange but even more so in the relationship.

It was a great pleasure for me to create a historical document with the advice and support of one of the most significant historical figures in the field, Zerka T. Moreno. Zerka was not only my encyclopedia of knowledge about the early days of action psychotherapy, but also my most important reader, the one who could truly amend all the awkward and false notes and support the true. I am blessed to have a foreword to my book written by Zerka.

I acknowledge my client, "Sally," a courageous person who taught me how to guide her through the tangle of eating disorder. I thank Andrew Gaines for help in developing the Role Checklist and my student assistants, Pam Edgar and Mary Hershkowitz, for help with the manuscript. I also thank Mary Catherine La Mar at Rowman & Littlefield for her gentle and professional shepherding of the manuscript.

And finally, I want to recognize the extraordinary community of colleagues and friends in the fields of action psychotherapy, who remind me regularly, even when I am unwilling to listen, that I am not alone.

Introduction

The proverb, "actions speak louder than words," sets up a dichotomy with actions as superior. Throughout the history of psychotherapy many have perpetuated this dichotomy, offering theoretical reasons to justify their points of view. In traditional forms of shamanic healing, action expressed through movement, mimesis, and drama prevails over words. In the early days of psychoanalysis, Freud invented a talking cure for patients manifesting a variety of neurotic symptoms, relegating action to the low status of a defense against feeling, a resistance needing to be overcome through a process of analysis. In 1914 Freud wrote that "the patient does not remember anything of what he has forgotten or repressed, but acts it out. He reproduces it not as a memory but as an action" (150). It was the job of the classical Freudian analyst to help the patient transform that action into words.

Some of Freud's early colleagues disagreed with him and promulgated more active approaches to healing. For them, action was not necessarily the opposite of language, but rather a concomitant, moving clients into other realms of expression through the body and emotions. These same analysts, however, depended heartily upon words to treat patients.

Over time, others, like J. L. Moreno and Fritz Perls, took a more radical stance, viewing words as resistances to expressing deeply affective and somatic states. As new approaches arose to challenge the orthodoxy of previous ones, splits developed both within a particular framework, such as psychoanalysis, and between orientations, such as psychoanalysis and psychodrama. And yet as time passed, the differences began to fall away. Contemporary psychoanalytic thinking has moved away from Freud's intrapsychic, drive reduction model, embracing relational and interpersonal perspectives. Some even refer to the transference/countertransference relationship in analysis as an enactment, suggesting dramatic action. Freud, who was trained as a neuroscientist, could only hint at the scientific veracity of his early neurological studies. He would be surprised and delighted to learn that current scientific evidence in the growing field of neuroscience has begun to uncover the complex relationship between the two hemispheres of the brain. He might be even more surprised and less delighted to learn that neuroscience points to the significance of working through the body in action to optimally repair damages wrecked on the brain by psychological trauma (see van der Kolk 2002b, 2002c).

This book is not intended to promote the polarity of action and words, but rather to explore how action approaches to psychotherapy grew out of Western verbal methods and even traditional shamanic practices, eventually coalescing into a theory and practice that is creative and holistic. As the central concept in the book, action refers to the therapeutic application of drama, play, and nonverbal expression in the service of engaging the body, mind, and emotions of clients in a process of healing. Although there are several forms of action psychotherapy, including Gestalt therapy, dance/movement therapy, somatic psychotherapy, and bioenergetic analysis, the focus of this book will be upon psychodrama and drama therapy.

The main purpose of this book is to make a case for the inclusion of the action psychotherapies into the mainstream of psychotherapy, mental health counseling, and clinical social work. This perspective is well supported by the addition of action psychotherapies within current mainstream anthologies in play therapy (see Irwin 2000; Landy 2003) counseling (see Corey 2001), and psychotherapy (see Johnson 2000a; Blatner 2001; Johnson, Smith, and James 2003). Action approaches will be seen as especially valuable for mental health professionals who envision their work within a holistic, creative, and relational framework.

THE STRUCTURE OF THE BOOK

The action psychotherapies are conceived throughout the book within a broad context. The book begins with shamanism, a traditional healing form with ancient roots, noted by its theatricality and use of song and dance, storytelling, and trance to harness the power of the spiritual world. This particular source is given to remind the reader that the healing arts began in traditional cultures where magic preceded science and where action preceded words. After describing a shamanic ritual in contemporary Korea, I cut across cultures to Vienna at the turn of the century to tell a story of the early days of psychoanalysis. I look especially at the work of Freud's colleagues, Carl Jung, Otto Rank, Sandor Ferenczi, and Wilhelm Reich, all of whom experimented with early forms of psychotherapeutic action.

In drawing a line from the early days of psychoanalysis to current practices in drama therapy, I visit several major psychotherapists who struggled with the limitations of verbal and cognitive methods and innovated expressive forms of action in treatment. Of special note is the work of J. L Moreno, who developed a fully dramatic form for healing not only the individual, but also the group. Henry Murray, Erik Erikson, and Fritz Perls are also featured in this brief history, as well as those working through psychotherapeutic models of constructivism, cognitive behavioral therapy, and brief models of therapy.

An overview of the dramatic therapies as practiced in the twenty-first century extends from this rich context, focusing in depth upon three major approaches—role theory/method, psychodrama, and developmental transformations. In discussing these approaches, I provide a model that highlights several common therapeutic polarities: emotion and distance, fiction and reality, verbal and nonverbal expression, action and reflection, directive and nondirective action, transference and countertransference.

Throughout this discussion, reference is made to a 2005 research film, *Three Approaches to Drama Therapy*, which features the theory and practice of three prominent drama therapists. In the film, the three therapists demonstrate their work in sessions with a common client. Transcripts of those sessions will be highlighted and analyzed to provide an in-depth, comparative view. This film was modeled after the classic film, *Three Approaches to Psychotherapy* (Shostrom 1965), featuring Carl Rogers, Fritz Perls, and Albert Ellis working with the same client whom they called Gloria.

After comparing and contrasting the three approaches, applications to several clinical disorders are given, some of which are well supported by research in neuroscience. The point will be made that action psychotherapies can be learned and used effectively by more traditional mental health professionals in the treatment of a range of clinical conditions including but not limited to trauma, posttraumatic stress disorder, addictions, and eating disorders. Specific applications of psychodrama, role method, and developmental transformations to these disorders will be featured.

In coming full circle, I question why the notion of drama has proven to be so resilient as metaphor and technique throughout the history of psychological healing. In the end, I return to the polarities in order to seek integration and to understand the continuity of ancient, classical, and contemporary forms of healing through word and deed, mind and body. If Shakespeare's most famous speech that begins, "To be or not to be," is really a question, the answer is: "To be *and* not to be." In accepting the continuity of life and death, of the actor who can only create when in role and of the role that can only exist when filled with the breath of the actor, each human being has the potential to live a fully integrated existence.

1

Shamans and Psychoanalysts

A GATHERING OF SHAMANS

In the spring of 2004, a dozen shamans, mostly women, gather at the seaside town of Yeon An Budoo, Korea, a fishing village on the Suh Hae Sea. A small audience reverently awaits their healing performance. The townspeople make their livelihood from the fruits of the sea. They often feel helpless when their catch is small or when unexpected natural disasters capsize their boats, and so they welcome this ritual moment of hope. The shamans will enact a wishful performance, the *Poong Uh Jae*, to relieve anxiety and reaffirm communion between the people and the gods. The *Poong Uh Jae* will assure the villagers that the gods will favor them with many fish and few accidents in the coming year.

On a makeshift platform, a young shaman appears, dressed in traditional costume—a white gown called a *gandi*, long black vest called a *kwaeza*, and black hat called a *gut*, tied under her neck. In front of her is a cleaned, uncooked pig, an offering to the warrior gods who, with luck and the help of the shaman, will bring the villagers a plentiful harvest of fish. Behind the shaman is a low table set with a white sheet, food and drink, flowers, and various props to use in her ritual performance, and behind that is a larger and higher table set with colorful fruits and cakes. Along the perimeter of the platform is a dazzling backdrop, painted with panels of various spiritual and mythological figures. A group of old musicians, attendants, and assistant shamans sits on the platform to the young shaman's left, ready to play their drums and cymbals, flutes and trumpets, on a cue from the young shaman.

At the beginning of the performance, the young shaman attempts to pierce the flesh of the pig with a trident. After several attempts she succeeds, and the pig is impaled on the trident, a sign that a healing god has been summoned. The shaman speaks directly to the people, and then over several hours time, she sings and dances and invites people up from the audience to whom she offers food and blessings. At the climax of her performance, she dances with two sharpened daggers, symbolically stabbing herself to mark the arrival of the gods within her body. She cuts a piece of flesh from the pig and symbolically ingests its power. After the dance, people approach the pig, take out paper money, and slap the bills on the carcass of the pig. They bow to the young shaman and receive her blessings. The cutting of the flesh and the giving of money symbolize the banishing of disruptive gods who might otherwise interfere with a successful outcome.

Throughout the day until late in the afternoon, other shamans perform. The highlight is the chief shaman, an older woman renowned for her ability to harness the power of the spirits. She is dressed in the brightest gandi of all, embroidered in blue and red and yellow and green. She creates an ongoing patter with the musicians and the audience, joking and laughing, teasing the spirits. She twirls and twirls, inviting the musicians to speed up the tempo and improvise freely, helping her to attain a trance state as she summons the gods. In an altered state, her patter takes the form of a story, *gong soo*, told by the gods inhabiting the old shaman. Other shamans approach the platform to speak to the gods and ask them the questions most important to the villagers: Will the catch be plentiful? Will the seas and winds be favorable? Will the accidents be minimal? And the gods within the old shaman answer in words and movement. The old shaman dances fluidly, shaking a bell and wielding a sword, raising her arms to the heavens to summon the healing powers of the gods. Toward the conclusion of her performance, the old shaman dances with a large puppet, entertaining the gods, the gathered shamans, and the celebrants.

At the end of the day, the shamans cook and eat the pig. They display all the money given by the audience, attesting to the success of the ritual performance. They form a procession, and with two puppet figures and a symbolic boat, they march to the edge of the sea. With music and prayers, they bless the fleet of ships and all the people, praising the good spirits, assuaging the evil spirits, and instilling hope in the villagers for a plentiful harvest.

As the shamans change out of their costumes, dismantle the stage, and load all the colorful props into their vans, they engage in small talk about the weather and the long trip home. All are tired from the healing performance. Many in their transition from healers to civilians with day jobs acknowledge that they are vessels that simply channel the spirits, for it is the spirits that will determine whether the villagers will prosper in the coming year.

Young Shaman Dancing with Daggers. Photo by Robert J. Landy

Chief Shaman at Work. Photo by Robert J. Landy

A GATHERING OF PSYCHOANALYSTS

In the fall of 1902, four physicians gathered in Vienna at the home of Dr. Sigmund Freud on Berggasse 19 "with the declared intention of learning, practicing, and disseminating psychoanalysis" (Freud in Gay 1988, 173). The small Wednesday Psychological Society soon became the Vienna Psychoanalytic Society. Over the years, its members included not only Viennese, like Alfred Adler and Otto Rank, but also such distinguished foreigners as C. G. Jung, Ernest Jones, Sandor Ferenczi, and Lou Andreas-Salomé. All the meetings adhered to a ritual structure that began with the reading of a scholarly paper, followed by coffee and cake, a social break of fifteen minutes, and then an intellectual discussion of the paper.

At the head of all gatherings was the prodigious Dr. Freud, teacher, mentor, and muse for many of the others. Freud's biographers have referred to the religious quality of the gatherings, viewing the leader, Freud, as both a pope of a new sect (Jones 1959, 205) and as a prophet (Gay 1988, 205). As the small group increased in membership, its members asserted their needs for power, independence, and ego gratification. As matters of theory and practice became contentious and as personalities and loyalties clashed, the group set up its own clandestine "Committee," a kind of inquisition to insure the sanctity of the central Freudian principles. Many who were at one time particularly close to Freud experienced a kind of excommunication from the inner sanctum, including Alfred Adler, C. G. Jung, Otto Rank, and Sandor Ferenczi.

The aim of Freud and his followers was to promote the classical principles of Freudian psychoanalysis and attempt to move its methods into the mainstream of psychiatry. They viewed themselves as scientists who had made important discoveries about the nature of the human mind and then invented a rational cure for irrational psychological disturbances. Despite attacks from the conservative medical establishment, Freud lived long enough to see a growing dissemination of his ideas. The guardian of psychoanalysis became the seminal figure in the newly developing field of psychotherapy. His free association talking cure, based in a psychosexual understanding of the human personality, would dominate the mental health professions for decades. Unlike the shamans and occultists and clerics of all kinds, Freud remained the rationalist, who insisted, like the Greek philosopher Protagoras, that man is the measure of all things.

Shamanism and psychoanalysis offer two distinct views of healing. The former centers in a spiritual worldview, which presents a confluence of body and spirit, natural and supernatural events. Shamans not only aid in the healing of physical illnesses, but also psychological ones, both of which they view as spiritually based. The training of the shaman involves learning

The Secret Committee, 1912: Otto Rank, Sigmund Freud, Karl Abraham, Max Eitingon, Sandor Ferenczi, Ernst Jones, Hans Sachs. Reprinted with permission from the Freud Museum, London

not only about the use of various herbal and medicinal remedies, but also about the healing properties of the performing arts as a means of moving spirits in and out of the psyche of patients. In describing the training and initiation of shamanic healers, anthropologist Mircea Eliade (1972) speaks of a figurative process of death and rebirth, where shamans engage in a symbolic journey to the spirit world. While there, they meet a spirit guide who offers medicines and wisdom. Because of the transformational nature of the journey, initiates are spiritually dismantled and reassembled, and then return to the material world endowed with the power necessary to heal those who are infirm and distressed. When they achieve the status of healer, they summon the positive spirits, offering hope to a community that events beyond their control will turn out well.

Shamanism has been practiced for many thousands of years on virtually every continent. It is still practiced among indigenous peoples in South America, Asia, and Africa and even among various new-age groups scattered throughout the Western world. Although leaders of organized religions have worked hard to destroy all remnants of shamanism, labeling it demon worship and witchcraft, its practice and imagery subsists. The modern symbol of medicine, the caduceus, two snakes wrapped around a staff, may well be a remnant from the shamanic past, predating the ancient Greeks. Some have argued (McNiff 1988; Pendzik 1988; Lewis 1993; Snow 2000; Glaser 2004) that the roots of contemporary expressive therapies are to be found in ancient shamanic traditions as shamans have regularly applied music, dance, narrative, and drama to heal the unquiet mind.

Psychoanalysis, as conceived by Freud and then amended by scores of depth psychologists, offers a seemingly different view of the human being. Many psychoanalysts see their work as scientifically based and amenable to empirical verification. Dark forces of the psyche certainly exist and can cause human beings great distress and pain. The pain is caused not by spirits but by early developmental experiences, some of which are traumatic and subsequently repressed. Repressed experiences find their way into the unconscious mind through psychological and neurological channels and are manifested in dreams, fantasies, wishes, spontaneous gestures, and verbalizations.

The initiation of psychoanalysts into practice is more scientific than symbolic. Their journey is through study, academic degrees, and supervised internships, as well as their own process of self-examination through analysis.

The traditional magical approach to healing had little in common with the modern scientific one, at least on the surface. Freud, himself, threw off all spiritual and magical associations, presenting himself as a rational scientist. And yet, in the early days of the Vienna Psychoanalytic Society, when the early founders were not only following the dictates of Freud, but making up their own rules, much experimentation was taking place. Carl Jung asked his patients to draw mandalas and dialogue with mental images. Otto Rank worked with myth and conceived the psychoanalytic process as a hero's journey. He was one of the first to relate the healing process to the creative process and to compare the experience of the client to that of the artist. Rank's collaborator, Sandor Ferenczi, experimented with a radical form of interpersonal therapy, mutual analysis, allowing his patients to take on the role of therapist and analyze his own psychological journey. Wilhelm Reich manipulated the bodies of patients, inviting some to dance and to engage in role play.

Let us take a deeper look at the practices and theories of these men who dared to risk ignominy by challenging their mentor and their more conventional colleagues. By taking the risk, these individuals paved the way for those who would overtly exclaim the profound therapeutic benefits of cathartic and creative expression through all channels of mind and body, imagination and spirit. Like both non-Western traditional healers and Western scientifically trained physicians and psychotherapists, these innovators would pave the way for those who would soon after pioneer the action and dramatic psychotherapies.

C. G. JUNG AND ANALYTIC PSYCHOLOGY

When Jung first met Freud face-to-face in 1907 at Berggasse 19, he was exuberant. Their initial conversation lasted thirteen hours with Jung doing most of the talking. The younger psychiatrist and researcher was enamored with his older mentor, whose ideas of unconscious dynamics, free association, and dream interpretation had greatly influenced his own. Jung's research on word association, done in Burghölzli sanatorium in Zurich and published in 1906, provided early empirical evidence for Freud's theory of free association, and the master was very pleased. Within a short time of their acquaintance, Freud was looking to Jung as his intellectual heir.

One major obstacle in their conversations, however, concerned Jung's interest in spirituality and the occult and Freud's scorn for the same. Things began to unravel during their voyage to America in 1909 where Freud accepted an honorary doctorate at Clark University in Worcester, Massachusetts. Before embarking from Bremen, Germany, Freud, Jung, and the young Hungarian psychoanalyst, Sandor Ferenczi, engaged in conversation over lunch. Jung spoke passionately about recent discoveries in Northern Germany of prehistoric human remains, the mummified peat-bog corpses. As was his practice, Freud interpreted Jung's remarks, offering the ominous remark that Jung's concern with prehistoric corpses masked a death wish toward Freud. Following his pronouncement, Freud fainted.

Three years later, as their professional and personal relationship deteriorated, Freud and Jung met at a psychoanalytic conference in Munich. While deeply in conversation, both attempted to take some responsibility for the rift. But then Freud accused Jung of publishing articles in Swiss journals without referencing him. Jung responded by arguing that doing so would be redundant as Freud's work was so universally celebrated. The conversation veered toward the Egyptian pharaoh, Akhenaton. One colleague said that the ruler resented his father and tried to destroy his father's legacy by carving out his name on his cartouches, somewhat akin to removing all references in a scholarly article. Jung rebutted by claiming that Akhenaton engaged in a common practice of revising cartouches once he ascended the throne and that the father fixation was exaggerated.

Freud interpreted Jung's remarks as defensive and again accused his colleague of harboring a death wish against him, fearing that Jung sought to deface his identity. As in the meeting in Bremen, Freud fainted. Jung picked him up in his arms and carried him to a nearby couch, where he revived.

One way to read these fainting episodes is that when his words failed, Freud internalized the perceived death wish and acted it out by pretending to die. But his performance did not fool Jung, who took on a counterrole of helper and ultimately judged his mentor for a failure to acknowledge his internal daimons.

The Child and the Man

At the heart of the conflict was probably the clash of two powerful figures, a father figure searching for a son to carry on his legacy, and a son figure looking for a father who would truly embrace his independent spirit. At a more theoretical level, the two disagreed on the effects of infantile sexuality on psychosocial development and on the form and content of the unconscious. Their clash was particularly pronounced in their different approaches to dream work. Freud's most influential work, *The Interpretation of Dreams*, provided a template for reading the unconscious and its repressed content of unfulfilled wishes. But when Jung presented to Freud his apocryphal dream of a house with many levels, its lower prehistoric cave scattered with bones and skulls, Freud yet again interpreted Jung's imagery as a death wish. For Jung, this was a pivotal moment. He finally realized Freud's personal limitations as an analyst and mentor, and his own independent understanding of the shape and scope of the psyche with its various layers representing not only personal unconscious experience, but, said Jung (1963): "a collective a priori beneath the personal psyche . . . I recognized them as forms of instinct, that is, as archetypes" (161).

Whatever personal struggles the two enacted, the professional rift led to a major innovation in analytic thinking and treatment. Jung embraced Freud's concept of repressed affects stored in the unconscious but offered an alternative path to traverse the royal road to the unconscious. As Freud proceeded through verbal language, Jung proceeded through nonverbal imagery, invoking the imaginative and creative capacities of the human being. As Freud acted out his unconscious fears of being deposed and disposed by fainting, Jung summoned his daimons. Like a shaman, Jung willingly embarked upon a spiritual journey of dismantling and reassembling. Engaged with his darkest dream imagery, Jung built an innovative approach to psychotherapy, one based in the creative imagination rather than the rational intelligence.

Jung's journey, as we learn in *Memories, Dreams, and Reflections* (1963), began in childhood with experiences of the spirit world recollected in dreams. When he fully separated from Freud in 1912, he wrote: "A period of inner uncertainty began for me. It would be no exaggeration to call it a state of disorientation" (170). During that time, Jung engaged in an imaginative dialogue with himself, searching for a means to move out of his crisis. Realizing that he no longer embraced the Christian worldview of his father and his culture, Jung attempted to explore his inner life. He first did this by transcribing a series of extraordinary dreams, mythic in nature. But when the dreams did not sufficiently ease his dark mood, he focused upon childhood memories. When he recalled a moment of playing with building blocks at the age of ten, he was unexpectedly filled up with emotion. He mused (1963): "The small boy is still around, and possesses a creative life which I lack. But how can I make my way to it?" (174).

Jung found a practical solution in taking on the role of child and building structures with stones and other found objects and in the process reclaiming his creativity. He called this the building game. Jung's notion of play as a therapeutic process was not a new one (see, for example, Spencer 1873, and Schiller 1875), but Jung approached his own childlike play as if for the first time. In taking on the role of the child and creating dramatic structures representative of inner psychic states, Jung came to recognize the profound healing power of play. As player, he was aware that he had a means of returning to unresolved past experiences, resolving current dilemmas, and anticipating the future. This discovery within the field of psychotherapy marks an early link between the child, the artist, and the creative individual, all of whom replay and rehearse significant moments of distress and confusion in order to discover effective ways of dealing with them. Jung (1921) discusses play within the context of fantasy and imagination, all three processes that would prove essential in his developing theory and practice:

> Every good idea and all creative work are the offspring of the imagination, and have their source in . . . infantile fantasy. Not the artist alone, but every creative individual whatsoever owes all that is greatest in his life to fantasy. The dynamic principle of fantasy is play, a characteristic also of the child. . . . Without this playing with fantasy no creative work has ever yet come to birth (par. 93).

Jung, beginning with his own play as a means of working through a troubling life crisis, discovered a therapeutic method that would be developed in later years by others who initially trained in psychoanalysis. Some, however, like Freud's daughter, Anna, and Melanie Klein, trace their play therapy approaches directly to Freud, who suggested that play was a way to reach children. Once the communication was established, Anna Freud and Klein, like their mentor, used play as a means of opening up verbal channels for interpretation.

Others, more indebted to Jung, saw play as the direct language of children and thus a therapeutic process in its own right. The nondirective psychotherapist Axline (1947) and the psychoanalyst Winnicott (1971) both believed that children could solve their own problems through their enactments in play. Neither, however, directly incorporated Jung's work with myth and archetype. That work in play therapy was developed by Dora Kalff, a student of Jung's, who created a therapeutic approach called sandplay. Kalff's (1980) work was preceded by Margaret Lowenfeld (1979), a pediatrician and child psychotherapist, who asked disturbed children to build pictures on a tabletop and in a sandbox with miniature objects, then analyzed their depictions. Encouraged by Jung, Kalff studied with Lowenfeld and integrated her methods with those of Jung to expand the field of sand-play into a form based in an understanding of the archetypal images created by the children. Sandplay has developed as a psychotherapeutic approach in its own right, practiced by Jungians and others, including drama therapists (see Landy 1994).

More than viewing play as a practical solution to a personal crisis, Jung discovered at this juncture an original alternative to the Freudian verbal method of accessing and analyzing the unconscious. The alternative was based in imagery and action, as clients not only invoke images of the personal and collective unconscious, but also act on the images.

Active Imagination

This discovery became Jung's operative therapeutic method, developed over a long career. The treatment method went by many names, beginning as the transcendent function, then picture method, active fantasy, dialectical method, technique of the descent, and finally, active imagination. The first time he referred to active imagination was in London in 1935, where he gave his famous Tavistock Lectures.

Jung was more articulate in lecturing about the method than in describing it in his writing, but in a publication edited by dance therapist Joan Chodorow (1997), *Jung on Active Imagination*, we find many of the published explications of the approach. One of the most straightforward descriptions is from his collected letters (Jung 1947 in Chodorow 1997):

> You start with any image, for instance just with that yellow mass in your dream. Contemplate it and carefully observe how the picture begins to unfold or to change. Don't try to make it into something, just do nothing but observe what its spontaneous changes are. Any mental picture you contemplate in this way will sooner or later change through a spontaneous association that causes a slight alteration of the picture . . . note all these changes and eventually step into the picture yourself, and if it is a speaking figure at all then say what you have to say to that figure and listen to what he or she has to say (164).

As Jung got older, he began to let go of vestiges from his earliest training as a psychoanalyst. Over time, he would occasionally resist verbally analyzing his patient's images, believing that the images carry their own meaning and healing potential. When properly contemplated, the images transform and lead to a shift of understanding on the part of the patient. The ultimate goal of the therapeutic process, according to Jung, is individuation, that is, becoming whole through an integration of conscious and unconscious experience. Active imagination is the method toward realizing that goal.

Chodorow (1997) speaks of two basic stages of Jung's method. The first concerns an activation of the unconscious and the second "coming to terms with the unconscious" (10). She mentions that once an unconscious experience is activated, it can take many years to work through. Jung himself devoted more than fifty years of work with images from his unconscious that first appeared early in his childhood (see Jung 1963).

Others have attempted to quantify the steps of active imagination. Jung's student and later colleague, Marie-Louise von Franz (1980), offered the following:

1. Empty the "mad mind" of the ego;
2. Let an unconscious fantasy image arise;
3. Give it some form of expression; and
4. Ethical confrontation.

At a later point von Franz called for clients to apply this work to their everyday lives.

A second attempt at specifying stages was made by Robert Johnson (1986). He proposed the following:

1. The invitation (invite the unconscious);
2. The dialogue (dialogue and experience);
3. The values (add the ethical element); and
4. The rituals (make it concrete with physical ritual).

Jung, himself, resisted such a reductive approach, keeping open all the expressive possibilities of engaging with imagery. As Jung's primary nonverbal means of expression was through visual art, we find most references in his writing to that form, especially in relationship to working with the symbol of the mandala (see Jung 1933/1950, 1950). And yet Jung also makes reference to clients and to himself engaging with imagery through dance (Jung 1928–1930, 304) and writing (Chodorow 1997). Although Jung does not make specific reference to drama as a form of engagement with images, he writes eloquently about the process of playing and dialoguing with images (Jung 1928; Jung 1933/1950; Chodorow 1997), two key aspects of the drama therapy process.

Many post-Jungians reported experiences in therapy working with clients through story, drama, and narrative (see, for example, von Franz 1980 and Hillman 1983a). In the work of Dora Kalff and many other Jungian-based sandplay therapists, we see a clear example of active imagination applied to the therapy of children and later, adults.

Although Freud and his earlier colleagues worked with and through the unconscious, attempting to reveal and transform repressed affects, they did so through verbal and rational means. Freud worked most closely with affective experience when collaborating with Breuer in investigating hypnosis as a therapeutic technique, a process Breuer learned from Charcot in Paris in the 1880s. However, Freud abandoned this approach, deeming it too shallow, with no evidence of a lasting effect. It could also be true that Freud distrusted and feared the cathartic effect of hypnosis as it released an uncomfortable and often dramatic expression of feeling.

The uniqueness of Jung's approach was not only in working through imagery, the content of the unconscious, but also in working directly with emotion. Again, he used his own process as an exemplar for further work with patients. During the period of crisis initiated by his break from Freud, Jung had a series of highly disturbing and prophetic dreams, which coincided with the beginning of World War I. At this time, in 1914, he attempted to make sense of his constant state of tension through recalling his dream images, playing the building game, and writing down his fantasies. When feeling quite overwhelmed by anxiety, he practiced yoga to calm himself down enough to continue his active engagement with his disturbing images.

At this point he realized that not only was it crucial to engage with the emotions, but also to search for the images that lay hidden beneath the emotions. Emotional experience, then, was a precursor to the invocation of imagery. The imagery would then be the object of engagement, and from that active engagement and dialogue, the person would begin to discover a greater sense of balance. It is important to note that Jung did not dismiss affective experience once it had opened the path to the imagery, but rather viewed the two parts of the process as complimentary and reflexive, with affect leading to imagery and engagement with imagery enriching and clarifying the affective experience. He criticized Freud for separating affect from cognition in his free association method (Jung 1916/1958):

> Fantasy must be allowed the freest possible play, yet in not such a manner that it leaves the orbit of its object, namely the affect, by setting off a kind of "chain reaction" association process. The "free association" as Freud called it, leads away from the object to all sorts of complexes, and one can never be sure that they relate to the affect and are not displacements which have appeared in its stead (par. 167).

Jung noted in his 1916 paper, "The Transcendent Function," that work with imagery generated through dreams, fantasies, and play, both begins in emotional experience and returns to the affective source, expanding and illuminating it. In his own way, he was refuting Descartes' dictum of *cogito ergo sum*, which privileged mind over affect and body, providing a legacy still in effect in the medical profession. As we shall see later, that legacy has been soundly challenged in contemporary studies in neuroscience, most notably by Antonio Demasio (1994) in *Descartes' Error*.

Archetypes and Personality Types

When Jung wrote about his personal experience and that of his clients, he often used language highly charged with archetypal symbols. In analyzing the symbols over many years and contemplating them in the light of his rich study of ritual, myth, spirituality, and culture, Jung developed his theory of a collective unconscious and its archetypes. This line of reasoning ran counter to Freud's understanding of an individual unconscious whose contents were repressed wishes and fears as well as life and death instincts. In Freud's system, these psychic contents appeared to be universally present in the mind of all human beings. However, their origins and symbolic referents lay in individual sexual development. The origin of archetypes, according to Jung, lay in the collective experience of all humankind and could be read in peoples' expressive actions and artifacts.

Reading a Jungian description of a dream or fantasy feels similar to reading a poem by William Blake or viewing a mandala sand painting by a Buddhist monk. It is symbolic, expressionistic, nonliteral, and nonlinear. Here is an example of a fantasy offered by one of Jung's patients (1928):

> I climbed the mountain and came to a place where I saw seven red stones in front of me, seven on either side, and seven behind me. I stood in the middle of this quadrangle. . . . I tried to lift the four stones nearest me. In doing so I discovered that these stones were the pedestals of four statues of gods buried upside down in the earth. I dug them up and arranged them about me so that I was standing in the middle of them. . . . Then I saw that beyond, encircling the four gods, a ring of flame had formed. . . . I said . . . I must go into the fire myself . . . The fiery ring drew together to one immense blue flame that carried me up from the earth (par. 366).

And here is a personal excerpt from Jung's (1963) earliest recalled dream, one that would occupy him throughout his life:

> I was in this meadow. Suddenly I discovered a dark . . . stone-lined hole in the ground. . . . I saw a stone stairway leading down. . . . I descended (12).

Jung discovered a mysterious room with a throne at one end. A huge phallus stood erect on the throne. A single eye sat on top, looking upward. Jung noted "an aura of brightness above the eye." Although the phallus did not move, Jung was frightened that it might attack him. Before he awoke, he heard his mother call out: "Yes, just look at him. That is the man-eater!" (12).

In analyzing these images of life journeys, the first, an ascent taken by a woman, the second, a descent taken by a child, Jung summoned his full knowledge of archetypes. That knowledge was taken from various sources—alchemy and its notion of quaternary, religion, mysticism, and etymology. In the first example, Jung pointed to the meaning of the climb as a journey toward a midpoint or alchemical "squaring of the circle" (Jung 1928, par. 367). He viewed the four points of the quadrangle and four gods as representing the personality with its four functions. Jung named these functions intuition, sensation, feeling, and thinking. Jung viewed the patient as moving toward individuation by overcoming the gods and daring to enter the fire of the unconscious. As in alchemy where base metal is transformed into gold, she was transformed through the mysterious experience and emerged intact.

In reading the second example, Jung recalled a dream he had when he was three or four. He saw the descent as one into his developing unconscious. The adult Jung compared the phallus to a subterranean god and reflected upon his early association of Jesus with death. He linked the bright eye of the phallus to its etymology from the Greek meaning shining and bright. And later, he connected the man-eater image to the symbol of cannibalism, an idea that he discovered while reading an interpretation of the Catholic Mass.

From these and thousands of fantasies and dreams, Jung abstracted certain recurring motifs present in the collective unconscious. Over time he categorized them according to their archetypal structures and functions. Several major archetypes identified by Jung included the self, the shadow, the persona, the anima and the animus, and the psychopomp. The self is a figure of wholeness and represents the full personality including the conscious ego and the unconscious. The shadow is the figure of the denied aspects of the self. The persona is the social mask that one plays in relation to others. The anima is the female side of the male, and the animus is the male side of the female. The psychopomp is a spirit guide who leads one into the underworld or links the natural and supernatural worlds.

Alongside the archetypes, Jung and many post-Jungians (see, for example, Hillman 1983a) identified a number of motifs or complexes integrating culture with psychology. They included the great mother, the father, the child or *puer*, the maiden, the wise old man, the hero, the quest, among many others. These elements further clarified Jung's approach to an archetypal understanding of the collective unconscious.

Throughout a career of more than fifty years, Jung was sometimes contradictory and confounding in his many conceptualizations, especially those pertaining to archetypes and complexes. It is very difficult to find a systematic presentation of these elements in Jung's writings and, in fact, he wrote (Jung 1969) that there are "as many archetypes as there are typical situations in life" (48). To fully appreciate Jung's worldview, it is important to note that he remained an iconoclast who would just as readily break with his own ideas as he would break with those of others.

Perhaps Jung's most lasting contribution to psychotherapy was his work on a typology of personality differences. Among his most important books was *Psychological Types,* published in 1921, and marking the end of his "confrontation with the unconscious," as he referred to his psychological crisis after splitting with Freud.

To understand Jung's prodigious work on psychological types, one needs to be aware of Jung's underlying notion of dialectic, the principal that typologies of all kinds are driven by the interplay of polar opposites. In *Psychological Types* and related work, Jung pointed to two basic attitude types: those of introversion and extroversion. Jung made the point that these attitudes are expressed in relation to an object and that one's expression of the attitude can be viewed in terms of its flow toward or away from its corresponding object. Consistent with his notion of collective experience, he viewed these attitudes as universally pervasive. He also viewed the attitudes as categories that are of a higher level than those of the psychological functions.

Typical extroverts are those connected to the world of objects in an open and accessible manner. They engage in an ongoing dialogue with the outside world, believing that their actions will influence others and the actions of others will in turn affect them in meaningful ways. They appear self-assured, open-minded, playful, and action-oriented.

Typical introverts tend to move away from external objects, withdrawing from dialogue and connection. Turning inward, they tend to be inaccessible and autonomous, deriving pleasure from an engagement with their own thoughts, feelings, and images.

But Jung went beyond establishing a dichotomy by pointing to the possibility of both extraverts and introverts living a more balanced existence. For Jung, the attitudes expressed in conscious behavior suggest counterattitudes at the unconscious level. To explain this idea of balance, Jung (1921/ 1971) offered the concept of compensation. He wrote:

> The more one-sided the conscious attitude, the more antagonistic are the contents arising from the unconscious, so that we may speak of a real opposition between the two. . . . As a rule, the unconscious compensation does not run counter to consciousness, but is rather a balancing . . . of the conscious orientation. . . . The aim of analytical therapy, therefore, is the realization of unconscious contents in order that compensation may be re-established (pars. 694–95).

Thus for Jung, a balanced life is marked by a self-regulating process that promotes a fluidity between conscious and unconscious experience, a movement that allows one type of person to build an internal attitudinal bridge that extends to the opposite shore. If there is a core understanding to be extracted from Jung's voluminous ideas, it may be based in his life-long quest to engage with the implications of difference, opposition, and paradox, the seeming contradictions when two objects or ideas intersect. One of his clearest statements (1955) is the following: "Just as there is no energy without the tension of opposites, so there can be no consciousness without the perception of differences" (*Collected Works* 14, par. 603).

Having created a typology based in two attitudes, Jung recognized its limitations. He (1921/1971) noted: "Strictly speaking, there are no introverts or extraverts pure and simple, but only introverted and extraverted function-types" (par. 913). Jung viewed function as a basic means of expressing intrapsychic, interpersonal, and extrapersonal experiences. He pointed, somewhat tentatively, to four basic function types, noting that his choice of types sprung from his many years of clinical observation. The four are sensation, intuition, thinking, and feeling. Drawing upon his notion of polarities, Jung noted the paired opposites, thinking and feeling, as rational or judging functions, and the pair of sensation and intuition as irrational or perceiving functions.

Thinking and feeling are rational and judging as they both concern one's ability to evaluate a situation. They are, however, different in their means of evaluating a situation. The former, thinking, evaluates a situation by means of objective, logical criteria. The latter, feeling, does so in a more personal way, judging by means of affective and subjective criteria. For Jung, all functions can be charged with emotion. The feeling function, then, is not only characterized by degree of emotion, but by a preference to engage with others, to openly express personal feelings, and to make sense of the world through subjective means.

Thinking types are more analytical and scientific in their worldview. They view the complexities of life as problems to be solved. They engage with others in a reasonable way, ever trying to understand personal, interpersonal, and even transpersonal experience in a logical, methodical fashion.

As to the irrational and perceiving functions, Jung pointed to one's direct experience of engaging with the world, regardless of one's need to make sense of it. The sensation function leads one to take in the world through the senses. It is primarily a conscious activity and is irrational by virtue of not requiring any thoughtful action on the part of the perceiver. Persons dominated by the sensing function are straightforward and practical. They tend to focus on what is observable and even obvious. They tend to carefully listen to what others have to say and to scrutinize all that lies within their visual field.

The intuitive type is more inwardly directed. This type is most connected to unconscious experience and thus maintains a privileged position in Jung's typology, as it best describes the dominant function of Jung, himself. Intuitives tend to be ones who think out of the box and rather than focusing upon the details of a problem, look for a fuller, more universal picture. As sensation is grounded and attached to the empirical world, intuition is noted by its flights of fancy and expression through imagery and symbolism.

Taken together, the four functions present a total view of the personality. In Jung's (*CW* 6) words: "Sensation establishes what is actually present, thinking enables us to recognize its meaning, feeling tells us its value, and intuition points to possibilities as to whence it came and wither it is going in a given situation" (par. 958).

When integrating the four functions with the two attitudes, eight personality types emerge. However, Jung's system was even more complex as he introduced the notion of auxiliary functions. By this, he meant that any given function can serve as superior when expressed consciously, in either its extroverted and introverted attitude. At the same time, its counterfunctions and attitude appear in the unconscious and serve to compensate for the superior functions and attitude. When pairing the conscious functions and attitude with their unconscious counterparts, Jung, embracing his dialectical point of view, believed functions can only be paired with those that are opposite. If one primarily expresses oneself in a feeling way, for example, the unconscious counterpart would be either sensation or intuition. Feeling and thinking, both rational and judging functions, can coexist when both are expressed as dominant or primary functions. But when one is primary, its secondary counterpart must be from an irrational and perceiving function, that is, from either sensation or intuition.

Given this complex system of personality types and its theoretical implications for an understanding of analytical psychology, how can it be applied to clinical treatment? One simple answer is that an understanding of psychological type can help inform the therapist's understanding of the client and point the way toward treatment strategies most suitable for that type of client. Knowing that a client is, for example, a dominant extraverted thinking-type with sensing, and assuming that there coexists an auxiliary, unconscious potential for the same person to express himself as an introverted feeling-type with intuition, the therapist would not necessarily dive right into expressive, symbolic work, but rather start at a more external and verbal level, slowly moving into an engagement of the active imagination.

On a more practical level, Jung's typology has spawned the birth of a major assessment instrument, the Myers-Briggs Type Indicator (MBTI), which has been used for decades as a personality test. MBTI is used with individuals and organizations including the military, businesses, and major corporations. Some have criticized MBTI as too reductive (see Spoto 1995), limiting the complexity of Jung's theory of types to its conscious applications only. A second assessment instrument, the Singer-Loomis Inventory of Personality (SLIP), is scored in a more open fashion, attempting to identify a cognitive type as extracted from Jung's original eight psychological types. Because of its open nature and often ambiguous results, SLIP is used much less frequently.

Taken as a whole, Jung's prodigious work presages later developments in many forms of expressive and action therapy, especially art therapy where aspects of the collective unconscious are expressed in visual form. As we will see, the theory and practice of drama therapy in its several forms owes much to Jung's notion of psychological types, polarities of attitude and function, archetypes of the collective unconscious, and active imagination.

OTTO RANK—BEYOND FREUD AND BEYOND PSYCHOLOGY

By 1905, the young Otto Rank had studied and developed a deep attachment to the work of Sigmund Freud. Barely twenty-one and a gifted autodidact and writer, Rank approached his intellectual mentor with his first manuscript in hand, *The Artist*, a treatise on psychoanalysis and the creative process. Within a year, not only was Rank a regular at the meetings of the Wednesday Society, but he was appointed by his beloved mentor as its secretary. Freud's almost parental affection for Rank shepherded him through his doctoral studies at the University of Vienna, his training as a lay analyst, and his prolific research and writing. In fact, Rank worked alongside Freud in revising all editions subsequent to 1911 of Freud's masterpiece, *The Interpretation of Dreams*. In doing so, Rank had access to the depths of Freud's own inner life as expressed through his dreams. In 1914, Freud commissioned Rank to write two chapters on myth as part of the latest edition of his book, and with that, elevated Rank as coauthor.

Rank died young, at fifty-five, just one month after Freud's death. In his brief lifespan, however, marred and/or buoyed by his split from Freud, he offered a legacy that would influence generations of existential and humanistic psychotherapists as well as practitioners of brief therapy and creative arts therapy.

Rank's final book, published posthumously, was called *Beyond Psychology* (1941). In the preface, Rank wrote:

> Man is born beyond psychology and he dies beyond it but he can *live* beyond it only through vital experience of his own—in religious terms, through revelation, conversion or re-birth. My own life work is completed, the subjects of my former interest, the hero, the artist, the neurotic appear once more upon the stage, not only as participants in the eternal drama of life but after the curtain has gone down, unmasked, undressed, unpretentious, not as punctured illusions, but as human beings who require no interpreter (16).

In is no surprise that Rank invokes a theatrical metaphor in introducing his final masterpiece, as his preoccupations were dramatic in scope. He began his career as a psychoanalyst thinking about the problem of creativity and the notion of mental illness as a failed attempt at engaging in a willful creative act. His interests took him into studies of the myth of the birth of the hero, the Lohengrin saga, the psychology of literary creation, the figure of the double as revealed in cinema and literature, and many other arenas related to mythology and creativity. In the end, as suggested by the above citation, Rank viewed the mythic and creative types as human beings after all, unmediated by all intellectual attempts to imprison them within theories and metaphors. It could be that toward the end of his life, reeling from his forced exile from his once beloved mentor and psychoanalytic colleagues, he viewed himself as both a revered and reviled actor who, once off the main stage of psychoanalysis, longed for the peace that only comes in letting go of all desire to perform and to be applauded.

The Trauma of Birth

The beginning of Rank's separation from Freud came with the publication of *The Trauma of Birth* in 1924. At the time, he and Freud were devoted to, perhaps even dependent upon one another. The publication coincided with two events. The first was the publication of Freud's *The Ego and the Id*. And the second was the hospitalization of Freud. The initial reason concerned surgery for cancer of the jaw, a debilitating condition that would leave him in great pain and would compromise his ability to hear and to speak. Secondarily, while hospitalized, Freud had another secret surgery, a vasectomy, which he imagined to be a form of castration but which he chose because it was considered by physicians of the time to be a method of improving vision and enhancing the healing of cancerous tissue.

Rank's published thesis was a direct challenge to Freud's concept of the Oedipus complex and its central figure of the castrating father. Freud expounded on the image of the father who appears from the oedipal nightmare ready to punish the guilt-ridden child who dared to desire his mother. Freud applauded Rank's thesis at first, assured that it was simply a supplement to his own opus. But behind the scenes, the master was less secure and jokingly expressed his castration fears by invoking the biblical characters of David and Goliath. In a letter to Rank (Lieberman 1985), Freud wrote: "And now everything falls into place around this point, that you [Rank] are the dreaded David who, with his *Trauma der Geburt*, will succeed in deprecating my work" (205).

Central to Rank's cataclysmic book was the notion that the moment of birth marks not only a physical separation of child from mother, but also tells a psychological and mythological story of the loss of innocence and the struggle for independence. Rank stated that the birth trauma and its manifestations in early forms of separation anxiety marked a pre-oedipal phase in the psychological development of the human being. Freud's inner circle perceived this theoretical innovation as a direct challenge to the orthodoxy of the Oedipus complex and its focus upon the primacy of the father. Although Freud as the father of psychoanalysis was overtly accepting of his younger protégé's radical ideas, he was persuaded by his secret committee that Rank's ideas were heretical. Eventually, the Goliath that was Freud rejected the David that was Rank, preserving his status and leading to a diminution of the legacy of Otto Rank within psychoanalytic circles.

And yet Rank's ideas persisted and were taken up by progressive therapists like Rollo May, whose concepts of existential anxiety and ontological guilt were recapitulations of Rank's notions of the dual fears of life and death. Paul Goodman (Perls, Hefferline, and Goodman 1951) acknowledged his debt to Rank in his early formulations with Fritz Perls of the creative method of Gestalt therapy. And Carl Rogers spoke openly of the influence of Rank on his developing ideas of a relational form of therapy that proceeds beyond the hierarchical and patriarchic structures of classical psychoanalysis.

On Theory and Practice

Rank has influenced the action psychotherapists in writing about both the theory and practice of psychotherapy. In terms of the latter, Rank (1996) outlined the steps in therapeutic treatment that proceed from his theory of the birth trauma and that, in part, remain close to the steps of classical psychoanalysis. The process begins with "the freeing of libidinal mother fixation" (72), then proceeds to strengthening the ego through a form of reeducation. This step occurs as the client engages in a transferential relationship with the therapist who analyzes the transference and encourages identification with himself as "an adjusted representative of the outside world" (72). Finally, the identification is sublimated by the client into a healthier image of himself.

Rank noted that to ensure that psychoanalysis has lasting results, not only must the dependency inherent in the transference be resolved, but also that the transformation from dependence to independence must be sustained over time. That is done by removing the conditions that have led to neurotic symptoms. Doing so, urged Rank, required more than verbal, cognitive means. Rank, like scores of action psychotherapists influenced by his example, called for an emotional reexperiencing through an active process on the part of the client. Like psychodrama and other forms of action therapy, where a client is encouraged to replay an unresolved issue, Rank (1996) believed "we expose a patient in analysis to his primal trauma and allow him to live through the experience again" (74). For Rank, the exposure occurs in the transference where the therapist takes on the role of the primal mother, and the therapist helps the client symbolically cut the "psychological umbilical chord" (74), thus freeing up new possibilities of positive ego formation and self-reliance.

Although Rank did not go so far in his technique to actually dramatize the symbolic cutting, he did recognize that the healing needed to occur in the irrational, unconscious part of the psyche. Rank rejected Freud's (*Standard Edition* 1933) notion that "understanding and cure almost coincide" (145). Rank pointed out the contradiction within psychoanalysis of a psychology of consciousness pretending to be one of the unconscious, of an art pretending to be a science. Like his predecessor Jung, Rank ultimately embraced paradox, affect, unconscious experience, and chance as factors that determine psychic life. And like those who later became existential and humanistic psychotherapists, Rank (1996) noted that insight and understanding do not precede change but rather follow "the emotional and actual working-out of a problem" (223). When a psychotherapist works the other way round, the life of the unconscious is diminished. For Rank, awareness sprung from action.

Unlike his analytic predecessors, Rank argued for a psychotherapy more centered in the emotional experience of the patient, the relationship of patient and therapist, the present moment, and the active participation of the patient in directing his own treatment. This latter point is reinforced by Rank's notion of the will (see Rank 1936/1978), which he viewed as the creative principle denoting the individuality of each person. Rank (1996) referred to will as "the supreme autonomic organizing force in the individual" (268). In reference to the creative principle, Rank referred to the artist as a willful personality type who has discovered a way to re-create and thus objectify himself through his works of art. The neurotic, on the other hand, is one who has the creative urge but is unable to find an appropriate form in which to re-create himself. His impulse to create remains stuck on his own ego. As such, it finds expression in negative symptoms and self-destructive thoughts of fear and guilt.

Rank's clearest discussion of the action-based practice of psychotherapy appears in a book coauthored by Sandor Ferenczi, *The Development of Psycho-Analysis* (1925/1986), which will be discussed below.

Although persuasively arguing for a theoretically neutral practice, Rank also presented a number of theoretical concepts that are crucial to an understanding of action psychotherapy. A central one is that of the double, a concept that links two of Rank's favorite roles, that of the artist and that of the hero.

The Double

In explaining the double as a symbol of both the immortal self and the harbinger of death, Rank (1941) set himself apart from Freud and Jung, looking beyond psychology to explain human behavior. Rank offered a worldview based in "the conception of the supernatural" (62). He rejected Freud's notion that behavior is driven by the intellectual ego and instincts. And although he recognized Jung's spiritual bias, he rejected Jung's notion of the archetypes of the collective unconscious. Rank argued that since the earliest civilizations, human beings needed to deny a biological, natural understanding of life because to do so implied an acceptance of death. To compensate for the reality of death, early human beings adopted a magical view to assure themselves of eternal life. For Rank, this magical worldview formed the foundation of culture, a process of building symbolic structures to pass on traditions and legacies and to assure immortality. As culture and "the civilized self" (Rank 1941, 63) developed, they assumed three layers: the supernatural, the social, and the psychological. All three are predicated on the ultimate human need to cope with the persistent awareness of death and fear of the eternal loss of the self in all its forms.

In coping, argued Rank (1941), human beings have split the "over-civilized ego" (65) in two, creating the double. The two parts of the double are symbolized in folk beliefs and tales, literature and film, religion and psychology. Rank mentioned the early split between the body and soul and pointed to traditional superstitions regarding the shadow, which many early cultures envisioned as the soul. These superstitions included a fear to be contaminated by another's shadow or to allow one's own shadow to accidentally fall on certain foods or people. Some believed that the shadow can be wounded, causing potential harm or death to its owner.

The shadow as double is a complex image, not only representing the death of its counterpart, the living self, but also its eternal life, as represented in the soul. Rank mentioned that in some traditional cultures, illness is diagnosed by the size of the shadow, a short one indicating sickness, a long one indicating vigor and health. He gave the example of a dying person who is brought out into the sunlight in order to cast a shadow, signifying the soul, so that he is prepared to depart into the spiritual world.

After an exhaustive review of folk and literary examples of the duality of the shadow, the soul and of the self, Rank concluded that human beings invented religion to contain their belief in the soul of the dead, and invented psychology to contain their belief in the soul of the living. These two disciplines intersect and deepen with the advent of Christianity. From the early part of the first millennium, the notion of immortality becomes irrevocably associated with morality, the touch of evil. Now, the soul is not only long *and* short, vital *and* mortal, but also good *or* bad, most often seen as an either/or proposition. The figure of evil becomes the devil whom Rank (1941) viewed as "a personification of the moralized double" (76).

similar to object theorists? godmother / Bad mother

The Artist

Rank described the function of artist in terms of his understanding of the double. The artist draws upon the traditional irrational superstitions and re-creates them in a rational form that mirrors his own fears of death, struggles with good and evil, and hopes for immortality. Rank made reference to classical literary works such as Goethe's *Faust,* Stevenson's *Strange Case of Dr. Jekyll and Mr. Hyde,* Poe's "William Wilson," and Dostoyevsky's "The Double." To highlight the meaning of the double in these literary sources, Rank cited a passage from a Dostoyevsky story, "The Youth," where the main character proclaims: "I seem to duplicate myself, to divide myself in two parts—actually double myself and I am terrified of this doubling" (1941, 82). Then later in the story, Dostoyevsky provided a commentary, almost clinical in scope, attesting to the modern function of the double:

> What is the double really? He is—at least according to a medical book of an expert that I consulted lately on this subject—nothing but the first stage of insanity which may end in disaster, a dualism between feeling and willing (82).

This modern interpretation views the double and its manifestations in splits between feeling and thought, irrationality and rationality, sanity and insanity.

Extending this discussion, Rank pointed to the concept of twinship, another manifestation of the spiritual foundation of human behavior. In ancient cultures, twins were venerated for their supernatural powers, especially their gifts of divination. They were also viewed as artisans whose responsibility was no less than founding cities and, indeed, originating cultures. Rank makes reference to the cult of the twins Castor and Pollux in the mythological history of ancient Greece, and to Romulus and Remus as the spiritual founders of Rome. Rank spoke of the magical birth of twins and their ability to create new objects and institutions in nature, including agriculture and cities. Twinship embodied in two beings, according to Rank, led to the figure of the singular hero who embodied both the mortal and the immortal soul.

Rank believed that the hero as doubly mortal and immortal became the primary subject of the artist in ancient Greece. He went on the say that the artist fashioned himself after the hero, becoming the hero's spiritual double. His function was not only to immortalize the deeds of the hero, but also himself as the one who immortalizes the hero's deeds in words and in stone.

Rank was preoccupied with matters of the spiritual origins of the human mind, especially in his later years as he looked beyond psychology for answers to questions of existence. In looking to the roles of the hero and the artist, in looking to concepts of the double and shadow, in looking to reli-

gion and mythology, to narrative and film as viable sources of existential in-
quiry, Rank moved beyond his mentor, Freud. To be sure, his interests and
concerns were more in keeping with those of Jung. But more so, Rank's concerns mirrored those of traditional shamanic healers who begin with an understanding of a dual reality, an intimate confluence of the material world
and its double, the spiritual world, and who practice their healing more as
intuitives who seek to repair a rupture in the whole fabric, than as thinkers
who seek to reduce the whole to its parts.

Although there is no evidence of a direct influence, Rank's ideas found
new life in the work of such action psychotherapists as Moreno, who developed a psychodramatic technique of doubling, Perls, who sought to integrate discrepant parts of the personality, and Landy, who attempted to
conceptualize balance as an integration of role and counterrole.

SANDOR FERENCZI AND OTTO RANK—
THE DEVELOPMENT OF PSYCHO-ANALYSIS

Sandor Ferenczi, a friend and collaborator of Otto Rank, was a Hungarian neurologist whose early medical and therapeutic interests were in working with disenfranchised people, notably prostitutes in Budapest in the late
nineteenth century. He became a close associate and friend of Freud, even
closer as Freud attempted to cope with the defection of Carl Jung. Ferenczi
held a privileged position within the inner circle of psychoanalysts as a regular member of the Wednesday Society, as a brief analysand of Freud, and
as a companion of Freud on his first lecture tour to America.

Some of Ferenczi's innovative ideas on theory and practice will be elabo-
rated below. For now, we will look at the major collaboration between Ferenczi and Rank, which marked another challenge to Freud's orthodoxy, especially in clinical practice. In daring to be clinically innovative, Ferenczi,
like Rank, was criticized by Freud's committee, of which he was an active
member. However, Ferenczi was not as vilified as Rank, whose theoretical
crimes were unforgivable. The ideas presented here are from the collabora-
tive book titled *The Development of Psycho-Analysis*, published in 1925. Ferenczi, intending to write a "state of the art" book, was responsible for most
of this brief volume, with Rank contributing a didactic chapter.

The authors began by setting a framework for practice, noting that Freud
and other early writers, immersed in theory, neglected the development of
clinical practice. Referencing Freud's 1914 article, "Remembering, Repeating
and Working Through," which they viewed as his most current technical
work, the authors critiqued Freud's insistence that the goal of psychoanalysis is remembering and that repeating is a resistance. For Ferenczi and Rank,
repetition was encouraged as it provided a path along which themes

emerged, and that as these themes were repeated, the client was led toward remembering and then understanding the nature of the theme. The major technical innovation offered by the authors was that in order to invoke the repetition and the working through of past distressing memories, the analyst took an active stance in relation to the analysand. In this early book, Ferenczi and Rank first referred to their technique as "active therapy," still many decades removed from the term "action psychotherapy," but clearly setting the stage for further innovations in clinical practice.

In describing the enactment and repetition of past wounds, the authors (1925/1986) expanded on Freud's notion of transference, discussing the process in dramatic terms:

> The analyst plays all possible roles for the unconscious of the patient. . . . Particularly important is the role of the two parental images—father and mother—in which the analyst constantly alternates (41).

Although their approach was verbal, it also implied a creative process as a client played out the same pathological action, like a painter or writer returning again and again to the same image or motif in order to discover the precise form of expression and thereby gain mastery.

Further distinguishing their approach from Freud's, Ferenczi and Rank referred to Freud's early work in catharsis, where the goal of treatment, often through hypnosis, was a mental catharsis, that is, a moment of vividly recalling the past. The recall, if sufficiently charged, sometimes led to a corresponding emotional discharge. For the authors, a more effective therapeutic approach was for the affective experience to precede the recall. By working this way, they argued, the "pathologic complexes are reawakened and translated into remembering by being made conscious during the experience without permitting the time and possibility for repression" (26).

Ferenczi and Rank, thus, do not diminish the power of memory; they reconceive it as another, deeper form of repetition and recall. Although they do not speak of their work in aesthetic terms, their analytic efforts compare favorably to the creative process, in that the artist often discovers something of the personal or collective past through a direct, active engagement with feelings and images in the present moment. In the performing arts, all aspects of performance are based upon repetition and rehearsal. Performing artists master an action through rehearsal before they are ready to repeat that action to an audience in present time, as if for the first time. If the artwork is a play based upon a known myth or story, as were all the ancient Greek dramas, the goal of the actor is to bring the old story to life in a new way, hoping not only to please an audience, but to awaken them to a deeper meaning of the story as it impacts their lives. Like the psychoanalytic process suggested by Ferenczi and Rank, the performing artist proceeds from a rehearsal process involving affective memory and repetition, to the presentation of a collective memory, enacted in present time.

The notion of the primacy of the present moment was a radical departure from Freud's theory of infantile sexuality and even Jung's theory of the collective unconscious. Although Ferenczi and Rank did not reject the importance of historical factors in causing certain pathological conditions, they made clear that these conditions were most available to treatment when expressed in the present moment of the transference. They explained:

> The past and the repressed must find their representative factors in the present and the conscious (preconscious) in order that they may be affectively experienced and develop further. . . . Affects in order to work convincingly must first be revived, that is made actually present . . . which means changing the attempts of the patient to repeat into remembering (37–38).

Not only does this point of view set the stage for many of the humanistic approaches to psychotherapy, such as Carl Rogers's client-centered therapy and Fritz Perls's Gestalt therapy, but also for the creative and action forms, such as psychodrama and drama therapy, where experiences from the past are reenacted in the immediacy of the present in order to revision and integrate the past. Psychoanalyst Daniel Stern, best known for his research in the psychological significance of early attachments (2000), champions the importance of the present moment in psychotherapy, drawing examples from narrative and drama therapy (D. Stern 2004).

Before departing from this significant collaboration, let us look at several other principles articulated by Ferenczi and Rank that presage further innovations in the action psychotherapies. The authors critiqued the primacy of verbal interpretation as the *sine qua non* of therapeutic techniques. They appeared to take on a postmodern perspective as they suggested that symbols need to be understood within a subjective, relativistic context. Furthermore, they pointed to the importance not only of the verbal content of the patient's expression, but also the nonverbal form: "In an analysis fine details, apparent incidentals such as voice, gesture, expression, are so important" (29).

Also, the authors pointed to the relationship of patient and therapist as a primary factor in therapeutic change. They noted the human qualities and foibles of the therapist, speaking directly to the dangers of narcissistic countertransference, that is, moments where the therapist takes on the mantle of infallibility and unconsciously blocks the patient from exploring certain threatening affects.

In speaking about the importance of working through the transference, the authors again returned to Ferenczi's notion of the active therapist. They characterized activity as a therapist's willingness to take on and even to play out certain "roles which the unconscious of the patient and his tendency to flight prescribe" (43–44). In this unconscious role-play, the therapist is able to experience with the patient past traumatic experiences and help the patient work them through in the present. Although there is no physical reenactment of the past trauma as in dramatic forms of psychotherapy, the action is marked by an ability of the therapist to understand it through taking on a counterrole in relationship to the patient, and from this perspective to help the patient better understand and then transform his dilemma.

Ferenczi and Rank also pointed out the limits of theory, again critiquing Freud for his focus upon ideas often at the expense of the needs of human beings. They wrote: "The theoretic analyst always runs the danger of looking . . . for arguments to prove the correctness of a new statement, while he thinks that he is promoting the process of curing a neurosis" (52). While supporting the importance of theory as a framework that informs practice, they also reminded the reader that for the process to remain fluid, insights gleaned from practice must also lead to revisions of theory.

They argued further against mandated prolonged periods of time in psychoanalytic treatment, taking the position that longer treatments should only be motivated by what is "necessary and unavoidable in obtaining a better result" (53).

As they neared the end of their brief book, Ferenczi and Rank returned temporarily to Freud's early work with Breuer in hypnosis. They reminded the reader why Freud ultimately abandoned hypnosis—because it did not appear to reveal "all the vital psychic motives" (61). And yet they pointed to a major advantage of hypnosis as a means of helping a client move quickly beyond cognitive resistances and into affect. Although they viewed Freud's methods of free association and analysis of transference as in-depth ways of exploring psychological motives, they speculated about the possibility of combining hypnosis and free association, blending an altered state of consciousness with a fully conscious state, blending experience with reflection upon experience, affect with cognition, imagination with reality. They looked to a time when psychoanalysis was practiced by nonmedical therapists, when biological and social factors informed its theory and practice, and when various disciplines collaborated on solving a central question posed by Freud—how can repressed unconscious experience be brought to conscious awareness?

Both shamans and contemporary action psychotherapists have answered this question by building a bridge between imagination and reality, inviting clients into an altered state of consciousness to gather the power necessary to meet the demands of reality upon their return. Like Freud, Ferenczi and Rank attempted to buttress the consciousness of wounded individuals. They differed from their mentor in their methods of treatment that pointed to both traditional healers and expressive therapists to come, all of whom use active, creative, and often cathartic approaches. In the final paragraph of their slender volume, speculating on the future of psychoanalysis, they wrote:

> Under the influence of this increase in consciousness the physician, who has developed from the medicine man, sorcerer, charlatan, and magic healer, and who at his best often remains somewhat an artist, will develop increasing knowledge of mental mechanisms, and in some sense prove the saying that medicine is the oldest art and the youngest science (68).

SANDOR FERENCZI

Ferenczi, as mentioned above, is credited with many of the ideas expressed in *The Development of Psycho-Analysis*. There are several other theoretical and clinical ideas that he advocated throughout his career that also serve as models for those who developed holistic, creative, and action approaches to treatment.

Ferenczi is best known for his technical innovations to classical psychoanalysis. Most significantly, he innovated the method of active therapy, developed over more than twenty-five years of analytic practice, as a complement as well as supplement to Freud's fundamental rule of free association. In writing about active therapy, Ferenczi took great pains to apologize to his mentor and colleagues for any breach of orthodoxy and to explain that his approach was a means toward the greater end of analysis of repressed infantile trauma. That notwithstanding, Ferenczi's work marked a radical departure from the image of the distanced analyst frustrating the patient's primitive desire to act out difficult or traumatic experience through physical and affective channels.

For Freud, as well as his staunch disciples, acting out during treatment was considered a defense. At best, the therapist analyzed any attempt to physicalize an impulse as a resistance to a strong transferential feeling toward the analyst. The *sine qua non* of treatment was for the client to verbalize a feeling rather than to act it out. For the most part, the analyst frustrated any attempt on the patient's part toward physical or emotional enactment. Ferenczi generally agreed with this point of view arguing that in acting out their impulses, clients might not be able to distinguish between thinking and doing and, in some cases, fantasy and reality. Ferenczi (1919) also made the point that analysts feared that they could not contain such enactment, and many felt compelled to retain the infallible and controlling persona of the expert.

Active Therapy

Ferenczi (1952) spoke of his own experience where patients jumped off the couch and gesticulated wildly, cursed, and attempted seduction. Generally,

Ferenczi remained cool and analytical with such patients, arguing that the analyst "must point out over and over again the transference nature of such actions, toward which he must conduct himself quite passively" (182). Further, in pointing out the complexities of the countertransference provoked by such acting out, Ferenczi noted that the analyst needed to fully engage in his own unconscious process, the "free play of association and phantasy [*sic*]," while at the same time retaining a "logical scrutiny" of the patient's material so that his communications were always in the service of the analytic process. In this early work with active therapy, Ferenczi (1952) took care to prescribe actions that were well within the bounds of classical psychoanalysis. He conceived of his active approach as "interference in the patient's psychic activities to help over dead points" (196).

In 1920 Ferenczi specified that activity is centered in the work of the patient, rather than the therapist. The therapist's job was to impose certain tasks that were often challenging and even painful for the patient in order to help her access repressed memories. This approach predated many of the more prescriptive methods of cognitive-behavioral therapy where clients are given homework, or, in the case of George Kelley (1955), given certain fixed roles to enact in their everyday lives.

In his 1920 paper, "The Further Development of an Active Therapy in Psycho-Analysis," Ferenczi presented the case of a sexually attractive female musician who experienced profound stage fright. She had been referred to Ferenczi by a colleague who was unable to help her, despite giving her highly developed analytical insights into her phobias and obsessions. In working actively, Ferenczi noted that she had made reference to a song taught to her by her sister, who appeared to tyrannize her. Ferenczi helped her not only to recall the words but also the melody and finally to sing the song, which she could only do with much encouragement. On further investigation, Ferenczi became aware that the sister had performed the song with great passion and invited the patient to do the same until she expressed the song in a full emotional and physical fashion. The shift into these expressive channels opened up her ability to recall repressed memories from her childhood.

As the patient began to master her fears, Ferenczi interpreted her process through classical psychoanalytic concepts, referring to penis envy, masturbatory fantasies, and anal-eroticism. Although psychoanalysis often draws its epistemological content from sexuality, it is more germane to this discussion to focus on the particular method of active therapy. In doing so we see how given actions can help move the process of analysis forward. On the part of the analyst, the actions are given as either prohibitions or commands. As for the patient, her part of either disengaging from habitual actions or engaging in new ones opens up new avenues to the unconscious.

Ferenczi (1925) discussed in some detail the indications and contraindications for activity. At one point, perhaps as an assurance to his mentor, he spoke of activity as simply "a makeshift, a pedagogic supplement, to the real analysis whose place it must never pretend to take" (208). He spoke of the beginning of the analytic process as inappropriate for activity as the early task was to foster the transference and that too much activity might scare the patient away. Ferenczi noted that the optimal time for activity was toward the end of the treatment when the patient is given tasks to perform beyond the scope of the analytic sessions. He also noted that some forms of dysfunction are very well suited for active therapy including obsessive-compulsive behaviors, phobias, and war trauma. The latter is often treated within a shortened period of time and therefore requires a more direct, active approach.

Relaxation and Neocatharsis

Building upon his work in active therapy, Ferenczi moved further away from the fundamental rule of free association. In a 1930 paper, "The Principle of Relaxation and Neocatharsis," Ferenczi referred back to Breuer's groundbreaking work in hypnosis and its ability to access repressed memories. But he also noted that Breuer abandoned his cathartic method once the catharsis became too emotional and irrational. Freud's biographer, Peter Gay, refers to a particular turning point for Breuer when one of his patients in a hallucinatory state accused him of fathering her child.

For Breuer, the working through of irrational psychological trauma was to occur through rational means. Ferenczi wrote that Freud went beyond Breuer in noting the presence of sexual trauma in most of his neurotic patients and in his willingness to deal directly with its manifestations in the treatment. However, Freud, too, adopted an intellectual approach to treatment, which he then deepened in his discovery of the transference relationship between analyst and patient, which contained its own quality of affect. Having rejected his earlier cathartic work with Breuer as too superficial, however, Freud handled affect in a cool, analytical fashion, discouraging strong emotional outbursts, forbidding all physical and verbal acting out.

Ferenczi described his first analytic encounter as anything but cool. He told the story of a desperate young colleague who implored him to help treat his severe asthma. Applying Jung's association test, Ferenczi quickly discovered a trauma in the patient's early life when he was subjected to anesthesia against his will. After communicating this information, the patient immediately embodied the role of the child struggling against the chloroform mask, unable to breathe. After a cathartic release of emotion while reenacting this experience, the patient exclaimed that he felt a full sense of relief from his asthma.

However, Ferenczi (1955) acknowledged the transitory nature of his early cathartic successes and learned to focus more upon the "analytical re-education of the patient, which demanded more and more time" (112). But soon he grew disenchanted with the conventional rituals and procedures of classical psychoanalysis. He recognized, for example, the needs of some patients to move off the couch and walk around, of others to work longer than the single one-hour session. He recognized the limits of the principle of frustration and the needs of some for moments of indulgence. From this point, Ferenczi developed the principle of relaxation, often directing rigid patients in relaxation exercises.

Further, Ferenczi (1955) noted that sometimes after a successful extended application of relaxation and analysis, leading to a "fuller freedom of affect" (118), some patients would spontaneously act out in a highly emotional and physical manner, as if in a trance. For some, these enactments would be followed by amnesia. Ferenczi noted that these cathartic moments of auto-hypnosis were qualitatively different from those described by Breuer and Freud and explained them as having a strong sense of reality corresponding to the actual conditions of the patient's recalled past. Given that these cathartic moments came toward the end of an analysis, Ferenczi (1955) depicted them as follows:

> The catharsis of which I am speaking is, like many dreams, only a confirmation from the unconscious, a sign that our toilsome analytical construction, our technique of dealing with resistance and transference, has finally succeeded in drawing near to the aetiological reality (119).

Ferenczi called this moment neocatharsis, distinguishing it from the more random, less focused and more superficial moment of catharsis as defined by Breuer and Freud. Daring to critique has mentor, Ferenczi offered the thought that the childhood trauma that has plagued the adult lives of many of his patients was not the fantasy of hypersensitive children, but an actual incestuous act on the part of adults. Ferenczi more fully developed this theme in his influential 1933 article, "Confusion of Tongues between Adults and the Child."

Through relaxation therapy and neocatharsis, Ferenczi was able to penetrate the trauma and help the patient not only recollect the trauma, but also work it through. At the very end of his article (1933), he evoked a theatrical metaphor underlining the transformational quality of the principles of relaxation and neocatharsis:

> After reconstructing the evolution of the id, the ego, and the super-ego many patients repeat in the neocathartic experience the primal battle with reality, and it may be that the transformation of this last repetition into recollection may provide a yet firmer basis for the subject's future existence. His situation may be com-

pared with that of the playwright whom pressure of public opinion forces to convert the tragedy he has planned into a drama with a "happy ending" (125).

Child Analysis with Adults

Before leaving Ferenczi, I would like to point to two more of his radical departures from classical psychoanalysis—child analysis with adults and mutual analysis.

In partly justifying his active therapy, Ferenczi made the point that in many cases one needs to work through the imaginative and expressive channels of the adult patient. However, given the cognitive, verbal demands of psychoanalysis, the analyst would be hard pressed to justify a direct appeal to nonverbal work through the emotions and the body. To solve the problem, Ferenczi (1931) informed his skeptical colleagues that he would apply action approaches generally used with children to work with adults. In doing so he discussed the limitations of free association in accessing the unconscious: "free association was still too much of the nature of conscious selection of thoughts, and so I urged the patient to deeper relaxation and more complete surrender to the impressions, tendencies, and emotions which quite spontaneously arose in him" (128).

Ferenczi noted that in this increasingly expressive, imaginative approach, somewhat akin to Jung's active imagination, patients became less inhibited and childlike, expressing themselves through movement and visual images, even through role-play. He gave an example of the latter by referring to a patient who transferred aspects of his grandfather onto Ferenczi (1931). While talking about the transference, the patient suddenly arose from the couch and embraced Ferenczi, uttering: "I say, Grandpapa, I am afraid I am going to have a baby!" (129).

Rather than analyzing this astonishing moment, Ferenczi turned to her, took on the role of the grandfather, and replied: "Well, but what makes you think so?" (129). By choosing to engage in the role-play, Ferenczi was actually creating an early form of drama therapy, although he referred to his intervention as a game of questions and answers and related it to the kind of therapeutic approach one would take with children. He also noted that when he called this kind of role-play a game or when he did not play his corresponding role in a believable manner, the patient would disengage from the interaction. But when he, indeed, engaged dramatically with his patient, the ensuing enactment would often reveal deeper levels of unconscious experience. Ferenczi (1955) noted that, at times, "they enacted before me traumatic occurrences, the unconscious memory of which lay, in fact, behind the dialogue of the game" (130).

Upon making his discoveries of the power of such childlike enactments, Ferenczi (1955), ever the Freudian apologist, reminded his readers: "The material reenacted in play or repeated in any other way has to be thoroughly worked through analytically. Of course, too, Freud is right when he teachers us that it is a triumph for analysis when it succeeds in substituting recollection for acting out" (131). But then, daring to take a small step beyond the shadow of his master, Ferenczi added: "But I think it is also valuable to secure important material in the shape of action which can then be transformed into recollection" (131). Thus, in the end Ferenczi acknowledged his difference with Freud who conceived of action as a defense against the recall of a trauma. For Ferenczi, action and enactment were positive means leading to the recall and working through of trauma.

Mutual Analysis

And finally, Ferenczi was credited with innovating a two-person paradigm for psychoanalysis, known as mutual analysis. We learn in Ferenczi's *Diary* (1988) that his analysis with the American, RN, led to a deep understanding of his own countertransference and a corresponding salubrious effect upon RN, leading her into a strong therapeutic bond with Ferenczi. In mutual analysis, both therapist and patient at designated times reverse roles, radically challenging the usual rules, rituals, and roles regarding power and control. As in conventional analysis, both parties involved in mutual analysis work to create a safe space that aids in exploring intrapsychic issues and working them through. Not only did Ferenczi experiment with this radical approach, but he also used radical techniques of role reversal, guided imagery, relaxation, and movement, all of which evolved from his notion of active therapy, and all of which would appear in later forms of action psychotherapy.

Ferenczi analogized the dyad in mutual analysis as two frightened children joined together by the need to share common experiences and hopes. In one of his early descriptions (Ferenczi 1988) of the process with a client whom he refers to as B, he wrote:

> I just wanted to show her what free association is, and she was to show me how the correct behavior of the analyst looks. I rejoiced at regaining my freedom and at the license it gave me. As a contrast to screaming and abuse I demanded tenderness and kindness (I asked her to caress my head and wished to be rewarded for all my exertions with affection, tenderness, embraces, and kisses (167).

Ferenczi (1988) was well aware of the ethical issues regarding psychological boundaries as well as physical and sexual ones, aspects of which he struggled with throughout his professional career. In considering how much he should personally self-disclose in the mutual analysis, he offered this: "Can and should one tell all this openly and really put all the cards on the table? . . . for the present, no" (35).

And yet, Ferenczi took many extraordinary risks, some of which led to censure and even excoriation by his colleagues. Some saw his radical role reversals as countertherapeutic and narcissistic, as a way to ease his failing health and personal demons. Others saw his experiment with mutuality as a logical extension of years of wrestling with issues of empathy, with rigid roles and definitions of mental illness, with rigid analytic techniques and theories that often did not respond to the human beings in treatment. For our purposes, Ferenczi's experiments late in his life point not only to the role reversals so inherent in many forms of action psychotherapy, but also to the attention to the intersubjectivity of the main players in the drama of psychotherapy. Finally, in experimenting with mutual analysis, Ferenczi stumbled upon a means of exploring that dynamic relationship not only through the logic of words, but also through expressive, creative channels that are often best revealed through action.

WILHELM REICH

Wilhelm Reich (1897–1957) was a psychiatrist, psychoanalyst, and member of the Vienna Psychoanalytic Society, best known for his radical focus upon the body as the locus of psychological healing. Over time, Reich's theories and clinical experiments developed in highly unconventional ways, incorporating not only psychological issues of human development, but also biological, cosmological, metaphysical, political, and parapsychological ones. He became more and more of a pariah within the psychoanalytic and medical communities for claiming to have discovered and harnessed an energy that could cure a myriad of psychological and medical diseases such as schizophrenia and cancer. In the end, feeling maligned and persecuted, he was hounded by the U.S. Food and Drug Administration, who eventually destroyed many of his controversial inventions and burned many of his books. Reich died in prison of a heart attack in 1957.

Character Analysis

Despite his wildly unconventional experiments and harsh treatment by European and American governments, Reich's ideas were original and at times brilliant. His most significant book, *Character Analysis* (1949), is still used as a text in some analytical training institutes. His notion that the full character of an individual, not only its parts or symptoms, was the proper arena of treatment led the way generally to holistic approaches to psychotherapy and more specifically to the subset of ego psychology. For our purposes, Reich's radical techniques of treatment through affect and enactment and especially through the body, provide a direction for bioenergetic analysis, somatic psychotherapies, as well as expressive and action psychotherapies.

Reich remained respectful of Freud, applauding Freud's progression from the cathartic cure through hypnosis, to the direct verbal interpretation of the unconscious, to the more indirect interpretation of resistances. Reich (1949) noted that the shift to an analysis of resistance marked a "turning-point in the history of analytical therapy" (10).

Reich wisely posed a major question springing from Freud's understanding that making the unconscious conscious, although necessary, was not always sufficient to bring about the desired therapeutic change. Reich's (1949) question was: "What further circumstances determine whether or not the becoming conscious of the repressed idea leads to cure?" (11). He believed that Freud's libido theory offered a path, even though his technique did not. He noted that Ferenczi and Rank (1925/1986) challenged Freud's purely verbal approach by encouraging the release of affect on the part of the patient. Reich in turn challenged their cathartic approach as being too limited in its lasting effects and boldly offered up his hallmark biophysical, somatic point of view. He argued that Freud and his followers could not answer the question, because their focus was only on the meaning of the patient's neurotic symptoms. For Reich, the question could only be answered by looking at the source of energy contained in the symptoms. When a symptom becomes conscious, argued Reich, its source, if dysfunctional, persists. Reich referred to this problem as libido stasis and the person who manifested this problem as the neurotic character. The cure was a somatic one, systematically removing the patient's body armor and thus transforming the neurotic character to the genital character who Reich saw as spontaneous and capable of achieving satisfactory sexual gratification.

In theory, Reich agreed with Freud at the time of the first publication of *Character Analysis* in 1933 that healing derives from an interpretation of early infantile experiences. At that time he also agreed that in treatment the therapeutic process starts in repetition and proceeds to memory, insight, and then affect. In his later work in orgone therapy, Reich's term for his bioenergetic approach, he amended this thought. By the early 1940s Reich believed that when the somatically based emotions are released from the muscular armor, and the patient is in the role of the genital character, then pathogenic memories are spontaneously acted out. Agreeing with Ferenczi and Rank, Reich argued that affect precedes memory. Reich's practice diverted radically from Freud's and from that of Ferenczi and Rank in that Reich worked directly on the body of the patient, manipulating posture and breathing, engaging in touch and role-play, all in the service of releasing affect and the subsequent memory and insight.

Although Reich for many years focused upon the historical issues of his patients, with a view that pathology begins in early infantile experience, he came to understand the limits of Freud's dictum that the proper sequence in treatment is from the present moment of acting out to the past moment of remembering and integrating infantile experiences. Reich (1949) believed that "Freud's rule . . . has to be complemented by the further rule that first that which has become chronically rigid must be brought to new life in the actual transference situation" (78). In his later work, Reich focused even more in the present, facilitating an opening of blocked energy in relationship with the patient.

Character Types and Body Work

Further, Reich came to care less about the content of the patient's verbal utterances and more about the form of presentation—the nonverbal behaviors, the breathing, the gait, and demeanor of the patient. In referring to his work as character analysis, Reich focused upon discrete character traits and helped patients understand how they presented themselves and how he could modify that presentation through opening up various somatically based blocks. As we shall see, the focus upon character traits rather than symptoms opens the way for a role-based treatment, common in drama therapy. In the role method of drama therapy, various role types, based upon characters from dramatic literature, exemplify discrete personality types. Although Reich viewed character armor as an ego defense mediating between the demands of the instinctual inner world and the frustrating outer world, he specified certain character types, the most significant of which are the neurotic character, incapable of expressing spontaneity and orgasmic potency, and the genital character, capable of full spontaneity and orgasm.

In a case titled "A Case of Passive-Feminine Character," Reich (1949) described his work with an anxious young man. In working with a symbolic dream, Reich encouraged the man to engage in action. Reich's step-by-step description of the action follows:

1. He thrashed around with his arms and legs, yelling: "Let me alone. . . . I'm going to kill you."
2. He grabbed his throat and whined in a rattling voice.
3. He behaved not like one who is violently attacked but like a girl who is sexually attacked: "Let me alone, let me alone" (88–89).

Reich encouraged a continuation of the action, which served to help him understand the complexity of the patient's resistance toward expressing aggression. Reich helped him understand the infantile source of his resistance and brought it back to the present in the transference relationship. Throughout the treatment, Reich did not focus upon the symptom of anxiety, but upon the character trait of the patient, expressed as a passive-feminine character resistance. Consistent with his theory, Reich believed the treatment was successful when the somatic core of the neurosis was eliminated and the patient was able to experience a satisfactory discharge of orgastic energy.

In other cases, Reich applied a dramatic metaphor to characterize the patient's character states. In presenting, for example, the case of an aristocratic character, Reich (1949) noted: "I told him he was play-acting an English lord, and that this must have a connection with his youth. I also explained the defensive function of his 'lordliness'" (181). In working with this case, Reich again concentrated on the form of his presentation, noting: "His movements were flaccid, his expression tired, his speech monotonous. . . . His intonation revealed the meaning of his behavior: he talked in a tortured manner, as if dying" (187). In resolving the patient's neurotic character structure, Reich noted that the analysis of the form of his behavior, "the way in which the individual acts" (188), was most useful in resolving the character armor and releasing the affects.

In treating a case of masochism, Reich, frustrated with his inability to effectively proceed through a verbal analysis of the patient's resistances, resorted to action techniques of mirroring and role reversal, both developed earlier by Moreno. Reich's (1949) description follows:

> Under these circumstances, the analysis made no progress. . . . So I began to show him a reflection of himself. When I opened the door, he would stand there with a drawn face, in an attitude of utter rejection. I would imitate his attitude. I began to use his infantile language, I lay on the floor and kicked and yelled as he did. . . . I repeated these procedures until he himself began to analyze the situation (225).

In a powerful case of a schizophrenic woman reported in the late 1940s, Reich fully transformed the distance of the classical verbal cure into embodied action. Not only did Reich move his patient off the couch, but, on occasion, he helped her to express rage by hitting the couch. As a warning, he added: "This is a dangerous procedure if the patient, especially the schizophrenic, is not in perfect contact with the physician. In order to secure this contact, one must explain to the patient that he must stop his rage action instantly when asked to do so" (409).

Later in the treatment, moving more to the edge, Reich again attempted to get the patient to experience rage through removing a block he noticed in her throat. He encouraged her to gag until the gag reflex was operative and she breathed fully. With this opening, she began to cry. Reich theorized that the patient's throat was constricted, because she was treated abusively by her nagging mother and had developed an impulse to choke her mother. When the patient asked Reich if she could choke him, he gave her permission to act out her fantasy. She acted out her rage cautiously, then let up, breathing fully. Although feeling better from her cathartic experience, she soon regressed into a psychotic state, which Reich expected.

Later the patient asked for a knife and when Reich inquired why, she responded: "to cut your stomach wide open" (424). Upon discovering that she actually wished to cut open her own stomach, Reich theorized that a schizoid murderer whose bodily sensations become unbearable will redirect the rageful impulse onto someone else.

Over time, she continued to play with the notion of homicide and suicide, but with greater distance. Once she put a noose around her neck but her actions, according to Reich, were mitigated by a humorous and playful approach to the mock suicide, an approach that as we will later see, is a hallmark of developmental transformations, a form of drama therapy. Through her expressive work with Reich, she was learning the difference between play and reality, the drama of the imagination and that of everyday life.

And yet again, several weeks later, the patient regressed to a psychotic state. In this state, she attacked Reich with a knife. Prepared for such episodes, Reich disarmed her and allowed her to safely purge her rage. Then she proceeded to cry bitterly, like a child. Reich commented that he expected such extreme behavior as she was close to the point of experiencing orgastic potency and was fighting against it. He noted that "sudden changes from a chronically low to a very high energy level constitute dramatic and dangerous situations because of the inability to tolerate strong sensations and emotions" (482).

Reich stayed with his patient over several years of relapses, hospitalizations, and remarkable moments of flow and potency. In the end, he proclaimed her well enough to live an independent life, separated from all therapeutic help. His controversial methods notwithstanding, Reich took great risks in working with this patient and in coming to a conclusion that has only been verified in recent years that schizophrenia is a biological rather than psychological condition. It is inconceivable that some of his methods of treatment, including irradiation in an orgone box and insistence upon the primacy of the orgasm, will ever be recognized as credible in a scientific sense. However, in his insistence throughout this and many other cases of working expressively and dramatically, Reich provided a clear model of a treatment beyond rational, verbal analysis.

Like Rank, Reich spoke about the primacy of the artist and of creative expression. Reich proclaimed that expression through words is limited in offering an understanding of human beings. Taking a biophysical point of view, Reich (1949) noted the linguistic and conceptual connection between expression and emotion. He wrote:

> The living expresses itself in . . . expressive movements. . . . The term means literally that something in the living system "presses itself out" and consequently, "moves." . . . The literal meaning of emotion is "moving out," which is the same as expressive movement. . . . The words which describe emotional states render, in an immediate way, the corresponding expressive movements of living matter. . . . Even though language reflects the state of plasmatic emotion in

an immediate way, it cannot itself reach this state. The living . . . has its own specific forms of expression which cannot be put into words at all (360–61).

Reich went on to note that musical and visual artists speak in an expressive language that transcends words. He related this to his theory of orgone biophysics, which he saw as an expressive, preverbal language. By this time, in the 1940s, Reich adapted a theoretical position close to that of contemporary expressive therapists—the body reveals that which verbal language conceals. In Reich's (1949) words:

Orgone therapy is distinguished from all other modes of influencing the organism by the fact that the patient is asked to express himself biologically while word language is eliminated to a far-reaching degree. This leads the patient to a depth from which he constantly tries to flee (363).

Reich's Legacy

In treatment, Reich helped patients understand and work through the depth of their pathological distortions. Words were not eliminated altogether, but the focus was upon the body and how it is armored against feeling and expression. Reich created a systematic approach to loosening the body armor by moving carefully from one segment of the body to another, releasing what he referred to as plasmatic streamings and emotional excitations.

Given the unscientific and sometimes bizarre nature of Reich's proclamations and given the political climates in which he boldly proclaimed his findings—fascist Europe in the 1930s and conservative America in the 1950s—his work was reviled by many. And yet, his radical innovations captured the attention of those who further developed his psychophysical approaches to therapy (see, for example, Janov 1970). One of the best known was Alexander Lowen who founded the method of bioenergetic analysis and offered a model for those in dance/movement therapy and drama therapy of healing through the body. His work will be discussed in the next chapter.

Likewise, Jung and to a lesser extent, Rank and Ferenczi, left their own legacies that would be further developed by a range of psychotherapists and creative arts therapists. The one central figure who seemed to have rejected all influences was a contemporary of Freud and the early psychoanalysts. His work would provide a clear link between old world Vienna and the new world of psychotherapeutic experimentation in the United States. His name was Jacob Levy Moreno.

2

Pioneers of Action Psychotherapy

EARLY HISTORICAL INFLUENCES ON
ACTION PSYCHOTHERAPY

Before delving into the prodigious work of J. L. Moreno, let us look briefly at some lesser yet important historical influences on the development of action approaches in psychotherapy. Casson (2004) reviewed many of the major historical therapeutic applications of action methods, specifically psychodrama and drama therapy. He first looked back to the influence of shamanism, referring to the theatrical devices of ventriloquism, masks, and puppets as means of invoking and enacting figures from the spirit world. He then made reference to theatrical plays where psychological issues are played out for the cathartic benefit of the audiences. Casson's examples include Greek drama and Shakespearian tragedy, but he especially focuses on the play *Lila*, by Goethe, written around 1775, concerning a form of psychodramatic enactment. The central character, Lila, fearing that her husband has died in battle, reacts by developing psychotic symptoms including delusions of being persecuted by ogres. Her doctor directs a number of her relatives to take on the roles of the ogres and to enact Lila's fantasies. The therapeutic dramatization helps Lila regain her sense of reality. In 1972 Moreno (Diener and Moreno 1972) cited a letter written by Goethe in 1818 referring to his play as a psychological cure.

Casson makes reference to early forms of therapeutic theater including the work of Goethe's physician, Johann Christian Reil, in the late eighteenth century. Reil not only encouraged mentally ill patients to enact their interpersonal conflicts, but also urged directors of mental institutions to construct theaters. In doing so, Reil questioned:

> Why could there not be written real plays for . . . mental patients, to be performed by the patients themselves. The roles would be distributed according to the individual therapeutic needs. The fool for instance, could be given a role making him aware of the foolishness of his way of behaving (Reil in Harms 1957, 807).

Theaters were built and mental patients performed plays for therapeutic purposes in many European countries throughout the nineteenth and twentieth centuries in France, Italy, Germany, and England. The most famous was in Charenton Asylum in France, where one of the patient-actors was the Marquis de Sade. An imaginary depiction of de Sade's theatrical experimentation is brilliantly rendered in Peter Weiss's 1963 play, *The Persecution and Assassination of Jean-Paul Marat as Performed by the Inmates of the Asylum of Charenton under the Direction of the Marquis de Sade.*

Casson further discusses the early action-based work in psychiatry leading up to psychoanalysis. He cites the French psychiatrist Pierre Janet, a student of Jean Martin Charcot, who was one of Freud's early mentors. Both Charcot and Janet practiced hypnosis to treat mental illness. Janet's work in hypnosis and hysteria actually predated by several years Freud's findings that unconscious factors lead to hysterical symptoms. In a description of Janet treating a patient through role-playing, Eigen (1993) writes:

> Janet could deal with a man who believed himself to be possessed by a devil by striking up a conversation with the devil to see what it wanted. In time it came out that the man began to see devils after a lapse into infidelity on a business trip away from his wife. . . . The devil was placed in the context of a personal (clinical) history and soon disappeared (71–72).

After his well-researched history of early therapeutic drama in theatrical and medical settings, Casson, like most others who have attempted such a review (see Lewis and Johnson 2000), reached the point where the single most important innovator of action and dramatic approaches to psychotherapy became clear. And so we move forward to J. L. Moreno.

J. L. MORENO AND PSYCHODRAMA

Although a maverick who never sought entry into the *sanctum sanctorum* of the Wednesday group, the physician J. L. Moreno walked similar though less elegant streets of Vienna in the early part of the twentieth century, engaging with homeless children, refugees, and prostitutes, helping them discover a sense of wellness through creative means. Possessing all the charisma and theatricality of the shaman, Moreno often imagined himself to be a spiritual redeemer. Possessing the academic credentials and scientific training of the physician, Moreno imagined the possibilities of transforming the modern practice of healing.

In his most immodest moments, Moreno imagined himself to be Christlike and to move beyond Freud and Marx in his attempts to heal the ills of individuals and societies. In truth, this larger-than-life figure was an early founder of group psychotherapy and the first of the early twentieth-century psychotherapists to fully conceive of dramatic action as the primary approach to healing. For Moreno, the health of humankind lay in its ability to be creative and spontaneous. Although his ideas were akin to his contemporaries Jung, Rank, Ferenczi, and Reich, who introduced means of working through the imagination, the spirit, and the body, Moreno rejected most of what he saw in psychoanalysis and medicine, finding his sustenance in the act of dramatic creation which to him was equivalent to taking on and playing the role of God (see Moreno 1941/1971). Like Reich, Moreno also offered a sweeping critique of all things political and spiritual, viewing his creations, psychodrama, sociodrama, and sociometry, as panaceas for the ills of a society burdened by repressive political, spiritual, and psychological forces.

Moreno's theory and practice of psychodrama and sociometry will be discussed in some depth in chapter 3, as this work represents the seminal action psychotherapy of the twentieth century. For now, let us look at some of the major developments of Moreno's work that ultimately led to his mature inventions and innovations.

Early Developments in Austria

As a young man and indeed all throughout his career, Moreno had a need to help those whom he saw as the underclass. During his days as a medical student just before the First World War, Moreno and a small group of followers founded the House of Encounter, a community center for refugees and immigrants to Vienna. Their work included helping the immigrants resettle, find jobs, and establish social networks.

Shortly after the center closed at the dawn of World War I, Moreno worked at the Psychiatric Clinic of Vienna University. During this time, between 1912 and 1914, Moreno, well aware of Freud's work, attended a lecture given by Professor Freud. According to Moreno, after his lecture Freud approached Moreno and inquired about his therapeutic approach. Moreno (1946/1994) replied: "Well, Dr. Freud, I start where you leave off. You meet people in the artificial setting of your office, I meet them on the street and in their home, in their natural surroundings. You analyze their dreams. I try to give them the courage to dream again. I teach the people how to play God" (5–6).

Moreno was not a modest man, and it is difficult to take the full corpus of his published writing literally. His articles and books, although full of original theoretical and clinical reflections, are often marred by imprecise and overblown prose. In many instances, he writes more as a poet than as a critical thinker. And yet he provided a clear and bold critique of classical psychoanalysis. In this early instance, Moreno criticized Freud for his rejection of religion, for his indifference to the politics of fascism and socialism, and for his inattention to group process in psychotherapy. Further, Moreno critiqued Freud for his purely cognitive, rational approach to psychotherapy, which he saw as limited to affluent, neurotic young and middle-aged adults.

Moreno did not stop with refugees and immigrants. He worked with children throughout his medical studies, whom he met in local parks and entertained through telling stories and playing games. He saw his games as revolutionary as he challenged the children to make up new identities and to move through the park in search of new parents who would be more permissive and spontaneous than their own. The next logical step for Moreno was to create a theater for children, and he did so by directing them in classical and improvised plays.

Further, in his wanderings through the streets of Vienna, Moreno befriended prostitutes and began to organize them in small discussion groups to share stories about their daily indignities and search for ways to improve their conditions. From this experience, Moreno developed his early formulations of group therapy and sociometry, the study of group process. Moreno, like Ferenczi before him, saw the value in forming a system of mutual analysis, although Moreno's (1963) notion was that of peer-to-peer counseling where "one individual could become a therapeutic agent of the other" (xxix).

Moreno's interest in group dynamics and sociometry further developed as he worked in refugee camps as a doctor during the war. It was there where he carefully observed the difficult living conditions of the displaced children and adults and made recommendations to the Minister of the Interior for sociometric ways to analyze and improve their conditions.

Alongside his social concerns, Moreno also pursued his passion for the theater, challenging what he called the cultural conserve of classical plays and conservative forms of presentation. Moreno viewed the cultural conserve generally as the status quo, the completed products and forms of any given culture. At one point, at the age of nineteen, Moreno and a companion went to see the play, *Thus Spake Zarathustra*, based upon the work of Nietzsche. As the lead actor was about to speak his lines, Moreno interrupted, loudly accusing the actor of artificiality and demanding that the only role he was fit to play was that of himself. As he was arrested, Moreno boldly announced the end of the conventional theater and the birth of a new art form where all played themselves. The new form, which was embryonic in his young and rebellious mind, became psychodrama, a form of therapy based upon the actor's dramatization of his own life stories.

Shortly after this outburst, Moreno (1915) published a philosophical treatise, *Invitation to an Encounter*, that well defined his thinking throughout his life. This philosophy is well articulated in a poem that would serve as Moreno's signature motto:

More important than science is its result.
One answer provokes a hundred questions.

More important than poetry is its result,
One answer invokes a hundred heroic acts.

More important than recognition is its result,
The result is pain and guilt.

More important than procreation is the child.
More important than evolution of creation is the
Evolution of the creator.

In place of the imperative steps the imperator.
In place of the creative steps the creator.
A meeting of two: eye to eye, face to face,
And when you are near I will tear your eyes out
And place them in place of mine,
And you will tear my eyes out
And will place them instead of yours,
Then I will look at you with your eyes
And you will look at me with mine.

Thus even the common thing serves silence and
Our meeting remains the chainless goal:
The undetermined place, at an undetermined time,
The undetermined word to the undetermined man (2).

This early statement of philosophy, written when Moreno was twenty-three, sets forth three basic principles. The first is the immutable principle of the individual creator who stands above his creation. The second is the principle of role reversal, the ability of one individual to experience the world from the point of view of the other. This principle would stand as one of the major innovations of psychodrama. The third is the principle of meeting or encounter, "the chainless goal" that became the basis of relational approaches to individual and group psychotherapy. According to Zerka T. Moreno (2006b), Moreno took the title of his book, *Invitation to an Encounter*, literally, inviting one and all to meet with him. His life and work was about facilitating relationships. As a physician and therapist, he did not wait for a patient to come to him, but rather he was the first to establish the meeting.

While living near Vienna in the provincial town of Bad Vöslau in the 1920s, Moreno attempted to innovate several forms of radical theater. As a local family doctor in a small town, Moreno at times invited his patients to reenact troubling scenarios from their lives or enact imaginary scenarios with others in their families in order to defuse potentially frightening experiences. One example concerned a patient who approached Moreno and asked for help in facilitating his suicide. Although he refused medical means, Moreno offered a dramatic solution. He helped the man move beyond his deep depression by encouraging him to enact scenes of preparation for the suicide. He and his assistant witnessed the man's enactments uncritically, often playing auxiliary roles, until the man was free of his need to carry out the action in reality.

Moreno called these therapeutic experiments *theatre reciproque* and directed them both in his office and in the homes of patients. But as a Bohemian in a very conservative Austrian village, more shaman than physician, Moreno evoked suspicion. Even in the city of Vienna, Moreno's motives were suspect. In the early 1920s, Moreno befriended a number of actors, some of whom, like Peter Lorre and Elisabeth Bergner, became prominent in German theater and cinema. Attempting his first sociodrama in 1921, with the goal of exploring possibilities of enlightened leadership of the state of Austria, Moreno rented a prominent theater, invited the literati and local politicians, and appeared alone on stage in the costume of a court jester. His props were a throne and a crown. In the role of the jester, Moreno told the audience that he was in search of the king and invited people up to take on the role of a wise and enlightened leader. But few responded. In fact, most left the theater either baffled or angry at such an audacious, bizarre performance. Moreno's attempt at creating a form of social encounter and political dialogue failed.

Undeterred, Moreno began another theatrical experiment, attempting again to subvert the cultural conserve of dramatic literature and create a form of spontaneous performance. He gathered a group of actors and worked with them to create improvisational forms of drama in response to ideas suggested by the audience and in response to the news of the day. He called the latter The Living Newspaper. This improvisational work, called *Stegreiftheater* or theater of spontaneity, was much better received by audiences and provided the impetus for Moreno to move his actors even closer to his notion of psychodrama.

The most notable moment in the early discovery of psychodrama came out of Moreno's work with the Stegreiftheater. As reported in detail (Moreno 1946/1994), this discovery occurred as Moreno was working with one of his cast members, Barbara. Barbara most often was cast in ingénue roles. During this time, Barbara became romantically involved with George, a young playwright who attended all of Barbara's performances. Shortly after their marriage, George approached Moreno and exclaimed that the woman he first admired in the theatrical role of sweet ingénue was, in fact, a shrew at home. George begged Moreno to help him find a way to live with the distress of his abusive wife.

Moreno, incubating the idea of psychodrama, decided upon a theatrical cure. He approached Barbara and convinced her to take on a different persona onstage. He said to her (Moreno 1946/1994): "People would like to see you in roles in which you portray . . . the rawness of human nature, its vulgarity and stupidity" (3). Barbara agreed enthusiastically. Encouraged by Moreno, she took on a character from the newspaper of a prostitute who is murdered on the street. Her performance was highly realistic and cathartic. She played many such roles and George reported to Moreno that the theatrical release had lead to more moderate behavior at home. Both George and Barbara discovered ways to catch themselves before their squabbles escalated into major marital conflicts. Furthermore, the experience of watching Barbara enact counterroles lead George not only to appreciate her more, but to begin to join her on stage in the spontaneous dramas directed by Moreno.

Over time, the stage dramas of Barbara and George recapitulated the stress in their daily lives and led to corrective experiences. Those experiences carried over to audience members who identified with the protagonists and shared their own experiences with the ensemble. Moreno's job was to shape the role-playing and then to help Barbara and George, as well as members of the audience, reflect upon the link between the dramatic reality and that of everyday life.

Moreno discovered further guiding principles in this early experiment. For one, a major function of theater can be therapy if the theatrical experience is both a recapitulation of and corrective to the challenges of everyday life. Also, unlike psychoanalysis, this early form of psychodrama demanded that action precedes reflection (see Marineau 1989). This principle of action remained paramount to all developments in Moreno's work.

The principle of catharsis is also clearly demonstrated in this early dramatic work in a way that is quite different from that described by Freud and Breuer. The aim of catharsis was not for the subject to remember a repressed experience from the past while in an altered state of consciousness, but to release affect while consciously role-playing in the present so that a given role would not have so much control over the role-player.

A final principle, embraced fully by Moreno throughout his career, is that therapeutic drama occurs within a group format and that one person's authentically enacted experience has universal implications. Moreno in his own way rediscovered a central tenet of theater, that of representation, which Aristotle referred to as an imitation of an action, and which Shakespeare referred to as holding a mirror up to nature. Moreno might have taken pleasure in noting that his early work was a reversal of Shakespeare's famous metaphor of the world as stage. For Moreno, the stage was a world.

Moreno in America

At the age of thirty-six, in 1925, Moreno immigrated to America. Although his experiments in sociometry and medicine, in theater and therapy, had been exciting and influential, he experienced a number of setbacks in the Old World. For one, the marriage of Barbara and George disintegrated, and several years later George committed suicide. While working with another couple through his early form of public psychodrama, that relationship also ended in divorce and the suicide of the husband. Moreno's actors, especially the most gifted ones like Peter Lorre and Elizabeth Bergner, were more interested in the art and economics than the therapy of theater and went on to professional careers. Lorre proceeded to work with an even more iconoclastic theater visionary, Bertolt Brecht, whose ideas of a social-political theater at times mirrored those of his contemporary, Moreno.

Moreno's large ideas never seemed to reach a large enough public. His design for a radical symbolic theater without an audience, which he submitted to the International Exhibition of New Theatre Techniques in Vienna in 1924, was eclipsed by that of a rival, Friedrich Kiesler. The townsfolk in his small village were becoming more and more suspicious of his unorthodoxy. Moreno, himself, was becoming confrontational and unsettled. And waiting in the wings, Europe was about to erupt in a storm of anti-Semitism and war.

Within a relatively short time, Moreno was able to reestablish himself in the United States, ultimately settling in Beacon, New York, where he opened up a sanatorium for treatment, training, and education and from where he wrote and disseminated his mature ideas concerning psychodrama, group psychotherapy, sociometry, and sociodrama. His work developed and was enhanced in his collaboration with and marriage to Zerka T. Moreno (2006a, 2006b).

Retaining his essential commitment to sociometry, Moreno worked in the 1930s at Sing Sing prison to implement a sociometric analysis of prisoners' preferences and needs, a project that influenced psychologists and criminologists in implementing therapeutic systems within the prisons. As a historical aside, Sing Sing has housed a theater and drama-therapy program since 1996 called Rehabilitation through the Arts.

As director of research from 1932 to 1934 at the New York State Training School for Girls in Hudson, New York, Moreno devised sociometric analyses of the delinquent girls' group behavior, improving living conditions. By introducing therapeutic sessions through role and action methods, he helped the girls modify their behavior and live more effectively with their peers and supervisors. According to Marineau (1989), this work "created a revolution that soon permeated other institutions and fields. Role-play training was born, and so was the systematic use of psychodrama and group therapy" (113).

Moreno left his mark on many other venues in the United States before finally settling into Beacon. He advised psychiatrists and army officials during the Second World War on matters of personnel and group dynamics. He successfully implemented training and therapeutic programs at St. Elizabeth's Hospital in Washington, D.C., where a psychodrama theater was constructed. In 1935 Moreno engaged in a sociometric analysis of the famous boxers Max Baer and Joe Louis and used his analysis to predict the outcome. He observed the boxers in training and devised quantitative systems of measuring their strength and endurance on somatic and psychological levels. In that he was observing well-conditioned athletes, Moreno commented on the body as a central focus in all matters concerning individual psychology and group dynamics. Later referring to the popular approaches to bodywork in the late 1960s, apparently innovated by the therapists Fritz Perls and William Schultz, Moreno and Moreno (1969) reminded his reader that it was he who began to work psychodramatically with the body of his clients.

In his research with boxers, Moreno devised a sociometric tool, the social atom, that became a trademark of his approach. The social atom was a diagram of important figures in a person's life, sketched in relationship to one another, so as to reveal the interpersonal dynamics. In working with the social atoms of the boxers, Moreno included family and friends, colleagues and trainers. Fortunately for Moreno, Joe Louis won the fight in 1935 in a fashion that justified the intricate webs of social relationships he charted so carefully.

In 1936, when Moreno founded Beacon Hill Sanatorium in Beacon, New York, he intended to treat patients with various psychiatric problems, many of whom were considered hopeless cases by others, and to train professionals and laypeople in the methods of psychodrama and sociometry. With funding from private donors, Moreno built his first psychodramatic stage with different levels to represent the stages of the process from warm-up to action to closure. In realizing this design, Moreno implemented his idea of a continuity between actor and audience, all being full participants in the therapeutic action. Beyond the immediate stage, the sanatorium also represented Moreno's notion of an integrated community, an early exemplar of a therapeutic milieu, where all staff and patients, family and visitors were encouraged to engage with one another openly and equitably. Moreno and his most important coworkers often encouraged those in the community to experiment with role-reversal, taking on another's point of view in order to enrich their own.

The sanatorium became a beacon for members of the psychiatric and lay communities who wanted to learn better ways of engaging in action

approaches to treatment. It was a meeting place of action psychotherapists just as Bergasse 19 was a meeting place of psychoanalysts and as
Yeon An Budoo was a meeting place of shamans. The hospital officially
closed in 1967 as Moreno spent more and more time traveling and lecturing. Moreno passed away in 1974.

In 1982 the Moreno Institute was sold, but the legacy continues undis-
turbed and intact under the guidance of Zerka T. Moreno, who keeps the light
shining throughout the world of psychodrama and action psychotherapy. *The
Quintessential Zerka* (2006a) is a collection of historical and contemporary essays, attesting to her status as codeveloper of the field of psychodrama.

In subsequent chapters, the specifics of psychodrama will be discussed in
depth. For now, it is important to acknowledge Moreno's seminal work in
challenging the conservative ideologies, practices, and theories of mental
health and theater practitioners. It was Moreno who first recognized the
primacy of action and drama in moving the treatment of a troubled person
from the past to the present, from the cognitive to the somatic and affective, from rational thought to imaginative thinking, from the unconscious
to the conscious, from detachment to encounter, from abstract reflection to
concrete action. And it was Moreno who insisted that these shifts in clinical approach should occur within a group setting and a theatrical environment where actor and audience alike are empowered to dramatize their life
stories.

Many of these paradigm shifts came to fruition in the turbulent 1960s
and 1970s as countercultural movements, excoriating the cultural conserve,
were born. During that time, Moreno influenced Eric Berne, the founder of
Transactional Analysis, and Fritz Perls, the founder of Gestalt therapy, both
of whom attended his open training sessions in New York City. Perls, and
to a lesser extent, Berne, played a part in moving forward the notion of action psychotherapy. But before looking at Perls' work in Gestalt therapy, let
us turn to an influential psychologist, Henry Murray, the designer of the
Thematic Apperception Test (TAT), who built a psychodrama theater at Harvard and who gathered around him some of the most exciting and creative
psychotherapists of his generation. Among that group was a young man
who experimented with dramatic approaches to psychotherapy named Eric
Homburger Erikson.

HENRY MURRAY'S EXPLORATIONS IN PERSONALITY

Henry Murray (1894–1988) was not, strictly speaking, an action psychotherapist, but more of a creative researcher, writer, and mentor who is
best known for his projective assessment test, the TAT, which he designed
with Christine Morgan, and for his eclectic and imaginative explorations in

personality. Murray was trained as a historian, physician, biochemist, and then psychologist, having been tutored and analyzed by C. G. Jung while at the same time studying and embracing the basic psychosexual theories of Freud. Like Moreno, Murray was attracted as a young medical student to misfits and pariahs. As a medical student, he wrote (Murray 1940):

> Whatever I succeeded in doing for them—the dope fiend, the sword-swallower, the prostitute, the gangster—was more than repaid when, after leaving the hospital, they took me through their haunts in the underworld. This was psychology in the rough (152).

Action Methods at the Office of Strategic Services

In the 1930s Murray was appointed director of the prestigious and eclectic Harvard Psychological Clinic, where he collaborated with other creative psychologists like Erik Erikson. His tenure at Harvard was interrupted by World War II when he worked for the Office of Strategic Services (OSS), the precursor of the Central Intelligence Agency (CIA), to screen individuals to work as covert operators and propagandists. Aside from paper-and-pencil tests of intelligence, Murray and his colleagues devised intricate action methods of evaluating potential operatives. One approach was to create scenarios involving both physical courage and imaginative problem-solving skills and to subject his applicants to improvisational role-playing where they had to, for example, forge a stream or climb a wall in order to accomplish their clandestine missions.

Murray saw his approach to creating a battery of tests as a holistic method as it attempted "to arrive at a picture of personality as a whole" (OSS Assessment Staff 1948, 28). Most relevant to this book was Murray's dramatic approach to the assessment. For one, he and his colleagues asked the applicants to begin by creating a fictional cover story and fictional identity designed to hide their true identities. Later, they were required to engage in a number of fictional role-playing games and performances, all serving to reveal aspects of their personalities hidden beneath the fictions.

The OSS staff referred to one of their assessments as a psychodramatic improvisation as it involved spontaneous role-playing in front of an audience. Two candidates were given roles, one defined as superior and the other inferior, and a scene involving a specific conflict. They were asked to enact the scene and attempt to resolve the conflict. Following the enactments, peers and superiors judged their performances in terms of their believability in role, personality characteristics, social attitudes, and effectiveness in resolving a difficult problem.

Although Moreno is not mentioned by name in the book describing the OSS assessment process, his influence is manifold. Aside from the improvisational test, the candidates were also asked to evaluate their peers sociometrically. Murray and his colleagues adapted Moreno's systematic approach to revealing social dynamics by asking each candidate to rate all his peers based upon such variables as leadership, social acceptance, and rejection. In evaluating the results, the OSS staff drew sociograms charting the relationships among the candidates.

Toward the end of the war, Murray and several other leading psychologists were hired by his boss, William "Wild Bill" Donovan, to write a psychological profile of Adolph Hitler to be used not only in understanding his complex personality, but also in speculating upon possible scenarios Hitler might implement in the final stages of the war. Murray's 1943 work provided a model of the psychological profile now commonly used in criminology to understand the mind, motivations, and strategies of serial killers and terrorists. In fact, Murray's name has been linked with serial killer Theodore Kaczynski, the Unabomber, who claimed to have participated in disturbing experiments led by Murray at Harvard where he was a student (see Chase 2003).

Murray's Research at Harvard

It was Murray's research at Harvard in the 1930s on personality, however, that is most relevant to tracing the modern history of action and creative approaches to psychotherapy. This research concerned subjecting a group of Harvard students to a battery of psychological tests, ostensibly to understand the nature of the human personality. He and his colleagues were theoretically eclectic, but because of Murray's background, they tended to rely most often on psychoanalytical interpretations of their findings. In determining criteria for assessing their subjects, most all of whom were Harvard undergraduates, they identified forty-four personality variables, which consisted of lists of needs, inner states, and general traits. These variables revealed a holistic conception of personality, including not only cognition, but also affective, somatic, social, aesthetic, and spiritual aspects. This holistic approach offers a useful model for drama and other action therapists not only for research purposes but also for conceptualizing the personality.

Murray and his colleagues worked with several small groups of subjects. Each subject was given a battery of some twenty-five tests lasting about thirty-six hours. Of note were procedures designed to elicit aesthetic, imaginative, and affective responses on the part of the subjects. These included the Aesthetic Appreciation Test, the Musical Reverie Test, the TAT, and the Dramatic Productions Test, which are most germane to our discussion.

The Musical Reverie Test

The subjects in the Musical Reverie Test were asked to listen to a number of classical musical excerpts and identify "dramatic occurrences" evoked by the music, which they did through storytelling and role-playing. From this experience, the experimenters concluded that the dramatic associations with the music provided useful information about the personality structures of the subjects. One young man, for example, told the story of a street beggar, forced by an exploitative bully to play his violin in the street for money. The beggar discovered an old violin master who took him in, protected him, and taught him to become a famous violinist. This rags to riches story, reminiscent of an old Horatio Alger novel, *Phil, the Fiddler* (1872), revealed to the researchers certain intrapsychic issues and family dynamics of the subject.

Some forty years after the publication of the Musical Reverie Test, Helen Bonny (1997), a music therapist and researcher, developed a similar approach to music therapy called Guided Imagery in Music. Through this approach, clients are asked to listen to various recordings of classical and contemporary music and to freely express images evoked by the music. The images are expressed verbally and through drawings of mandalas on paper. Bonny thus moved the earlier version of the Musical Reverie Test further into the realm of action psychotherapy by means of an art form.

The Thematic Apperception Test

For the TAT (Murray 1938), the subjects were shown a series of pictures, which portrayed characters in provocative situations such as the following: "A short elderly woman stands with her back turned to a tall young man. The latter is looking downward with a perplexed expression, his hat in his hands" (537). As in the Musical Reverie Test, subjects were asked to respond to the projective stimulus by means of a dramatic story of their own, offering their sense of the events preceding and following the moment in the picture.

Paving the way for the projective aspects of drama and other action therapies, this experience provided subjects with a distance from their everyday lives. In creating fictional roles and stories in response to the pictures, the subjects safely re-created aspects of their actual lives. The premise of aesthetic distance not only defines the act of making art, but also the experience of drama and related arts therapies where clients, once removed from their everyday experiences, are encouraged to act within an imaginative frame in order to reveal certain unconscious experiences.

Murray's projective approach to exploring the unconscious was certainly not new. A number of projective tests, include the Rorschach Inkblot Test, preceded his own TAT. However, given his sensibility and openness to the full spectrum of personality expression, the reading of his projective test was not limited to a classical psychoanalytical interpretation. Rather, Murray's example provided a model for those who worked directly with fictional roles and stories to help clients discover a deeper understanding of unconscious dynamics.

Erik Homburger Erikson and the Dramatic Productions Test

And finally, let us look at the Dramatic Productions Test devised by Erik Homburger, who later changed his name to Erik Erikson. Homburger, a lay analyst of children, took his inspiration, as did Ferenczi, from the playful, nonverbal expression of young people. Homburger was familiar with the work of the early psychoanalysts in play therapy, as well as that of the pediatrician and psychologist Margaret Lowenfeld (1979), mentioned earlier, who devised a projective approach called World Technique where children re-created their inner worlds by means of toys and play objects. In Homburger's active test, subjects were asked to construct a dramatic scene on a tabletop with miniature objects provided by the researcher. As in the previous projective tests, the researcher intended to explore unconscious dynamics implicit in the dramatic story. In interpreting the dramatic constructions, Homburger noted some pronounced trauma expressed in symbolic forms. He made his determinations based on the form and content of the dramatic constructions, looking at such elements as roles, boundaries and borders, themes, plot development, and commentary from the subjects.

One figure that Homburger noted was chosen repeatedly by the subjects was that of a little girl, and one repeated theme had to do with an accident that befalls this character, often having to do with cars or vehicles. He speculated that the figure of the little girl, as the youngest among the toys presented to the subjects, might represent the archetypal role of child and that the repeated theme of the accident might represent that which happens to children. From a more psychoanalytic perspective, he reasoned that the accident experienced by the girl might represent the related themes of violence and sex.

At the end of his speculations, Homburger made a distinction between dramatic and traumatic moments, both of which threaten the integrity of the ego. In drama, individuals are confronted with existential choices which, when resolved, can lead to expanding their ability to negotiate external reality as well as their own internal demons. In doing so, they become heroes. In trauma, free choice is removed as an option, transforming people into victims rather than heroes and diminishing the resiliency of the ego.

Homburger as Erik Erikson went on to create a model of human development that proved to be highly influential to the field of developmental and ego psychology. Erikson postulated eight stages throughout the life cycle, completing Freud's psychosexual stages that began in infancy and ended in latency. More attuned to Shakespeare's poetic ages of man from *As You Like It* than Freud's scientifically based stages, Erikson embraced a dramatic version of development as one heroically moved through the life cycle by resolving conflicts along the way.

Like his mentor, Murray, who wrote a psychological profile of Hitler, Erikson wrote psycho-biographies of Martin Luther and Mahatma Gandhi. His last work in specifying the final stage of the lifespan inspired many in arts therapies who work expressively with the elderly. But it is his early work in dramatic constructions, similar in many ways to the work of Jung, that proved most influential to art and drama therapists who developed similar projective means of working with children and adults through miniature objects.

In concluding his ambitious personality study, Murray mentioned that intuition was omitted as a variable because intuition is a quality that permeates all major personality functions. Then he went further, emphatically stating that action should stand in the place of intuition, noting action was minimized in the writings of his mentor, Carl Jung. Murray (1938) defined action as "the practical and effective manipulation of the physical or social environment, its aim being tangible achievement, power and possession" (727). Like Moreno and others who conceived of action as an essential form of psychotherapy, Murray left his own mark in defining an approach that empowered individuals and groups not only by assessing their personalities, but also by changing them.

FRITZ PERLS AND GESTALT THERAPY

Fritz Perls (1893–1970), the founder, with his wife Laura Perls, of Gestalt therapy, was a contemporary of Murray and Moreno, all born within a few years of one another. Although he might have been aware of Murray's work at Harvard, he was much more of a kindred spirit to Moreno. Both had a similar background as middle-class German-speaking Jews. Both graduated medical school in Europe in the 1920s and eventually made their professional reputations in the United States. Both studied psychoanalysis and rebelled against the orthodoxy of Freud. Both were iconoclasts who associated with Bohemian artists and envisioned their work and indeed their lives as more art than science. Both were charismatic and at times grandiose and assumed the mantle of the guru. And both played seminal parts in forging and popularizing a psychotherapeutic approach based in action.

In drawing the line from the early psychoanalysts to Perls, one recognizes clear connections. Perls, for example, studied with and was analyzed and supervised by some of the stellar analysts of his time including Wilhelm Reich, Karen Horney, and Otto Fenichel. The language of his early book, *Ego, Hunger and Aggression* (1947), written in collaboration with Laura Perls, whose contributions Perls does not fully acknowledge, is steeped in Freudian concepts of ego and instinct, resistance, introjection, and projection. But when the Freudians rejected his paper on oral resistances at a conference in Marienbad in 1936, he counterrejected the Freudians.

Liberated from conventional psychoanalysis, Perls embraced other models. One, the organismic approach of Kurt Goldstein, was also highly influential to the work of Henry Murray in its holistic view of the personality. Perls assisted Goldstein at the Institute for Brain-Injured Soldiers in Frankfurt in the 1920s. Through the influence of his wife, who was a colleague of Goldstein, Perls also became interested in the earlier work of the Gestalt psychologists, Wertheimer, Kohler, and Koffka, although his notion of Gestalt therapy was far removed from the cognitive underpinnings of Gestalt psychology, which dealt primarily with issues of perception and problem-solving.

When he published his first book in 1947, he had incorporated some of the ideas of his predecessors in conceiving a holistic view of personality and of a balanced relationship between the figure and the ground of the perceptual Gestalt. More significantly, Perls moved away from the cognitive and rationalist focus of both Gestalt psychology and classical psychoanalysis, favoring instead the somatic focus of an earlier mentor, Wilhelm Reich. And in abandoning Freud's conception of the instincts of eros and thanatos, the latter being the source of aggression, Perls reconceived aggression as a means of survival which, once fully expressed, restores balance. The expression of aggression became not only the hallmark of Perls's therapeutic approach, but also of his abrasive personality. Further, in rejecting Freud's "archeological complex," that is, his insistence on revisiting historical experience as the source of neurotic behavior, Perls focused on the present moment, the here and now, as the locus of transformation.

Before developing his signature Gestalt therapy approach through engaging the client in role-play and role reversal, Perls (1947) settled on a form that he called concentration therapy. Within this form Perls developed the following techniques: visualization, expressive speaking, emotional discharge, internal silence, speaking in first person singular, body concentration, and awareness. For each technique, Perls proposed many specific exercises. Summing up his goals, Perls (1947) stated emphatically: "The curative steps to be taken are obvious: you have not only to become fully aware, what emotion, interest or urge you are concealing, but you must also express it by words, art, or action" (257).

As Perls found his niche at the Esalen Institute in Big Sur, California, in the 1960s, he was best able to realize his therapeutic mission of expression through action. Much of this work appears to be psychodramatic in nature, and Perls was certainly influenced by Moreno. But Perls, as Moreno, needed to find his own path, and so he not only reconceived some of Moreno's signature techniques, but also invented many of his own. Like Moreno, Perls became associated with a poetic aphorism. It is cited at the beginning of his book, *Gestalt Therapy Verbatim* (1969):

I do my thing, and you do your thing.
I am not in this world to live up to your expectations
And you are not in this world to live up to mine.
You are you, and I am I,
And if by chance, we find each other, it's beautiful.
If not, it can't be helped.

But Perls's dictum, a celebration of the supremacy of the individual over and above the relationship, is quite different from that of Moreno and Ferenczi before him, who offered a vision of mutuality through role reversal and encounter. In many ways, Perls captured the spirit of the existentialist thinkers more than of the Gestalt psychologists in his understanding of the alienation of human beings, alone in the universe and subject to the vicissitudes of chance.

Perls's theoretical ideas were mostly derivative, not only from the existentialists and the Gestalt psychologists, but from the early psychoanalysts. And yet his insistence on working holistically in the here and now was radical for its time, as was his direct engagement and encounter with his patients. Perls, like Freud, came of age in a historic moment that was on the cusp of change. He transitioned as a psychoanalyst in the conservative, buttoned-down 1950s to a Gestalt therapist in the explosive 1960s, a time of human-potential movements, sensory awareness, rampant narcissism, and radical experimentation with altered forms of consciousness. It was a good time to be Fritz Perls, on the barricades of bourgeois life, attacking those poor unexpressive individuals cut off from their bodies and their most intense feelings.

The greatest contributions of Perls to action psychotherapy were technical as he blended the biophysical ideas of Reich and the psychodramatic ideas of Moreno into his own unique form of Gestalt therapy. Perls was not a prolific writer, and most all of his publications after *Ego, Hunger and Aggression* were descriptions of his therapeutic process. It is in these descriptions that we can clearly see his action-based therapeutic process as modeled after psychodrama and leading toward drama therapy.

Some of Perls's most compelling contributions appeared in 1969 in *Gestalt Therapy Verbatim*. As is customary with many of the therapists whom we have explored, Perls, too, needed to discredit Freud, especially his overemphasis upon verbal analysis. Perls (1969) wrote:

> Verbal communication is usually a lie. The real communication is beyond words. . . . [J]ust listen to what the voice tells you, what the movements tell you, what the posture tells you, what the image tells you. . . . You don't have to listen to *what* the person says: listen to the sounds. *Per sona*—"through sound" (57).

Unlike Freud's approach to analyzing dreams and connecting the symbolic content of the dream to repressed wishes and early psychosexual stages of development, Perls viewed the dream as a stage and worked with dreamers as if they were not only the playwrights of their dreams, but also the actors. Their job, coached by Perls, was to play out conflicting parts of themselves as represented by objects and roles in the dream. The goal was to help clients discover a balance, "a oneness and integration of the two opposing forces" (74). In distinguishing his approach from that of Moreno, Perls noted that in Gestalt therapy, the client plays all the roles. In psychodrama, others in the group play auxiliary roles in the client's drama and thus, claimed Perls, often bring in their own baggage. Perls also noted that in Gestalt therapy, clients were encouraged to give action to all objects, human or otherwise, whereas in psychodrama clients worked primarily with reality-based human roles.

A Session with John

As an example of the specific action approach used by Perls, let us turn to a brief session with John. John volunteered to work on a dream with Perls, but Perls, in character, proceeded to frustrate John. In reaction, John accused Perls of being hostile. Perls (1969) invited John to work with the image of the hostile figure through the techniques of the empty chair and role reversal, two methods he borrowed from Moreno:

> Perls: Put Fritz on the chair. Say "Fritz, you seem to be a little bit hostile." Play Fritz.
>
> John: Play Fritz. . . . Play you. . . . I can't play you. . . . I think you're so omnipotent. . . . I'm trying to be Fritz. . . . I'm telling you to be open. I'm telling you to bend to my will. . . .
>
> Perls: OK, switch chairs. Answer this.
>
> John: I don't want to bend myself to your will. I think you're a pompous old shitty crappy bastard.
>
> Perls: Could you go on a little bit with your mud-slinging. I like that. . . .

John: OK. . . . You want to be God, you want to show off your whole production to this group here. I'm not convinced that this is better than analysis. You know, maybe you're just a big pompous ass who is satisfying his own omnipotence by being up here. . . .

Perls: So now can you play that role? Play a pompous ass, omnipotent. Play that Fritz that you just spoke to.

John: That's what I'm afraid I'll be. If I really—am me. A goddamn pompous ass like you are. . . . All right. I'm Fritz Perls, I know everything. . . .

Perls then encouraged John to take on the pompous qualities, and he turned to the audience and said: "I'm more important than all of you—you aren't anything." Following that, John offered his dream of coming to Esalen and feeling competitive with three men on horseback. In that he had trouble telling his dream in the present tense, Perls scolded and insulted him. In counterattacking Perls, John became aware of the pompous, arrogant part of himself and realized that he felt very small in stature, dissociated from his body, a man who could not sit up tall on a horse like his competitors. Perls pointed out a polarity between the pompous ass and the insignificant John and asked John to play out an encounter between the two roles. As the insignificant role, John said:

"I'm nothing. . . . I don't even feel my own body—because you, you pompous ass, won't let me (voice begins to break)—you goddamn bitch. You try to run everything and I'm squelched. . . . You won't let me exist, you won't let me feel that I'm real" (225).

In taking on the pompous role, John countered:

"You don't deserve to exist, you goddamn nincompoop. . . . You're too afraid to exist. . . . You aren't here and you never were here, you never will be here, and I hate you!" (cries)

And finally, as the insignificant John, he concluded:

"God, I hate you because you won't let me exist. You're stamping me out. But it's me. I know it's me" (226).

As the dialogue concluded, Perls pointed out that John had been playing out his polarity of omnipotence and impotence, with no center. And then Perls encouraged John to play both the insignificant and the pompous roles again and at the end of each sentence to add the rejoinder, "and this is a lie." In doing so, John began to let go of his attachment to the extremes, to reclaim his body and to let go of his grandiosity. In the end, John referred to the two empty chairs representing the polarities and asked, with some degree of distance: "Does it have to be just a constant dialogue . . . between two parts of yourself? Can't you be someplace somewhere in between? Can't you feel real. . . . I want to have a center" (229).

Here we see the mature Perls who used the reality of the here and now to help John become aware of his polarities and to work them through. The method of work is a dramatic one as John identifies the qualities of each role and engages in a series of monologues, deepening an understanding of each role, and dialogues, looking at the dynamics between the polarities.

Perls (1969) saw the basic conflicting aspects of the personality as polar roles that he called topdog and underdog. The former is a bully, a pompous, controlling, and righteous part of the personality that manipulates through threats and demands. For John, the topdog was the pompous ass. The underdog is the defensive, weak, whiny part of the personality that manipulates through cunning and apparent helplessness. The underdog was the insignificant John. Neither extreme role can win the dramatic battle. As Perls well illustrated, the dilemma is only resolved as the extremes seek a balance. For Perls, that balance was best realized in releasing feeling associated with an extreme role and then becoming fully aware of one's body. As we shall see later, the notion of role and counterrole and the search for balance between polarities will become a hallmark of the role method of drama therapy.

As part of Perls's technique, he invited John to "put Fritz on the chair," that is, reverse roles with the therapist. By using role reversal, Perls provided an opportunity for clients to view a dilemma from another point of view and reown their projections. In John's case, the empty chair held the grandiosity not only of the pompous Perls, but also of the pompous John, just as a second empty chair held its polarity. This technique, so common to psychodrama, will also become a staple in drama therapy.

A Session with Gloria

Another example of Perls's action approach is taken from the film, *Three Approaches to Psychotherapy*, produced by Everett Shostrom in 1965. As mentioned above, Perls is one of three featured psychotherapists, all of whom work with a common client, Gloria. The film is important to this book as it provides a model for the film, *Three Approaches to Drama Therapy*, which will be discussed in some detail later.

When Perls first appears on film, he states his goals and methods in working with Gloria. Although somewhat obliquely stated, he implies that he will encourage authentic expression in the here and now, focus upon the relationship between himself and Gloria, and help her to "integrate conflicting polarities" (Perls in Shostrom 1965). Perls characterizes his work as "a safe emergency," implying that he will provoke a kind of crisis, ameliorated only by its distance from everyday life. Perls also notes that he will focus upon nonverbal behavior, helping Gloria to become aware of her body language.

Ironically, it is Perls's nonverbal behavior at the beginning of the session that is most expressive. He appears uncomfortable in his seat. He spends time searching for his cigarettes and matches, as if he is distracted by the setting and needs to calm himself down. Rather than providing a comfortable space for Gloria, he leans into her, almost obtrusively. His fidgeting and intrusiveness appear to be his warm-up to taking on the role of topdog, provoking Gloria into the counterrole of underdog.

In response to Perls's nonverbal cues, Gloria says, "Right away I'm scared." Perls jumps right in, focusing upon Gloria's nonverbal expression: "You say you're scared, but you are smiling. I don't understand how you could be scared and smiling at the same time." Right from the beginning, Perls puts Gloria on the defensive and she, in her own way, attempts to counter, noting his arrogance, like John in the above example. But then she verbalizes her fear that Perls will corner her. Perls picks up on the image and notes that when Gloria speaks of her corner she touches her chest, as if to protect herself. Perls wonders aloud whether she is embodying the corner through this gesture and asks her to speak openly about her feeling of being trapped. Gloria goes to the past, evoking the role of herself as a little girl who retreated to a safe corner when distressed. Perls responds in attack mode, attempting to bring her back to the here and now: "Are you a little girl? Are you a little girl?"

In response, Gloria returns to the present, asking Perls for help and comfort, noting that Perls could easily make her feel dumb. Perls counters by asking how playing dumb, a quality of the underdog, benefits her. Gloria is unable to respond so Perls amends his question and asks how playing dumb affects Perls. Throughout, Perls does his best to frustrate Gloria. As much as she retreats, he attacks, calling her a phony repeatedly, accusing her of performing rather than staying with her feelings, pointing out the discrepancies between her words and gestures. At the height of Perls's attacks, Gloria counterattacks, expressing her strong displeasure with Perls' behavior. At this moment Perls congratulates her, although he does so in a mocking way. Despite his performance, Gloria is able to take in his praise and admits to feeling embarrassed. She becomes aware of hiding her embarrassment through physical gestures, such as smiling.

But soon again, Perls attacks, and well into her anger, Gloria accuses Perls of egotism, of demanding so much respect. In turn, Perls asks her to take on the role of a respected person. Gloria admits her difficulty in taking on this role, especially in relation to Perls, for fear that he will demean her and banish her to her shameful corner. Perls then takes on the demeaning persona and responds, sarcastically: "You need to have someone pull out little mam'sell in distress out of the corner." Adding insult to injury, he accuses Gloria of being phony for not pulling herself out of her self-imposed corner.

Although Perls's manner was confrontational, he attempted to provoke Gloria into a foreign role, that of the assertive, powerful woman, one who inspires respect. In doing so, he was working toward helping her integrate an imbalance of polarities.

On the whole, this session was only modestly successful, unlike that of John. It appears that Perls was able to realize some of his goals by fostering authentic expression in the here and now, an awareness of nonverbal behavior, and at least a cursory ability to integrate polarities. It is less clear if the "emergency" provoked by Perls was safe enough for Gloria to come to some kind of clear resolution.

At the end of the session, one rather dramatic moment occurred that, if further explored, might have led to further awareness of the polarities. Throughout, much of the struggle between Perls and Gloria was about intimacy and the complexity of relationship. Both at times withdrew to their various corners and attacked the other for not providing what he or she wanted. Both accused the other of being too distant and emotionally inaccessible. In a soft moment, Perls responded to Gloria's need for intimacy by asking, "How should I be? How could I show you my concern?" He added that if she were to cry, how would she like him to respond? Gloria responded by saying that she might be able to accept Perls's comfort. And then, pointedly, she became aware of the possibility of playing the dual roles of the child, accepting the parent's comfort, and the parent, able to comfort the child. Finally, she imagined herself in the role of the parent and boldly pronounced that if Perls were a baby in distress, she would provide comfort. In response, Perls suddenly ended the session, some six minutes before his allotted time, leaving the viewer to imagine what might happen if they played out Gloria's fantasy.

Later, during his summation, Perls criticized Gloria for avoiding a deeper level of encounter with her pain and with Perls. But is it possible that Perls missed the opportunity to engage more dramatically in role reversal? What might have happened if he had actually assumed the role of baby or even of parent? But then again, Perls did not overtly engage in role playing with his patients. His method was about empowering them to play out all their roles, alone. This last point might reveal both a major strength and weakness of Gestalt therapy. By playing all the roles, people like John and Gloria have the chance to integrate several split-off parts of themselves. But by doing so alone, in the presence of a frustrating therapist, they lose the opportunity for support and comfort.

Few were as influential as Moreno or even as Murray, Erikson, and Perls in providing a clear understanding of the theory and practice of action and drama in psychotherapy. But aspects of others' work merit some brief discussion before we move into a fuller presentation of the three main action approaches featured in this book. In an article titled "The Emergence of Role Playing as a Form of Psychotherapy," Kipper (1996) focuses mainly on three therapeutic modalities: psychodrama, fixed-role therapy, and behavior rehearsal. As psychodrama is discussed in depth in other chapters, we turn our attention briefly to the latter two.

GEORGE KELLY AND FIXED-ROLE THERAPY

George Kelly (1905–1967) was a psychologist who was among the first to implement a psychotherapeutic approach based in the principles of constructivism. Constructivism is a philosophy that seeks to understand the ways that individuals and groups act upon the world through language, gesture, and symbolic action in order to construct their own realities. Kelly lived in Kansas during the Dust Bowl and the Great Depression of the 1920s and 1930s and was devoted to helping rural farming families in distress. He had a background in speech and drama, two disciplines that shaped his developing work.

Initially applying psychoanalytic techniques in treating rural families, Kelly began to realize the futility of providing psychosexual explanations for problems embedded in living in a harsh environment. He developed an approach originally called constructive alternativism, which concerned exploring the way his patients constructed their realities and searching for alternative solutions to their problems. By the 1950s, he wrote his influential book, *The Psychology of Personal Constructs*, laying out his mature theory and practice.

Kelly's most important development for our purposes was that of fixed-role therapy, an approach that arose from his work with rural clients during a time of crisis. It was clear that Kelly treated clients for brief periods of time and that he required a down to earth and efficient approach. Combining his psychological talent for analyzing the personality with his theatrical talent for creating a character and directing a scene, Kelly devised a systematic role method.

The method began by asking the client to write a self-characterization, an autobiography of sorts. Kelly and his colleagues aided in the writing by asking clients to sort a group of cards upon which were written various skills and personality qualities. Rejecting a medical approach to diagnosis, Kelly (1955) firmly believed: "if you do not know what is wrong with someone, ask them, they may tell you" (Vol. 1, 241).

Kelly and his team studied the self-characterization and from that developed a fixed-role sketch, which provided the outline of a fictional character different from the client yet similar in some essential ways, mirroring, for example, the economic circumstances of the client. Throughout the treatment, usually lasting several weeks, the client took on the fictional role and played it out both in therapy and in everyday life.

During treatment, Kelly helped clients deepen their commitment to the roles through improvising potential scenarios, sometimes with Kelly enacting auxiliary roles. In addition to developing their roles with the therapist, the clients played out the roles in all aspects of their everyday lives for the remainder of the treatment.

Kelly was most likely aware of Moreno's work in psychodrama, as it was readily available in published form, and less likely aware of Perls' work in Gestalt therapy. By engaging in role-play with his clients, he was certainly practicing techniques common to both, although his particular role method was uniquely grounded in the theoretical model of constructivism.

In follow-up discussions, client and therapist evaluated the effectiveness of the new role. As such, the fixed-roles were constructions that had the potential of changing the way clients related to habitual circumstances. Like actors with new parts, clients in fixed-role therapy reported an ability to not only view themselves in new ways, but also to view the world anew. Consistent with the notion of constructivism, they took an active part in devising the role behaviors that lead to a change in perspective. In working through fixed roles, Kelly was one of the first to practice a form of brief therapy, much in keeping with Rank and Ferenczi's notion of a shorter time frame of treatment.

Like Moreno, who devised sociometric tests, Kelly invented his own assessment instrument, the role construct repertory test, better known as the rep grid. The test proceeded as clients identified some ten to twenty people who are important in their lives. When administered by a therapist, the choice might not be random but based upon responses to certain questions such as, Who is someone in your life whom you loved?

Once all the choices were made, the therapist chose three figures at a time and asked the client to determine which two are similar and which one is different. From these choices, the therapist created a similarity pole and a contrast pole, representing a construct in one's social interactions.

From a series of directed questions and answers, the therapist helped the client identify some ten to twenty constructs that served as a map into the personality of the client. The rep grid has been used in therapy, assessment, and research with individuals, small groups, and large groups. As we will see later, this personality test predates drama therapy instruments, such as role profiles, used for similar purposes.

BEHAVIOR REHEARSAL AND MULTIMODAL THERAPY

Kelly's role approach, although based in constructivism, very much foreshadows the development of cognitive-behavioral therapy. Unlike the more cathartic and existential role approaches of Moreno and Perls, fixed-role therapy looks more toward modifying behavior and rethinking options. In fixed-role therapy the role becomes the mediator between thought and action.

Joseph Wolpe

Joseph Wolpe and Arnold Lazarus, two major figures within the tradition of behavioral therapy, used a form of role-playing to help clients modify their behavior in relationship to stressful and overpowering life circumstances. Their particular approach was called behavior rehearsal.

Wolpe (1990) speaks of this approach as follows:

> The therapist takes the role of a person towards whom the patient has a neurotic anxiety reaction and instructs him to express his ordinarily inhibited feelings toward that person. Particular attention is given to the emotion infused into the words. . . . The patient is made to repeat each statement . . . being constantly corrected until the utterance is in every way satisfactory (68).

Through the behavior rehearsal, patients slowly move from the expression of inhibited feelings toward more direct feelings that relieve their anxiety and satisfy their needs in relationship to the other. Wolpe became known as developing behavioral approaches of systematic desensitization, reciprocal inhibition, and assertiveness training. In practicing these approaches at times through role-playing, he established the compatibility of action with behavioral therapy.

Wolpe was also known to use other action and expressive approaches toward changing behavior, including imagery and eye movement. The work in eye movement later evolved into an approach to treat trauma and related conditions, called Eye Movement Desensitization and Reprocessing or EMDR.

Kipper (1996) specifies four basic stages in behavior rehearsal. The first involves preparing clients to accept the premise that role-playing can be useful in developing new ways of relating to embedded problems. The second concerns focusing upon the particular problematic situation that requires a new response. At this stage, the therapist creates a hierarchy of new behaviors required, ranking them from least to most difficult. In stage 3, the actual enactment of the new behaviors begins. At this point, the therapist and client engage in role-play, rehearsing the desired behaviors step by step through the hierarchy, until the client has mastered the most challenging impediment. Often the therapist will model the desired behaviors or coach clients toward a given level of competence.

In the final stage, clients implement the behaviors in everyday life. After this is done, clients write up their experiences and reflections, which are later shared with the therapist. In their continuing collaboration, therapist and client work to modify the behaviors to obtain the optimal results.

Arnold Lazarus

Arnold Lazarus collaborated with his mentor, Wolpe (Wolpe and Lazarus 1966), in developing behavior rehearsal and behavior therapy. Like Wolpe, Lazarus believed that action approaches to psychotherapy allowed clients to construct, rehearse, and implement effective roles essential in moving through certain psychological blocks. But Lazarus also realized the limits of behavioral approaches to certain entrenched anxiety and mood disorders. In response, he incorporated cognitive approaches and then, aware of the need to view the person more holistically, he isolated seven interrelated modalities of personality. The modalities included behavior, affect, sensation, imagery, cognition, interpersonal relationships, and the requirement of drugs or biological interventions. Lazarus developed an assessment instrument, the Multimodal Life History Inventory (Lazarus and Lazarus 1991), which identified the strength of each modality and pointed to treatment strategies. The acronym for the results, applying the first letters of each modality, is BASIC ID. Influenced by Lazarus, drama therapist Mooli Lahad (1992) later developed a similar multimodal model based in storymaking. This model uses the acronym BASIC Ph to represent styles of coping with stress. Lahad's styles include coping through beliefs, affect, social relationships, imagination, cognition, and physical means.

Lazarus applied action methods to treatment more frequently than Wolpe, extending from behavior to the full compliment of modalities. In the second version of the film, *Three Approaches to Psychotherapy* (Shostrom 1977), for example, we see Lazarus working directly through role-play.

Although the work of Kelly, Wolpe, and Lazarus was couched in theoretical models of constructivism and behaviorism that do not, at first glance, suggest dramatic methods of treatment, all three found ways to effectively reach their therapeutic goals through action. Lazarus's approach was the most far-reaching in that he not only incorporated role-playing, but also extended his theoretical frame from behavior and cognition to affect, sensation, and imagery, all domains addressed directly in drama therapy and psychodrama. The one modality omitted by Lazarus was that of the body. In looking at a latter-day approach to working somatically, extending the ideas and practices of Wilhelm Reich, we turn to Alexander Lowen.

ALEXANDER LOWEN AND BIOENERGETIC ANALYSIS

Alexander Lowen was originally a lawyer who became interested in psychotherapy and attended a series of lectures given by Wilhelm Reich in New York City in 1940. Inspired by the lectures and the notion that healing occurs through removal of body armor, Lowen engaged in therapy with Reich. He (1993) described his first encounter as follows:

I went with the naïve assumption that there was nothing wrong with me. . . . I lay down on the bed wearing a pair of bathing trunks . . . I was told to bend my knees, relax and breathe with my mouth open and my jaw relaxed. . . . After some time, Reich said: "Lowen, you're not breathing." I answered, "Of course I'm breathing; otherwise, I'd be dead." He then remarked: "Your chest . . . isn't moving. Feel my chest." . . . I lay back and resumed breathing. . . . Reich said: "Drop your head back and open your eyes wide." I did as I was told and . . . a scream burst from my throat. . . . I was not connected to it emotionally. . . . I left the session with the feeling that I was not as alright as I had thought. There were "things" (images, emotions) in my personality that were hidden from consciousness, and I knew that they would have to come out (17–18).

Lowen went on to become a psychiatrist, extending the principles and techniques of Reich into his own form of somatic psychotherapy that he called bioenergetic analysis. Like Reich, Lowen worked with methods of deep breathing and body motility, developing a series of psychophysical techniques to release tension and restore emotional expression. Lowen (1967) wrote about work with individuals he characterized as schizoid, helping them to reconnect to their social worlds and to experience a greater sense of integration.

Lowen frequently asked patients to sketch their body images. Working with the sketches, he guided his patients toward understanding the genesis of their defensive armoring in their early relationships with their parents. Like Reich, Lowen in part framed his theoretical understanding in Freud's theory of infantile sexuality. In practice, however, his approach became more and more action based. In facilitating the release of tension through the body and voice, Lowen developed a series of expressive movements. Examples included kicking and beating the couch while uttering a simple text such as: "I won't! I hate you! No!" At times, Lowen engaged with the patient by verbalizing, for example, "You will!" At other times, Lowen intervened physically, clasping, for example, a patient's wrist to provoke a deeper emotional expression.

Lowen prescribed many positions of expressive movement in response to an immediate affective need, such as striking the couch with a tennis racket to relieve anger, banging the head against a mattress to release frustration and, as an example of an affirmative gesture, reaching up with arms outspread for one's mother.

Like drama and movement therapists who made use of related forms of action, Lowen at times characterized his patients according to roles, such as witches and victims, clowns and dolls, seducers and innocents. However, unlike many later drama therapists who deconstruct the notion of a core self, Lowen took a traditional humanistic position of viewing role-playing as false and inauthentic, a distortion developed in childhood of one's true authentic being. For Lowen, the authentic self, seen most clearly in the infant, is one marked by flow and spontaneity in body and affect.

Lowen's work inspired many dance/movement therapists, somatic psychotherapists, and primal therapists, all of whom believe that healing proceeds through forms of action that unblock the body and release repressed affect stored in the body. For the treatment to have a lasting effect, Lowen, like his mentor, Reich, believed that patients needed to integrate their present experience of somatic and affective relief with an understanding of their early trauma.

OTHER EXPERIMENTS IN PLAY AND ACTION PSYCHOTHERAPY

As we have seen, psychotherapists from various orientations work at least in part through action. There are many more examples, too numerous to discuss in depth, but worthy of mentioning. In play therapy, for example, J. Solomon (1938) developed a form called active play therapy. Virginia Axline (1969), working in the tradition of client-centered therapy, often engaged in role-play with children. In a later version of Axline's approach, Landreth (1991) categorized play objects and toys according to their creative-expressive and emotional-release qualities. Landreth makes sure that the child has access to a plethora of creative media including visual art and performing art materials.

D. W. Winnicott

Among the post-Freudian psychoanalysts, D. W. Winnicott is one who has made a lasting contribution to understanding the theory and practice of action psychotherapy. When working with children, Winnicott applied a relational approach to psychoanalysis based in the primacy of play. Winnicott developed the influential concept of transitional space and the related one of the transitional object. The transitional phases come into play as the developing child separates from the mother and takes on an independent existence even as it clings to dependency. While moving into a new developmental stage, the child requires a transitional space in order to negotiate the pull to and from each side of the psychological border.

Like the notion of aesthetic distance, transitional space is the psychological gap that stands between one stage of development and another and between inner experience and the outside world. Winnicott (1953) described transitional space as located "between the thumb and the teddy bear, between oral eroticism and true object relationship" (89). The thumb and teddy bear are both transitional objects as they sooth the child, just as the child is about to reach out into the wide world alone, by recapitulating the safe attachment to the mother's body. Winnicott's theory of play as a bridge between the inner experience of the child and the external reality is a dramatic one in that the child does not only repeat problematic experience in play, but also resolves it through imaginative, symbolic action.

Action Approaches in Brief Psychotherapy

Action approaches are also used regularly in brief psychotherapy. Since the advent of managed care, the trend has been for psychotherapists to achieve greater therapeutic benefits in less time. Echoing the sentiments of Rank and Ferenczi calling for a shortened course of psychoanalytic treatment, Harry Stack Sullivan (1954) looked forward to the kind of therapy that "has a high probability of achieving what you're attempting to achieve, with a minimum of time and words" (224).

Transactional analysis innovated by Eric Berne (1961) is one example of a brief psychotherapy based in part in dramatic action. Berne identified three ego states of child, parent, and adult. In working with clients, Berne used role-playing as a means to explore these ego states as they are played out in social relationships. Berne (1964) also conceptualized human interactions in terms of repeated dramatic scenarios, referring to these scenarios as games and helping people to identify and work toward modifying ineffective games in their lives. As mentioned earlier, Berne was influenced directly by Moreno, having attended his open psychodramas in New York City, even though he was loath to acknowledge Moreno's influence (Z. T. Moreno 2006a).

Another brief approach, more clearly dramatic, was that developed by Robert and Mary Goulding (1978) called redecision therapy. The Gouldings theorized that clients got stuck in dysfunctional patterns as children, developing attitudes to help them survive often difficult or traumatic conditions in their families. They helped clients revisit the child role and discover ways to revise their old patterns. In therapy clients made use of the psychodramatic and Gestalt technique of the empty chair, often taking on the dual roles of child and parent. Through role-play, clients were able to review and then revise the decisions they made in the past. An example, called "The Case of the Woman Who Stood Up for Herself," concerns an anxious and insecure twenty-five-year-old woman named Maria, who recalled a moment at age six when she was scolded by her father for spilling a glass of juice. The redecision therapist gave the following directions:

> Let yourself be 6 years old again and go back there. See the room and the juice on the rug and all the details, and let yourself feel yourself being that scared 6-year-old girl (Hoyt 2003, 370).

In her work, Maria was able to take on the role of the young girl as well as the father and discover that the scary father was hardly the beast that she thought he was. In the child role, aided by her therapist, she was able to stand up for herself and say to her father: "I'm only a little kid and I make mistakes, but I'm not bad and you shouldn't yell at me" (Hoyt 2003, 370). As an adult in brief psychotherapy, Maria was able to create a new model of herself as one who despite her shortcoming had the power to question authority and take a stand. According to the redecision therapists, it is the action approach that facilitates this process as it moves directly into an identified problem, empowering clients to respond through expressive enactment to the question: "What are you willing to change today?"

Given this rich history of action in psychotherapy, let us now take a more in-depth look at the two action psychotherapies that are the beneficiaries of this legacy—psychodrama and drama therapy.

3

An Overview of the Dramatic Therapies

We have already seen how J. L. Moreno developed his understanding and implemented the practice of sociometry, psychodrama, and sociodrama. In addition to these forms, Moreno innovated group psychotherapy, which stood in marked contrast to the psychoanalytic model of individual treatment. Moreno's action-based work radically challenged the ideas of the early psychoanalysts and crystallized many of the action-based experiments of the psychotherapists reviewed above.

Moreno's legacy is intact more than thirty years after his death. Several generations of trainers, practitioners, researchers, and writers have passed on the classical structures of theory and practice to successive generations (see, for example, Holmes, Carp, and Watson 1994; Karp, Holmes, and Bradshaw-Tauvon 1998; Blatner 2000; and Gershoni 2003). Many (see Hare and Hare 1996; Blatner 2000), however, have written that Moreno's theories of role, spontaneity-creativity, and sociometry are unsystematic and lacking in empirical validation. But, undaunted, the same critics embrace the subjective, even poetic nature of the field and the aesthetic-spiritual vision that was articulated and then implemented by Moreno.

Moreno's contributions to the theory and practice of action psychotherapy are vast. Some of the specifics will be discussed in chapter 5. Unlike the multiple pioneers in drama therapy, Moreno, in collaboration with Zerka T. Moreno, remains the founder and central figure in psychodrama. Others have taken his work in new directions, especially in terms of populations served (see, for example, Bannister 1997, on work with abused children; Hudgins 2002, on work with PTSD; Casson 2004, on work with people who hear voices; Dayton 2005, on work with addicts). Blatner (1996, 2000) has expanded upon Moreno's role theory and has linked psychodrama to a wide variety of approaches in applied theater (see Blatner with Wiener 2007). Dayton (2005) has looked at the connections between Moreno's action work and major research findings in neuroscience that speak to the confluence of mind and body, emotion and cognition. Although few have significantly challenged Moreno's central concepts or classical techniques, there have been several innovations that presage the later developments in drama therapy. The ones we will look at are centered in two major themes that Moreno pursued throughout his personal and professional life—the spiritual quest for creative expression and the social quest for tolerance and survival.

Psychospiritual Roles

When Moreno originally developed his role theory (1946/1994; Z. T. Moreno 2006a), he identified three kinds of roles:

1. Psychosomatic or physiological roles, which refer to the body
2. Psychodramatic or fantasy roles, which refer to the imagination
3. Sociocultural roles, which refer to relationships with others within their particular environments

Psychodramatist Natalie Winters felt that Moreno had omitted a whole category, which she called psychospiritual roles. Winters felt it was particularly important to offer this role designation as Moreno often expressed his ideas in spiritual language, comparing acts of God with the inherent potential of all human beings to create their own roles and realities. For Winters (2000) psychospiritual roles have to do with spontaneity and the act of creation, two major concepts in Moreno's role theory.

Although Moreno provided examples of specific roles within the three categories, he did not fully define them or speak of their functions within human life. Further, he did not develop a full theoretical framework to contain such roles. Winters (2000) goes beyond Moreno in identifying nine role types within the general category of psychospiritual roles. And to add further dimension to these role types, she discussed the function of each role. The roles listed are the imaginer, the mediator, the rememberer, the receiver, the giver, the artist, the channeler, the believer, and the prayer.

As we shall see in our discussion of role theory in drama therapy, Landy (1993) developed a comprehensive Taxonomy of Roles that also includes descriptions of the role type and its function. The one role common to both Winters and Landy is that of the artist. Winters (2000) description follows: "The artist aligns with aesthetic values and produces that which evokes sensuality, insight, foresight, and pleasure for all to share. He or she works from an intuitive nature with connection to a higher self" (21). Landy (1993), serving as a bridge between Moreno and Winters, links the aesthetic and spiritual qualities of the artist. He characterizes the artist as sensitive and creative and writes that this role type functions "to assert the creative principle, envisioning new forms and transforming old ones. Because of the spiritual demands and responsibilities of the aesthetic process, the artist often pays an emotional price" (241).

As noted in chapter 2, Moreno was critical of Freud, accusing him of failing on two accounts—by rejecting religion and by rejecting social processes. In addressing the former, Moreno (1946/1994) wrote: "It remained for psychodrama to take the God-act seriously and to translate it into valid therapeutic terms" (8). In redressing the latter, Moreno went on to say: "and for sociodrama to take the groups seriously—as a process *sui generis*—and so to broaden and deepen the scope of analysis beyond any visions Freud ever had on the subject" (8). In his life and work, Moreno attempted to cover the full spectrum of human experience. He began at a very young age with the spiritual and as he grew older, spent more and more time attempting to solve the social ills of humankind.

Sociodrama

Moreno originated the notion of placing social issues onstage in the early 1920s. Over the next twenty years he developed his conception of sociodrama. According to Moreno (1943): "Sociodrama is based upon the tacit assumption that the group formed by the audience is already organized by the social and cultural roles which in some degree all the carriers of the culture share" (438). Sternberg and Garcia (2000a) provide more specificity: "Sociodrama is an action method in which individuals enact an agreed upon social situation spontaneously" (196).

Moreno attempted to dramatize some of the most crucial social-political issues of the day. His goal was first to explore the issues improvisationally. But with his characteristic utopian zeal, Moreno (1946/1994) also thought of sociodrama as being able to "cure as well as solve, that it can change attitudes, as well as study them" (363). The cure was to occur through a form of social catharsis brought about by establishing a collective identity in the room, as all actors and spectators become protagonists in a shared drama.

Moreno's sociodramatic-like experiments began in Vienna with The Living Newspaper, where actors improvised scenes based upon current events in the news. After he immigrated to America, Moreno continued performances of The Living Newspaper that extended to more ambitious sociodramas enacted with large groups at professional conferences around such issues as the

1948 race riots in Harlem, the trail of Adolf Eichmann in Jerusalem, and the assassination of John F. Kennedy in Dallas.

Others have extended the form of sociodrama. Sternberg and Garcia (2000b) acknowledge Moreno's structure and theory of sociodrama, linking it to his work in sociometry and psychodrama. But going beyond Moreno, they apply the work to a wide range of populations including people with developmental, hearing, and visual disabilities as well as speech and language impairments. In terms of the latter, they provide a clear example of sociodrama with an aphasia group. Both Sternberg and Garcia have also used sociodramatic training in the field of corrections. Garcia's (Sternberg and Garcia 2000a) early work, for example, encompassed the instruction of police trainees in dealing with family crisis, sex crime investigation, and suicide.

Lewis Yablonsky, a student of J. L. Moreno, also worked extensively in the field of criminal justice, writing articles and books on violent gangs and juvenile delinquency. Yablonsky, like Moreno, was attracted to fringe elements in society, as well as highly charged political issues. In 1996 he conducted a large sociodrama at the World Congress of Psychotherapy in Vienna. Aware that he was in the birthplace of his mentor, Moreno, he also realized that Vienna was the birthplace of Freud and Hitler. While warming up a group of more than 1,000, Yablonsky (1998) invited three people to take on the roles of Moreno, Freud, and Hitler. Gong Shu, who had been trained by Zerka T. Moreno, and wrote a book (2003) linking Chinese medicine with psychodrama, agreed to take on the role of Moreno. A psychoanalyst took on the role of Freud. And a young man from Romania, who had lived under the dictatorial regime of Ceausescu, took on the role of Hitler.

After a heated dialogue among the three, the director engaged with the audience, and many strong feelings were expressed. Although tempted to deal psychodramatically with the pain of individuals who revealed their holocaust trauma, Yablonsky stayed focused upon the group issues. He even dared to give voice to a small segment of the audience that supported a neo-fascist ideology, thus revealing a more complex group sociometry than expected. Another unexpected reaction was that of collective guilt, which came from a younger segment of the group, some of whom were psychotherapists from Vienna. One person expressed his guilt by pointing to the potential crimes of his parents during Nazi times and the effects of their unwillingness to talk about their part in the war machine.

Yablonsky noted that the sociodrama took on an even larger dimension when a psychiatrist from Africa spoke of his own trauma, living with a past legacy of the atrocities of slavery. The emotionality of this man's story evoked a catharsis within the group, relating more to the present issues of racism within the United States and Europe. Upon reflection, Yablonsky noted the positive influences on the group of the figures of Freud and

Moreno, but that the emotional impact centered in the figure of Hitler. For Yablonsky, the legacy of Hitler and others, like Ceausescu and the slave traders, continued to cast a pall over all attempts at social harmony and reconciliation.

In a final example of a newer approach to sociometry, Peter Kellermann (1998) defined the field as "an experiential group-as-a-whole procedure for social exploration and intergroup conflict transformation. As such, sociodrama can be regarded as an action oriented and structured counterpart to group analysis with large groups" (179). Kellermann's position is that Moreno and others have taken too much of a utopian, atheoretical point of view, especially in claiming that sociodrama is curative. For Kellermann (1998), who is Israeli, sociodramatic directors need to consider not only psychological problems, but also "intergroup clashes" and "increased polarization between various subgroups of society" (31). Kellermann calls for an integrative approach to conflict management. He critiques Moreno and the later humanist psychologists for rejecting Freud's notion of aggression out of hand and for their failure to recognize a complexity of factors that determine aggression such as instinct, drive, genetic make-up, environmental and social factors. Kellermann argues that those practicing sociodrama should heed Freud's (1930) dark assessment of the human condition:

> Men are not gentle creatures who want to be loved . . . they are on the contrary, creatures among whose instinctual endowments is to be reckoned a powerful share of aggressiveness. As a result, their neighbor is for them . . . someone to cause him pain, to torture and to kill him. . . . Who, in the face of all his experience of life and history, will have the courage to dispute this assertion? (111–12) . . . It is always possible to bind together a considerable number of people in love, so long as there are other people left over to receive the manifestations of their aggressiveness (114).

In applying his integrative model of sociodrama to conflict management in general and peace making, as one element, Kellermann (1998) offers a three-part approach. He calls the first part crisis sociodrama, which concerns a response to a calamitous event of great social significance. Examples include assassinations of major political figures as well as terrorist bombings. Other examples are of crises of longer duration, such as economic, social, or political upheavals. Through sociodrama, heterogeneous groups are able to reenact the crisis, express their emotions, and bond in their universal struggle to deal with their shared sense of loss, helplessness, and hope.

Kellermann's second application is political sociodrama, based on a view of society as perpetually wrestling with conflict and crisis that ultimately leads to growth. The themes of this form of sociodrama include inequities among classes and the consequences of social disintegration. Political sociodrama aims to allow many voices of the community to be heard, but is often based upon a leftist ideology, similar to that which informed the agit-prop theater experiments of Bertolt Brecht and Clifford Odets in the early twentieth century, as well as the more contemporary theater experiments of Augusto Boal.

Kellermann's third application is that of diversity sociodrama that concerns issues of prejudice and the struggle of minorities for equal rights. Sociodramas of this type include enactments between black and white, Muslim and Christian, Jew and gentile, disabled and able-bodied. These enactments attempt to explore intergroup tensions and search for ways to realize the goal of tolerance.

Given the ambitious goals of all three forms, Kellermann recognizes that Moreno's utopian agenda of human survival will not be met by sociodrama alone. And yet he acknowledges the more realistic goal, certainly inspired by Moreno, of "bringing large groups of different people together and opening up new channels of communication between them" (Kellermann 1998, 46). Kellermann's work is extended in a new volume, *Sociodrama and Collective Trauma* (2007), which responds to traumatic events of the early twenty-first century.

Bibliodrama

As an imaginative child on the way to developing a spiritual/poetic sensibility, Moreno was imbued with a sense of destiny. At the age of fourteen, standing before a statue of Jesus, Moreno had a vision. In his autobiography (1985) he wrote: "I wanted Jesus to move out of the stone and act out his life there in the park for the people of Chemnitz. . . . Standing before the Christ in Chemnitz, I began to believe I was an extraordinary person, that I was here on the planet to fill an extraordinary mission" (1). In 1920 Moreno published his first book, *The Words of the Father*. In this poetic book, Moreno imagined himself in the role of God. Central to the book is a poem, which begins:

I AM GOD,
THE FATHER,
THE CREATOR OF THE UNIVERSE.

THESE ARE MY WORDS,
THE WORDS OF THE FATHER.

and ends:

I AM UNNAMED.
I ONLY AM TO BE.
I WAS UNNAMED
UNTIL YOU SPOKE TO ME (49–57).

Moreno undoubtedly was moved by his deeply felt epiphanies, experiences that informed his search for helping people in need to find a place of expression, if not enlightenment. On another level, Moreno's visionary experiences can be seen metaphorically as God, the Creator, represents the creative capacities of human beings. In the early 1920s, before he coined the phrase "psychodrama," Moreno (1934/1978) used the term "axiodrama" to refer to "the activation of religious, ethical and cultural values in spontaneous-dramatic form" (xxvi).

Axiodrama as a concept and a method has been long replaced by psychodrama and sociodrama. It does appear, however, as a topic in conferences and publications concerning the exploration of moral and ethical issues (see Lindkvist 1994). In the 1970s, an alternative form developed, that of bibliodrama. Bibliodrama returns to Moreno's spiritual roots, though not in such an extreme way. Like psychodrama, sociodrama, and even axiodrama, bibliodrama involves a process of enactment through role-playing, but in this case, the roles to be played are taken from the Bible or other spiritual volumes such as the Mahabarata (see Condon in Blatner 2007). The religious figures are most often those named in the holy books, both human and divine. But they can also be inferred figures, such as Noah's wife, or even objects and locations such as Noah's ark, Jesus' manger, or the Garden of Eden.

Peter Pitzele (1998), one of the pioneers of bibliodrama in the United States, was trained by Zerka T. Moreno. For Pitzele, the goal of bibliodrama is to help groups find wisdom and comfort by bringing the old Bible stories and images to the present through enactment. Pitzele views biblical stories as sketches of a narrative, leaving much to the imagination of the reader and the actor. He notes that the stories from the Old Testament have been subject to scholarly interpretation, transformed from an ancient oral tradition into a written commentary called "midrash." In its more modern form, midrash has evolved into new interpretations of the old stories. Bibliodrama is one means to enliven the tradition of midrash.

In bibliodrama, many of the classical aspects of psychodrama are employed, starting with a narrative, a director, a protagonist, and auxiliary egos. The narrative comes from the Bible or other spiritual text, and the work begins as all read and discuss a given passage. The work proceeds as people are chosen from the group to play figures in the story. The story is enacted, led by the director, and following the enactment, the group reflects upon the meaning of the story in their professional and personal lives.

Bibliodramas are conducted both in Europe and America using Old and New Testament stories, among others. As an example, Pitzele worked with a woman who had taken on the role of Miriam, prophetess and sister of Moses, on her deathbed. Pitzele (see Wilensky 2005) described the process of dramatization, reflection, and the aftermath of the biblio-drama as follows:

> The woman received the farewells of her brothers, and of the young women who have danced with her. Then, alone, she reflects on what her death will mean to the Israelite people. Miriam is aware that she has been their water-finder, their dancer, their mother. She fears that without her, the tradition will become too priestly, too hierarchical. She is afraid too that her concern for the natural world will not be carried on. Later, I got a letter from the woman who played Miriam. She has started an ecological movement in her synagogue. They call themselves the Sisters of Miriam (NP).

In this example, one woman is the focus as she takes on the role of Miriam. Generally speaking, however, in bibliodrama, many participate in enacting figures in the Bible stories in order to reveal relationships. Pitzele and others work continuously with clergy, with congregants, with children and adolescents in religious schools, and with all groups who are open to exploring their own midrash through not only cognitive means, but also through action.

Playback Theatre

Jonathan Fox, the founder of Playback Theatre (PT), like Pitzele, trained in psychodrama with Zerka T. Moreno. Like Pitzele, Fox conceived of a new form, related to but separate from the classical form of psychodrama. As Pitzele's work is related to Moreno's vision of a spiritual dialogue, Fox's work is related to Moreno's vision of a social and cultural dialogue, articulated originally in *Who Shall Survive?*

In the original Playback company, founded in 1975, Fox was joined by Jo Salas, a musician and music therapist, who added a significant musical element to the work, echoing another of Moreno's (1946/1994) visions, that of psychomusic, the spontaneous expression of feeling and thought through music. PT is a modality that has grown substantially since its founding. At the turn of the century, Salas (2000) identified eighty registered groups in more than thirty countries.

PT is a form of nonscripted, improvisational performance. It has been performed in thousands of venues including a maximum security prison auditorium in New York, a church in New Orleans shortly after Hurricane Katrina, a street corner in southern India, a wedding ceremony in Sydney, Australia, and a center for mentally ill people in Japan. In PT, a group gathers within these and other specified spaces and individuals tell stories from their experience. A trained group of playback actors and musicians then perform the stories, playing them back through sound, movement, and dialogue.

PT proceeds in a basic sequence that begins when someone in the group volunteers to tell a story. The storyteller is called the Teller and the director is called the Conductor. The Conductor invites the Teller to come up and sit in a designated chair. Near the chair are a group of playback actors and a second group of playback musicians. The Conductor interviews the Teller to learn of the circumstances of the story. After the story is told, the Conductor asks the Teller to choose actors from the playback company to represent characters in the story. When the preparation is complete, the Conductor says, "Let's watch." The actors and musicians then improvise the story. For closure, the Conductor checks in with the Teller, asking if she wishes to amend or correct a moment in the story. At times, the Conductor will ask the actors to replay a part of the story. At times, the Teller will comment upon the enactment, sharing a thought or feeling, or ask the audience to comment. At the conclusion of the sharing, the Conductor thanks the Teller and invites another to tell a story.

There are various goals of PT groups. Some claim that PT is more of an aesthetic form and less of a therapeutic one, as it meets the theatrical criteria of entertainment, enlightenment, and pleasure. At times, however, it clearly satisfies therapeutic goals of catharsis and integration, understanding and empathy. At best, PT integrates both aesthetic and therapeutic goals. In addition, it often incorporates sociodramatic goals of exploring significant social or political issues.

As an example of the work with social and political issues, Hutt and Hosking (2005) reflected upon experiences working in countries at war. They spoke of work in Fiji just following a military coup in 2000, and they tried to understand "how playback theatre can contribute to reconciliation by generating a communal setting where people can come into meaningful relationship and give expression to their deep concerns" (NP).

At the beginning of the PT experience, the Conductor asked the group: "What was it like getting here today? What is one word to describe your week?" As they responded, the actors transformed the words into fluid movements and sounds, playing back the essence of the Tellers' intentions. Having warmed up the group, the Conductor moved into the stories. In Fiji, some months after the coup, which had the consequence of deeply dividing the indigenous Fijians from the Indian Fijians who made up 48 percent of the population, the following story was told by a Fijian man:

> For weeks before the coup, the radio had been talking up a case against Indian Fijians. They were presenting a view of Indians taking over the businesses, employment and now the government. I came to accept this view. I was feeling angry and resentful about this situation and then I got caught up in the excitement generated by the coup and the temporary breakdown of the law and order. Along with a couple of friends I wanted to do something to "get back" at the Indians. We decided to go a village some distance away from our own

community where we would not be recognized. Here we spent time throwing stones and rocks at the houses of Indian villagers. This went on for some time until a group of Indians came towards us brandishing long cane knives and began chasing us. I was frightened for my life but in the end we got away okay. However as we arrived back to the outskirts of our village, my friends and I saw an Indian man in the middle of the road up ahead. He was striking a cane knife on the surface of the road. We were again very frightened and we decided to attack him. I suddenly recognized this man as someone I knew quite well, but I was not able to tell my friends. They picked up a big rock and threw it at this man injuring him quite badly. At this moment I suddenly woke up, I sort of came to my senses. This man was not some impersonal stereotype "Indian," he was a neighbor. I realized that I had been caught up in doing something, I felt terrible. I still feel badly about this, and I have not told this story to anyone (NP).

After the actors played back the story in a sensitive fashion, the Conductor, aware of the powerful impact upon the group, encouraged people to respond to the story through verbal sharing. Many identified with the Teller, letting him know that he was courageous in daring to share such a painful memory. Some shared stories of their own violent actions. Many expressed remorse and compassion. More stories were told of prejudice and brutality and of forgiveness. The actors were careful to play back the stories in a stylized fashion, distancing the group from the harsh realities of their experience. As the session ended, someone sang a Bob Marley song that had been taught to the group earlier by a Fijian man. The refrain was: "Peace, perfect peace. I long for peace in our neighborhood."

Reflecting upon this and related PT experiences in traumatized communities, Hutt and Hosking cite two powerful references, the first asserting that this kind of work is about "small moments of redemption, in which meaning emerges out of a sharing and listening to injurious memory" (Krondorfer 1995, 133). The second affirms the notion that "reconciliation is the creation of time and space in which to find new ways of dealing with past grievances" (Villa Vicencio 2001, 1).

Writing about the power of this experience in PT, Hutt and Hosking reiterate the values of telling, listening to, and performing stories—creating a sense of empathy and community. Jo Salas (2000) well articulates these values, which serve as clear goals for many PT practitioners:

The profound affirmation and validation of having your story enacted according to your subjective perception; the certainty that you have been fully heard by performers and audience; the relief from aloneness that comes from bearing witness in a public or semipublic setting; the sense of distance or mastery in relation to a difficult past experience; new perspective or insight into a life situation; the catharsis of laughter or tears (290).

In many ways, PT provides a bridge between psychodrama and drama therapy, a modality that, like PT, is based upon the telling and enactment of stories. Salas's goals could just as well apply to drama therapy. The history of drama therapy is the story of several pioneers. And although Moreno invented his own unique form of action psychotherapy, he is clearly part of the developing tradition of drama therapy, an action approach to healing the whole person and the groups within which people gather.

DRAMA THERAPY

The significant figures reviewed in chapters 1 and 2, all of whom had an impact upon the most explicit forms of action psychotherapy, were trained primarily in the medical and psychological professions. With the modest exception of George Kelly, none had extensive training in theater. Despite his early theatrical experiments (see Scheiffele 1995), Moreno was a psychotherapist who used elements of theater to express his notions of individual and group therapy.

Many of the pioneers in drama therapy came to the profession with a background in the art form of theater and/or educational theater. Some went on to train in psychology and related social sciences. But for the most part, the field attracted theater artists who wished to extend their work beyond the conventional forms of art and entertainment. For the early drama therapists, therapeutic goals ranging from symptom relief to transformation were more important than art and entertainment. Unlike theater, drama therapy privileges the actor over and above the role, the person over and above the persona. And yet, for many drama therapists past and present, the creative process remains paramount. Drama therapy, like the related creative arts therapies of dance, music, poetry, and visual arts, is distinct from other psychotherapeutic forms in that it proceeds through art making, an engagement with imagery generated in movement and sound, words and visual images.

International Influences on Drama Therapy

Drama therapy as an organized profession took root most firmly in England and the United States in the 1970s, although there is evidence that two Russian theater artists, Nicolas Evreinoff and Vladimir Iljine (see Jones 2007), experimented with therapeutic theater in the early 1920s. Evreinoff was a theater director and playwright, a contemporary of Stanislavski, who conceived of the process of acting as not only aesthetic, but also as a means of overcoming psychological and physical blocks. Evreinoff viewed theatricality as an essential human quality, a taking on of various personae as a means of expression and of transformation. He went so far as to refer to his approach to theatrical role-playing as theatrotherapy (see Evreinoff 1927). Like George Kelly, he believed in the curative power of constructing and playing out new roles.

Iljine had his own approach which he called therapeutic theater, centered in play production as well as improvisation, based somewhat in Stanislavski's exercises in actor preparation. He worked with mentally ill patients in Kiev in the early part of the twentieth century through a three-part structure where problematic themes were identified, dramatized, and then reflected upon (see Petzold 1973; Jones 2007). For Iljine, there was a clear connection between the fictional dilemmas of theatrical characters and the real life ones of actors. Iljine (1910) conceived of his therapeutic theater as a holistic form of healing as can be seen in the title of his article, "Patients Play Theatre: A Way of Healing Body and Mind." Iljine was exposed to the ideas of the early European psychoanalysts, actually meeting Sandor Ferenczi in Budapest in 1922. He was also influenced by Moreno's ideas and in fact translated Moreno's *The Theatre of Spontaneity* into Russian and later had the opportunity to meet Moreno at the first International Congress of Psychodrama in Paris in 1964.

Augusto Boal and Drama Therapy

There are many other international influences on the field of drama therapy. One that certainly merits attention, as it has engaged many drama therapists since the late 1970s, is Theatre of the Oppressed, developed by the Brazilian theater artist, Augusto Boal (1979). Boal began by creating political theater, an extension of the dramaturgy of Bertolt Brecht. As many drama therapists are drawn to the field as a means of transforming not only personal issues, but also social and political ones, Boal's theater held a special appeal. The work began as a means to place larger social issues upon the stage and to empower audiences to act upon them.

Boal's work developed into a form called Forum Theatre where spectators are invited onstage in order to influence the dramatic action by presenting their particular point of view. Over time, Forum Theatre developed further into an approach called The Rainbow of Desire (Boal 1995), where personal as well as political and social issues are dramatized and transformed. At this point, Boal's work became less about creating a theater aesthetic and more about creating a therapeutic theater.

The transition from political to therapeutic theater came about in 1989 when Boal was invited to address the International Association of Group Psychotherapists on the occasion of the 100th anniversary of J. L. Moreno's birth. Following his address and meeting with Zerka T. Moreno, Boal published *The Rainbow of Desire* (1995) outlining his ideas linking theater and therapy and providing examples of his therapeutic work. Although Boal at one time separated himself out from Moreno and his therapeutic community, his ideas of spontaneous action, aesthetic space, staged action, and catharsis place Boal well within the Morenian tradition (see Feldhendler 1994).

A Brief History of Drama Therapy in the United Kingdom

The most significant developments in the new field of drama therapy occurred in the UK and the United States, where several pioneers moved the profession forward. Dramatherapy (one word) in England can be traced to the work of Peter Slade. Slade was initially an actor who developed a research interest in the play of children. In his influential book, *Child Drama* (1954), Slade laid out a theoretical and practical framework for understanding the development of children in terms of their relationship to their bodies, to space, and to roles. In his work, Slade made a clear distinction between child drama, the spontaneous play of children in everyday life, and scripted theater. Although Slade was most influential in the development of the young field of educational drama, he also was the first in England to apply his drama-based ideas to therapy with children and adults. In the late 1930s, Slade collaborated with William Kraemer, a Jungian psychotherapist, to treat a range of psychological problems. In 1939 Slade was the first to lecture on dramatherapy at the British Medical Association. That lecture, "The Value of Drama in Religion, Education and Therapy," was published in 1940 by the Guild of Pastoral Psychology. The first known publication in the field to use the term "dramatherapy" was that of Slade's 1959 monograph, *Dramatherapy as an Aid to Becoming a Person*.

From the 1940s until his death in 2004, Slade remained committed to drama in education with children as well as dramatherapy with those suffering war trauma, juvenile delinquency, and various mental and physical disabilities.

Slade's work had a strong influence on Marian Lindkvist, one of the first generation of dramatherapists who defined the parameters of a unique discipline. Lindkvist developed the idea of bringing performing companies to hospitals and institutions to entertain young people with medical and psychological infirmities. Around the same time, in 1964, she founded Sesame, one of the first organizations devoted to the research and study of dramatherapy, as well as the training of practitioners for the new profession. Lindkvist (1998) based her work on her personal experience as a mother of an autistic child and later as a researcher studying the movement and drama of schizophrenics. In founding Sesame, Lindkvist developed a training program to integrate the work of Peter Slade in child drama, Rudolf Laban in dance and movement, and C. G. Jung in archetypal psychology.

Sue Emmy Jennings has been the most prolific of the British dramather-apy pioneers. She began her career as a performer and dancer and then worked extensively in drama in education. At that time, in the 1960s, drama in education, extending from the work of Peter Slade, was establishing itself within the school system in the UK. Such seminal figures as Dorothy Heath-cote and Gavin Bolton experimented with in-depth forms of role-playing and extensive improvisational stories based in current events that chal-lenged conventional educational theater approaches. Both influenced gen-erations of drama educators to work precisely within a cognitive frame, de-veloping problem-solving strategies through drama.

Jennings, noting that many children with special needs were underrepre-sented, began her own center, in collaboration with Gordon Wiseman, called the Remedial Drama Group, to treat these children. In doing so, Jen-nings commenced a life's work that extended to various populations, ages, cultures, and nationalities. Jennings was instrumental in forging the profes-sion through founding professional organizations, most notably, the British Association of Dramatherapists (BADTh) in 1976, and a series of university and private dramatherapy programs throughout the UK, and then through-out the world in such locations as Greece, Israel, Norway, and Romania.

Jennings sparked a number of dramatherapy initiatives in the fields of trauma, disability, corrections, and infertility, among many others. She is also a prolific thinker, creating theory and practical resources through her teaching and publications. Of note is her creation of a theoretical model of the drama therapy process—embodiment, projection, role (EPR), which is developmental, beginning with the early experience of embodiment and extending to projection of the self onto objects and then to the playing out of roles. In recent years, Jennings, influenced by research in neuroscience, has been refining her model, exploring the concept that drama is at the core of human development. Further, she returned to her roots in theater, pri-marily as an actor and storyteller. At the same time, she has developed a program in Romania to work with the Roma people (gypsies) and has en-gaged in a study of mythological goddess figures.

The second generation that extends directly from Peter Slade, Marian Lindkvist, and Sue Jennings has moved the field in their own unique di-rections. Alida Gersie (1991, 1997; Gersie and King 1990), with a back-ground in comparative mythology, developed an approach called thera-peutic storymaking, applying classical myths to the treatment of a number of populations including refugees and delinquents as well as those experi-encing bereavement. Phil Jones (2007) and John Casson (2004) have pro-vided strong historical research for the field and have described work with emotionally disturbed children and psychotic adults who hear voices. Roger Grainger (1990, 1995), trained as a minister and theater artist, has developed theoretical and practical work based in the constructivist theories of George Kelly. Grainger (1990) has systematically described dramatherapy procedures with schizophrenics as well as presented a study of the spiritual dimensions of dramatherapy, echoing the ideas of Moreno, Winters, and Pitzele.

Ann Cattanach (1993, 1994, 2003), a student and colleague of Sue Jennings, has done groundbreaking research in the related field of play therapy with traumatized children, providing a model for dramatherapists who work with abused and neglected young people. Many others, part of the early growth of dramatherapy in the UK, have extended the work of their mentors and taken it in newer directions. Examples include Dorothy Langley (1989) in psychodrama, Steve Mitchell (1996) in adapting Grotowski's paratheatrical ideas to dramatherapy, and Ditty Dokter (1994, 1998), in discussing applications to eating disordered individuals, refugees, and migrants.

The journal *Dramatherapy* has been published in the UK since 1977 by the British Association of Dramatherapists. Also, Sesame publishes its own *Sesame Journal*. The following definition of the field is posted on the web site for the British Association of Dramatherapists: "Dramatherapy has as its main focus the intentional use of healing aspects of drama and theatre as the therapeutic process. It is a method of working and playing that uses action methods to facilitate creativity, imagination, learning, insight and growth." Also on the web site is a research register, compiled by Kim Dent-Brown, which lists both completed and ongoing research in the field.

Peter Slade passed away in 2004. Many of the first tier of dramatherapists have retired from active academic work, including Sue Jennings, Marian Lindkvist, Alida Gersie, and Ann Cattanach. But most continue their research and teaching and new generations carry on their pioneering spirit, looking for newer ways to implement action methods.

A Brief History of Drama Therapy in the United States

The history of drama therapy (two words) in the United States begins just a few years later, as individual pioneers, working in different parts of the country, made similar discoveries about the healing potential of drama before organizing into a profession. Like Sue Jennings, some came directly from a theater background. Others, like Peter Slade and Marian Lindkvist, came in part through theater and in part through drama in education. And still others came from related disciplines, forming a rather eclectic mix.

The first publication in America that referred directly to drama therapy as a practice separate from psychodrama was published in 1945 out of Beacon House, the publishing arm of Moreno's institute. The article, "Drama Therapy," was written by Lewis Barbato (1945), a major in the United States Marine Corps, who described a series of treatments within the neuropsychiatric department of a general hospital in Denver, Colorado. The treatments were run by a team comprised of a theater director, a psychiatric nurse with acting experience, and a stenographer. This team worked to help World War II veterans cope with psychotic and neurotic symptoms related to war trauma. The techniques described are surprisingly contemporary, quite in keeping with current practice in PT, psychodrama, and various forms of drama therapy. There are even references to cognitive-behavioral approaches as later practiced by Wolpe and Lazarus.

In one example, patients were encouraged to reenact traumatic incidents from their combat experience, desensitizing themselves from the trauma. In another, patients engaged in a form of behavioral rehearsal, preparing themselves for reentry into the family or workplace. The stenographer recorded the extemporaneous dialogue and action, which was later replayed by the patients, with modifications based on more appropriate role behaviors. This approach has some resonance with the fixed-role therapy of George Kelly as does a third example, where patients were asked to play roles and emotions against type, opposite their natural inclinations. As we shall see, the use of roles and counterroles becomes a hallmark of the role method of drama therapy.

Some thirty-four years after this article appeared, the professional organization, the National Association for Drama Therapy (NADT) was founded in 1979, just three years after the founding of the British Association of Dramatherapists. Among the founders was Gertrud Schattner, a Viennese actress from the 1930s who worked with concentration camp survivors in Switzerland after the war through writing, drama, and performance. Schattner (1981) writes that her work with performance especially provided enough containment and stimulation for many to regain their will to live. Settling in the United States after the war, Schattner went on to study psychotherapy and to work with various populations in need through children's theater, theater games, and eventually, drama therapy.

Ramon Gordon, a director and playwright who created a theater organization for prisoners and ex-offenders called Cell Block Theatre, was another founder of the NADT. A third was Eleanor Irwin, formerly a speech therapist, creative drama specialist, and psychodramatist who retained her passion for spontaneous drama as she trained as a psychoanalyst. In addition to her psychoanalytic practice, Irwin became a researcher and educator who incorporated her vast knowledge of play and drama in all her work.

David Read Johnson was another of the early founders of the NADT. In the mid-1970s, he was a graduate student in clinical psychology at Yale University, experienced in both theater and dance therapy, who went on to do significant research in the field and develop a unique approach to theory and practice. The initial group also included Barbara Sandberg, an educator with a background in theater and educational drama.

As this group began to talk, they reached out to others who were doing similar work, recognizing that unlike psychodrama, the new profession of drama therapy had many founders. In fact, within a short period of time, some entrenched in the psychodrama camp embraced their drama therapy neighbors. Over time such well-known psychodrama figures as Adam Blatner and Nina Garcia established their identities within both action therapies.

Some of the American pioneers, like Eleanor Irwin and David Read Johnson, were represented in the first published anthology of drama therapy writings, *Drama in Therapy* (in two volumes), edited by Gerturd Schattner and Richard Courtney in 1981. Interestingly, several of the papers chosen for the two volumes of this work were written by well-known drama-in-education specialists, among whom were Peter Slade, Brian Way, Nellie Mc-Caslin, and Richard Courtney. The implication was that the field was still closely connected to those in education and had yet to fully distinguish its own identity. In fact, there were many debates on how to write the title of the book, some arguing for *Drama Therapy*, suggesting a field in its own right, rather than the chosen, *Drama in Therapy*, suggesting a field that has not yet arrived. Virtually none of the early writers were fully based in the art form of theater, and some, like Sue Jennings, Brian Way, and Richard Courtney were British (Courtney, born in England, was at the time a Canadian citizen), representing earlier developments in the UK.

But in the next fully realized anthology of papers from key American figures in the field, *Current Approaches in Drama Therapy*, published in 2000, the field of drama therapy had arrived. All of the writers called themselves drama therapists, and although several came from an educational drama background, they tended to write about their work with clinical populations. Let us now look at some of the pioneers represented in this volume in terms of their influences and in their continuing influence on new generations of drama therapists.

Among the major figures highlighted in this volume are Eleanor Irwin, Robert Landy, Renée Emunah, and David Read Johnson, all of whom were instrumental in developing either the NADT or the two major academic programs in the United States. As mentioned above, Irwin (2000b) integrated her expertise in drama therapy with that of psychoanalysis, creating a psychoanalytic approach to the field. As such, Irwin (2000a) specified that the goal of drama therapy is "to make changes in personality, which implies dealing with unconscious aspects of functions" (28). It is interesting to note that Irwin's citations of psychoanalytic figures do not include those mentioned in chapter 1. Instead she makes reference to later developments in psychoanalysis including attachment theory, especially as practiced by John Bowlby, infant research, especially that of Daniel Stern, object relations theory, especially that of Margaret Mahler and D. W. Winnicott, and self-psychology, represented by Heinz Kohut. In a later article

(2005) Irwin stresses that her theoretical position is most fully centered in relational theories. She points again to Winnicott as significant in his linking of play, self-development, and creativity. With a nod toward drama therapy, she cites Winnicott's (1971) statement: "It is in playing and only in playing that the individual child or adult is able to be creative and to use the whole personality, and it is only in being creative that the individual discovers the self" (54).

Irwin worked mostly with children and drew upon her experience in play therapy as well as puppetry. In fact, she developed an assessment instrument called the puppetry interview (see Irwin 1985), where children choose puppets from a basket and express their current dilemmas through the guise of the puppets. Irwin influenced a number of drama and related creative arts therapists who studied with her to integrate drama therapy and psychoanalysis, including Elaine Portner and Rosalind Kindler.

David Read Johnson trained as a clinical psychologist, writing his doctoral dissertation on drama therapy. Johnson studied avant-garde theater in the 1970s, especially the approaches of Artaud and Grotowski, and performed with an improvisational theater company. He also studied educational drama in England, based in the work of Peter Slade. While working at the Yale Psychiatric Institute, where he practiced an early form of drama therapy, he collaborated with a dance therapist, Susan Sandel, deeply exploring the process of integrating body movement and drama. Johnson created his own particular mix of theater and psychology, developing the method of developmental transformations, which will be discussed in depth below.

Johnson's interests in dance/movement therapy, especially the work of Marian Chace, and in the theatrical experiments of Jerzy Grotowski remained constant, as did his interest in the work of such developmental and object relations psychologists as Jean Piaget, D. W. Winnicott, and Daniel Stern.

In creating an institute for his work in New York, Johnson mentored scores of drama therapists who practiced developmental transformations and wrote about their work with a number of clinical populations including homeless mentally ill (Schnee 1996; Galway, Hurd, and Johnson 2003), Vietnam War veterans (Dintino and Johnson 1996; James and Johnson 1996), the elderly (Johnson, Smith, and James 2003) and sexually abused children (James, Forrester, and Kim 2005).

Renée Emunah is the founder and director of the Drama Therapy Program at California Institute for Integral Studies in San Francisco. She studied drama therapy in London at Sesame and was influenced by Audrey Wethered (1973), who published one of the early texts in drama therapy. Emunah also trained in psychodrama and theater and from her eclectic background developed an integrative approach to theory and practice. She counts among her most important theoretical influences Erik Erikson and the humanistic psychologists, Abraham Maslow and Carl Rogers.

Emunah wrote one of the most influential texts in the field, *Acting for Real* (1994), describing her signature work with emotionally disturbed adolescents from whom she developed her integrative five-phase model of drama therapy. Emunah's model well incorporates aspects of child drama, theater, psychodrama, and ritual. Phase 1, that of dramatic play, draws from child drama and theater games to help clients develop trust and spontaneity. Phase 2, that of scene work, draws from theater and helps clients expand roles and emotional expression through working with fictional scenes. Phase 3, that of role play, focuses on a preview and review of current personal issues, building awareness of self in relation to role and a certain flexibility among roles. Phase 4, that of culminating enactment, is psychodramatically oriented as clients explore their core themes. This exploration leads at times to the presentation of self-revelatory performances.

In the final Phase 5, that of dramatic ritual, clients move toward integration, embracing the totality of their play, scene work, role-play, and enactments. This stage is marked by a review and validation of all the previous stages and a celebration of the process. Emunah has influenced generations of students who have studied with her in California and in workshops and trainings throughout the world.

Among others represented in *Current Approaches in Drama Therapy*, some, like Penny Lewis, a dance and drama therapist, and Stephen Snow, who began his career as a theater artist, were highly influenced by the archetypal focus of Carl Jung. Snow (2000), who founded the first drama therapy program in Canada at Concordia University, also points to the influence of anthropologists whose research illuminated the dramatic nature of ritual and shamanism (see Eliade 1961 and Turner 1982), and to those in performance studies, like Richard Schechner (1985), who applied anthropological research to a reconceptualization of performance.

Moreno has a pervasive influence on the drama therapists represented in *Current Approaches*, as noted in chapters on psychodrama by Nina Garcia and Dale Buchanan, and sociodrama by Pat Sternberg and Nina Garcia. PT is also represented in a chapter by Jo Salas.

Taking the position of combining drama therapy with narrative therapy, Pam Dunne (2000) makes frequent reference to the work of Michael White (1990; White and Epson 1998). Dunne, like others represented in this volume, began her career as a theater artist and drama educator, then studied psychodrama, drama therapy, and psychology, taking a fully eclectic view of the field before focusing in on a particular approach which she calls narradrama. Dunne developed her own training institute in Los Angeles where she has mentored a host of drama therapists.

Robert Landy is noted for his work in role theory and role method, which will be discussed in detail below. His influences, like those of many of his colleagues, come from psychoanalysis, theater, and drama in education. His first experience as a consumer of therapy was in psychoanalysis, and his connection to the early analysts came from a period of Jungian analysis with Edward C. Whitmont, a graduate of the Vienna University Medical School and a student of Carl Jung's. Although he struggled with the somewhat esoteric orientation of this particular practitioner, he learned to appreciate the therapeutic system in its relationship to the archetypes of the unconscious.

He also studied psychodrama with Lewis Yablonsky and Jim Sacks, both trained directly by J. L. Moreno, and Gestalt therapy with George Brown, who was trained by Fritz Perls. Landy worked in theater as an actor, director, and playwright, performing in classical Shakespearian drama, experimental theater and performance art. He studied and apprenticed with members of the original Group Theatre, a company inspired by the psychological acting approach of Stanislavski and the political sensibility of the radical leftist movement of the 1930s. While directing a number of plays written by Bertolt Brecht, Landy developed an understanding of theatrical distance. That understanding was further shaped by the sociologist Tom Scheff, who introduced him to models of aesthetic distance (see Scheff 1979). These experiences led to the development of distancing theory in drama therapy.

And finally, Landy engaged directly in conversations and trainings with three seminal drama in education figures—Richard Courtney, Dorothy Heathcote, and Gavin Bolton. Courtney's 1968 book, *Play, Drama and Thought*, and a series of interviews and dialogues with Courtney led him to an interdisciplinary path linking drama and theater to psychology and related social sciences. Dorothy Heathcote first introduced him to the idea of extending the borders of time and space to create profound explorations of contemporary social issues through drama. Gavin Bolton helped him understand the process of making meaning through role and story.

Like Emunah, Landy developed a major graduate program in drama therapy, this one at New York University. In that role, he trained many generations of students, some of whom became his collaborators in research and publication (see, for example, Landy, Luck, Conner, and McMullian 2003; and Landy, McLellan, and McMullian 2005). In creating the Center for Creative Alternatives, a training institute in New York City, in collaboration with Emily Nash, artistic director of Creative Alternatives of New York, this influence extends to professionals in the creative arts therapy, mental health, and theater.

Three Approaches to the Dramatic Therapies

With a plethora of approaches to drama therapy, it is difficult to clearly define a field that includes the work of Moreno, Slade, Jennings, Gersie, Irwin, Johnson, Emunah, Landy, and others. As noted above, definitions have been offered by the British Association of Dramatherapists and likewise by their American counterpart and many individuals. No one definition is complete in itself given the range of differences. However, there are three approaches that appear to be more developed than others in terms of theory, clinical practice, and research. The first is psychodrama, which is a discipline unto itself, but as it is so integral to drama therapy, it can also be seen as a subset of the more generic dramatic or action psychotherapies. Given the vast output of J. L. and Zerka T. Moreno and the extensive list of descriptive and research studies, psychodrama is clearly among the leading approaches in the field.

The other two approaches most represented in the descriptive and research literature, at least in the United States, are role theory/role method and developmental transformations. The former has been developed over twenty-five years and taught in some depth at New York University, and the latter is represented by private training institutes in New York and other sites internationally. Many scholarly articles and books have been written about both approaches by their founders and their students. Those in the UK might well choose other approaches as part of the triumvirate, such as the Sesame approach, Jennings' EPR, or Gersie's therapeutic storymaking, but there does not appear to be a significant body of publication, research, and training projects in these areas.

In the following three chapters, we will take an in-depth look at role theory/role method, psychodrama, and developmental transformations, noting the relevant historical influences and pointing to the continuing influence of three unique methods linked by their commitment to explore embedded problems through action.

4

Role Theory and the Role Method of Drama Therapy

INTRODUCTION

When the film *Three Approaches to Psychotherapy* was produced in 1965, it featured three of the best-known psychotherapists of the time—Carl Rogers, Albert Ellis, and Fritz Perls. In the film, all three discussed their particular approach, led a session with a common client named Gloria, and reflected upon their work. At the conclusion of the film, the producer, Shostrom, himself a psychotherapist, interviewed Gloria and asked her to choose which approach she found the most compelling. She chose Perls because she felt him to be the most provocative, not necessarily because of his technique, but because of his intrusive personality. But if we look at the techniques for a moment, we find that among the three, Perls's Gestalt therapy is the only action approach, one that focuses upon the body, the emotions, and the projection of parts of the self onto roles.

Perhaps Shostrom, as a filmmaker, chose Perls because of his abrasive personality and his ability to provoke strong responses from a client. Or perhaps he chose Perls because his approach was unique, not as dependent upon verbal discourse and conscious, cognitive decision making as was the case for Rogers and Ellis. The film has had a broad impact upon psychotherapy training in the United States. More than forty years after its release, it is still screened regularly in university classes as both a historical document and a model for teaching students the process of psychotherapy. And despite the waning influence of Gestalt therapy, with each screening students learn that a valid method of psychotherapeutic practice is through action.

In 2005, looking for a way to bring the dramatic action psychotherapies to the attention of the broader community of psychotherapists, this author modified Shostrom's concept and produced a similar film, *Three Approaches to Drama Therapy*. The film features three drama therapists also working with a common client called Derek. Landy's innovation was to film the piece in front of a small group of drama therapy graduate students who interviewed both the client and the therapists following each of the three segments. As in the Shostrom film, each drama therapist introduced his/her approach, led a session with the client, and then reflected upon the session. At the conclusion of this three-part process, following Shostrom, the graduate students asked Derek to discuss which approach he found most compelling.

Shostrom's film has generated considerable research, the most comprehensive of which is *The Hidden Genius of Emotion* (Magai and Haviland-Jones 2002), a study of the effects of the personalities of the three upon Gloria. Landy's film, intended as a research piece, has already generated several thesis studies, exploring the psychological, cultural, and methodological effects of the approaches on the client.

In the following chapters, I will explore the three approaches in depth. I will look first at each in terms of its place within the historical framework given above. I will then look at the theory of each action approach, specifying its basic assumptions, concepts, therapeutic goals, role of the therapist, view of wellness and illness, and methods of assessment and evaluation. Following the theory I will discuss practice which will be illustrated through the case of Derek. The practice will be further clarified by viewing each approach according to several polarities: emotion and distance, fiction and reality, verbal and nonverbal expression, action and reflection, directive and nondirective action, transference and countertransference.

The common client, Derek, a pseudonym, agreed to engage in a series of four sessions: one in role theory/role method, one in psychodrama, one in developmental transformations, and one follow-up discussion with a group of drama therapy graduate students. At the time of the filming, Derek was a thirty-year-old African American man. He was raised in a working-class home in an inner city, growing up with immigrant parents and one brother. Money was scarce as the father made a meager salary and gambled away much of it. As a result, the family often did not have enough money to buy proper food and necessities. The mother worked at menial jobs to make up the money lost by the father.

Throughout his childhood, Derek was humiliated and verbally abused by his raging father. His father physically abused his mother, sometimes in plain view of the children. Derek, his mother, and brother were unable to contain the father's violence but attempted to support and comfort one another. As a child Derek was anxious and frightened at home and in school. He struggled to grow into his identity as a black man, feeling at times either too black or too white. While in school, Derek was ridiculed by his peers for being too black and sometimes acted out against weaker peers, humiliating them as he had been humiliated. He compensated by doing well in school, eventually going to college and then on to graduate school for a master's degree. Derek attributed his resilience and success to his Christian faith, to the support and love of his mother, and to his wife who provided a stable and loving relationship. Derek noted that his father has changed radically in recent years, abandoning his violent and profligate behavior and embracing religion.

ROLE THEORY

Historical Overview

Derek's first session was in role method, an approach developed by this author and extending from his understanding of role theory. Although Landy's role theory is based upon the work of both Moreno and several early twentieth-century sociologists, it finds a clear precedent in the early days of psychoanalysis. Freud, who first specified the psychological effects of the therapeutic process, understood that in transference the patient projected past role relationships onto the therapist. Freud, however, did not use the language of theater to speak about the transference relationship, but in 1925, his colleagues, Ferenczi and Rank, seeking to explain their development of an active therapy, did. As cited above (Ferenczi and Rank 1925/ 1986), they wrote:

> the analyst plays all possible roles for the unconscious of the patient. . . . Particularly important is the role of the two parental images—father and mother—in which the analyst constantly alternates (41).

Rank, himself, began his psychoanalytic career embracing the role of the artist as a neurotic figure who harnessed his ability to create as a means of healthy expression and, indeed, transformation. He referred to that role throughout his career, adding another archetypal one, that of the hero, to explain the complex struggle for integration and transformation. Although Rank died young, banished from the inner circle of his peers, these two roles might have given him solace. They certainly provided a legacy that lives in all forms of psychotherapy that embrace dramatic and archetypal notions of existence.

In the early history of psychoanalysis, there are many examples of therapeutic role-playing. In chapter 1, we learned of Ferenczi and Reich's experiments with forms of role-play and role reversal through mutual analysis and character analysis. In chapter 2, we find reference to the French psychiatrist Pierre Janet, who worked in treatment through role. Even Jung's struggle to resolve a major life crisis involved a regression to the role of the child and an active creation of imaginary worlds with inanimate objects. This approach is repeated in the later work of Erik Erikson and others working with Henry Murray in the 1930s and 1940s. In the Dramatic Productions Test and other projective tests, these researchers explored personality functions through observing people's projective play while in role. Murray's approach to screening potential double agents during World War II involved the creation of fictional roles and stories.

Kelly, Perls, Berne, and others also contributed to an understanding of role. Perls' work with the polarity of topdog and underdog was a precursor to work in role and counterrole. Kelly's work in fixed-role therapy presaged later developments in drama therapy. Further, Kelly's projective Role Construct Repertory Test (rep grid) was, in fact, a card sort, similar to role profiles developed by Landy some forty years later.

But the most significant historical figure in conceiving of a role theory was Moreno. Although his role theory was never fully realized, Moreno saw role as central to psychodrama. In the next chapter, Moreno's ideas will be discussed in more depth, but for now it is important to note the centrality of role in his understanding of action psychotherapy and in its influence upon Landy's role theory. Moreno (in Fox 1987) wrote:

> The concept underlying this approach is the recognition that man is a role player, that every individual is characterized by a certain range of roles which dominate his behavior, and that every culture is characterized by a certain set of roles which it imposes with varying degrees of success upon its membership (65).

For Moreno, role was both a psychological and a social-cultural construction. However, his understanding was distinct from that of the early twentieth-century sociologists in that it developed out of clinical contexts, on the one hand, and out of theater, on the other. Moreno's conceptual language became the mainstay of Landy's understanding of role and counterrole, role-player and role-playing.

Moreno, ever the iconoclast, was in character when making the point (in Fox 1987): "Many American sociologists have monopolized the concept of role" (62). However, those same sociologists were highly influential in popularizing the metaphor of life as theater and in analyzing social events from a dramatic point of view.

The sociologists in question included Charles Cooley (1922), George Herbert Mead (1934), Ralph Linton (1936), Erving Goffman (1959), Theodore Sarbin (1962; Sarbin and Allen 1968), and Thomas Scheff (1979). From Cooley and Mead emerged the idea of a multidimensional personality comprised of many roles. Cooley's central metaphor was that of the looking-glass self, that is, the self as a reflection of others in one's social world. For Mead, actors in everyday life take on individual and collective roles from models in their social world and learn to act toward themselves as the models have acted toward them. Goffman went beyond Cooley and Mead in imagining the full interplay of individuals and groups in terms of a dramatic performance.

Sarbin, who studied with Moreno in the 1940s, conceived of the term "role enactment." Role enactment involves, first, the number of roles available for taking on and playing out. This idea was later quantified by Landy in developing his Taxonomy of Roles. It also involves the amount of time one plays out a particular role. Further, role enactment concerns organismic involvement or the style of one's enactment, having to do with the degree of affect expressed through a given role. Sarbin (Sarbin and Allen 1968) set up a continuum that begins with a noninvolved style of role-playing and proceeds through casual role enactment, ritual acting, engrossed acting, classical hypnotic role-playing, histrionic neurosis, ecstasy, sorcery, and witchcraft.

The idea of affective involvement in role-playing was expanded by Thomas Scheff, who conceived his own continuum of emotion and distance. Although an academic sociologist, Scheff was a scholar of drama and theater, as well as of psychoanalysis and related forms of depth psychotherapy. He was very much aware of the development of catharsis in psychotherapy from the early experiments in hypnosis of Breuer and Freud to the radical experimentation in the 1960s with forms of primal screaming and acting out. In fact, he viewed catharsis as a balanced position between the two poles of overdistance, a state of repression marked by a lack of emotional expression, and underdistance, an overabundance of emotionality. For Scheff (1981), the overdistanced person remembers the past while the underdistanced one relives it. He referred to the midpoint on the distancing continuum as aesthetic distance, a moment of balance when the past can be remembered with a degree of feeling that is not too overwhelming, where intense emotional expression can be tempered by cognitive reflection. The paradigm of overdistance, aesthetic distance, underdistance proved significant in the development of role theory in drama therapy.

Over and above the sociological sources, Landy's role theory is supported by theatrical influences. There are several modern performance theories that dovetail with the distancing paradigm. These theories stem from the actor's preparation to play a theatrical role. The first, developed by Stanislavski (1936), the director of the Moscow Art Theater in the early part of the twentieth century, had to do with an acting method based in affective memory, the recall of actual emotions associated with a theatrical stimulus. For Stanislavski, the actor's job was to behave on stage as if the dramatic moment was real. The reality of the moment was expressed emotionally, linking the past of the actor to the present of the role. Influenced by Freud, Stanislavski attempted to develop intuitive actors, open to dynamics of the unconscious. In the language of psychoanalysis, the raw emotional experience of the id was to be mediated by the ego, grounded firmly in reality.

As his work developed and he internalized the ideas of his contemporary, the Russian psychologist Ivan Pavlov, Stanislavski focused more upon the actor's physical actions and less upon recalled emotion. But his early work had a profound influence upon generations of American actors who translated his affective approach to the American hunger for psychological realism. Stanislavski's early approach can be likened to Scheff's notion of underdistancing, where affect is privileged over intellect.

The second approach is that of Bertolt Brecht's epic theater, marked by the alienation effect, a conscious awareness that theatrical performance is artificial, a separation of stage and world, actor and role, actor and audience, feeling and thought. Brecht's goal was less psychological and more sociopolitical. His was a revolutionary theater, akin to Moreno's sociodramatic experiments, intended to change the world. In training actors, Brecht encouraged them to consider the social conditions that led to their characters' dilemmas and to present the role as a problem to be solved rather than as a living, breathing human being. In using character types, masks and puppets, exaggerated scenery and props, Brecht created a theater of ideas and an acting style intended to distance audience members from an easy identification with the emotional lives of the characters. His ideal audience was, thus, an overdistanced one, moved more by their intellectual outrage of the general condition than their emotional identification with the individual case. Although the role theory of drama therapy is more attuned to Brecht's ideas than to Stanislavski's, it still aims toward providing an experience of aesthetic distance, where both feeling and thinking are available. In Morenian terms, this approach combines elements of psychodrama and sociodrama.

Basic Assumptions of Role Theory

Role theory begins with the assumption that life is dramatic; that is, a central feature of existence is dramatic action. Dramatic action is different from reflexive and instinctual action, such as quickly withdrawing a hand from a hot surface or reacting to an aggressor by fleeing or fighting. Dramatic action implies a degree of distance from the initial stimulus and the mediation of role. If the hand lingers too long on the hot surface, the person might be injured. When burned, the person needs to take some action. The kind of action the person seeks is related to the role taken. He might choose to deny his pain and play the martyr. Or he might choose to play the patient and seek a doctor for medical assistance. The relationship between action and role, however, is reciprocal. Roles emerge as much from action as action does from role.

Role theory embraces the *theatricum mundi* metaphor of life as stage and people as actors and is based on the assumption that human beings live a double existence. Although hardly the first to characterize the double life, Shakespeare popularized it in Jacques's speech from *All's Well That Ends Well*, which begins: "All the world's a stage." Extending this idea to the social world, the sociologist Goffman stated in *The Presentation of Self in Everyday Life* that "All the world is not, of course, a stage, but that crucial ways in which it isn't are not easy to specify" (72).

Most often, the dramatic worldview implies a relationship between a protagonist and an antagonist or self and other. Such a relationship can be external, as an aggressor attacks an innocent, or internal, as one decides whether to react passively or actively to an aggressor. Dramatic action is motivated by either conflict or tension between two figures, each of whom sees the other as blocking its way. In role theory, these two figures are called role and counterrole.

In that life is dramatic, human beings are natural role-takers and role-players. To take on a role means that people internalize the qualities of their role models, and to play out a role means that people act in ways similar to the role model. Role-taking and role-playing are actions that are unlearned. Further, in the interplay of internalization and externalization, of role and counterrole, individuals struggle with their contradictions. They are not motivated, as in cognitive dissonance theory, by the need to resolve them, but to discover ways to live in and among them. The dramatic worldview rests upon an acceptance of the inevitable doubleness of life and the human struggle to seek balance among contradictory tendencies and roles.

A final assumption underlying role theory is that an individual is not one thing, a core self, but a multitude of roles that exist in relationship to their several counterparts. Thus role theory is more postmodern than humanistic. At the center is not a God-like edifice that is essentially good and whole, but a principle, a potential of all human beings to play out one essential quality of the gods—to create new life out of old, to create something out of nothing through the action of the imagination. In role theory there are no false selves and false roles masking real and authentic ones. All roles are real and playable; and all roles are essentially amoral, given moral weight as they are played out in relationship to others.

In the film, Landy (2005) makes the assumption that in playing a variety of parts human beings achieve a greater sense of wholeness. Echoing both Jung's notion of individuation and Perls' notion of integration of the Gestalt elements of figure and ground, Landy says: "To be whole is not about being essentially one true, authentic thing. To be whole is about being many things at the same time, even when these things contradict each other and cause dissonance."

Basic Concepts of Role Theory

Role and Counterrole

Role theory begins with the concept of role, originally derived from theater as the scroll-like document upon which was inscribed the dialogue of a play. Over time role became associated with the character who speaks the dialogue. In theater and in role theory, the terms "role" and "character" are generally used interchangeably. Throughout the history of theater in Western as well as traditional cultures, roles have tended to be archetypal, representations of character types rather than fully blown human beings. The convention of role as complex character only came into being in the late nineteenth century with the advent of psychological realism in theater.

Role, then, is a crucial concept in characterizing both the actor on stage and the actor in everyday life. In its latter meaning, role is a personality construct, representing specific qualities of a person, rather than the totality. This understanding helps to inform the practice of drama therapy where clients are asked to work on parts of themselves rather than the whole.

The sociological and theatrical meanings of role complement one another in drama therapy. In drama therapy, a role is one of many parts of the personality that is animated as one acts in the mind and in the world. Roles represent specific types of behavior, more prototype than stereotype, that are distinct from other types. Like theatrical heroes and villains, heroic and cowardly roles serve a particular function in drama therapy and are played out with a particular degree of emotion and distance.

Roles adhere to their counterparts, called counterroles, creating dyads that are dynamic in nature, flowing toward and away from each other as the situation demands. Counterroles are not simple opposites, as villain is to hero, but can also represent a quality that one perceives as existing on the other side of the role. For example, the counterrole of hero can be mother, if one perceives mother as very much less than heroic. Any role can have many counterroles, and although this dynamic has a universal quality, as we see in the polarity of beauty and beast, it also has a subjective quality, as any one person in the role of beauty might perceive other nonbeasts as counterroles.

The dynamics of role and counterrole can be understood in terms of Jung's concept of polarities where the two attitudes of introversion and extraversion intersect with four function types: thinking and feeling, sensing and intuiting, themselves polarities. In creating his complex typology of personality types, Jung provided a model that informs Landy's role typology called the Taxonomy of Roles.

Taxonomy of Roles

The Taxonomy of Roles is a systematic view of many of the potential roles available to be taken on in theater, therapy, and everyday life. The role types are similar to some of the specific archetypes delineated by Jung and his followers, such as the puer or child, the psychopomp or spirit guide, the maiden, the wise old man, and the hero. Jung chose his archetypes from his readings in mythology, art history, anthropology, archeology, alchemy, theology, and philosophy. As Landy envisioned the art of theater as the most essential source of drama therapy, he turned to theater as the repository of archetypal roles, scanning the *dramatis personae* of hundreds of classical, modern, and contemporary plays in search of repeated role types. Landy expanded the four Jungian functions into six domains to contain the roles somatic, cognitive, affective, social, spiritual, and aesthetic. The affective and cognitive domains are similar to Jung's functions of feeling and thinking. The somatic and aesthetic domains, although similar to Jung's sensation and intuitive functions, are more broadly drawn, containing aspects of age, sexual orientation, appearance, and health, as well as creativity. Landy's additional social and spiritual domains, though not necessarily polar opposites, contain certain contradictory types such as tyrant and saint.

Role Qualities, Functions, and Styles

In the Taxonomy, Landy (1993) identified and categorized eighty-four role types and seventy-four subtypes. The roles types are organized, first, according to their qualities or distinguishing characteristics. Next the roles are specified by their functions that can be best understood in terms of Propp's (1968) definition of character function within his classic study of Russian folk tales: "an act of character defined from the point of view of its significance for the course of the action" (21).

Finally, roles are organized in terms of their styles. Style of enactment is "the behavioral form in which the role is enacted, whether reality-based and representational, abstract and presentational, or somewhere in between" (Landy 1993, 169). Reality-based enactments imply a greater degree of emotion; presentational styles imply a greater degree of cognition. Thus style of presentation relates well to the distancing model given above, with overdistance as the most stylized cognitive form, and underdistance as the least stylized and most emotional. At the midpoint of aesthetic distance, where both affect and cognition are available, the style of enactment has qualities of both realism and abstraction.

Role, Counterrole, and Guide

Neither the domains nor the roles within each domain are conceived as paired with their opposites. Rather, each role is capable of adhering to any other role in the Taxonomy as a counterrole. Going along with Jung's notion of balance, role theory posits a third dramatic form serving as a bridge between role and counterrole. That form is called the guide. Structurally, role theory recapitulates the form of many classical epic poems and dramatic tragedies. The basic structure is of a hero, also known as the protagonist, who is on a journey; a villain, also known as the antagonist, who blocks his way; and a guide figure, either god or mortal, who steers the hero through the dangers of the journey. Examples include Odysseus, whose voyage from Troy to Ithaca is blocked by many villainous figures but who is ultimately guided by the goddess Athena; Dante, whose descent into hell is marked by many circles of dread, but is lead through it all by the dead poet Virgil; and King Lear, whose journey toward awareness is blocked by his blinded vision and the villainous figures around him, only to be transmogrified by the steadfastness of his daughter Cordelia.

In role theory, the guide is a transitional figure that holds together the role and counterrole, offering the possibility of integration. It functions also, as in epic drama, to lead protagonists through the psychic dangers of coming to terms with all their resistances and fears. In terms of the therapeutic encounter, the therapist initially takes on the qualities and functions of the guide, standing in for less effective guide figures in clients' lives, until they are able to internalize this capacity and guide themselves along the way toward recovery.

Every role in the Taxonomy operates within the structure of role, counterrole, and guide. Any one role type, such as Fool, can serve as protagonist/role, antagonist/counterrole, and/or guide within an individual's therapeutic drama.

Role System

The role system is the totality of roles available to be enacted within any given actor at any given moment in everyday life. Like the theatrical character actor who has the ability to play a broad repertory of roles, the everyday protagonist has the capacity to realize a range of roles from all of the domains, even though some roles might appear contradictory. An incarcerated murderer might be a loving father. The class clown might be a sensitive artist.

The role system, a representation of the personality, contains both those roles that are available to consciousness and ready to be enacted and those that are less available due to psychological, social, and/or environmental factors. Given special circumstances, such as a new relationship or a natural disaster, dormant roles often are activated. These roles, however, appear in relationship to other, more known roles. The role system is dynamic and all roles, whether new or old, tend to seek their counterparts. In the case of a person with a healthy and fluid role system, the parts will fit in such a way as to tolerate paradox. In the case of a less integrated person, the combination of role and counterrole might create undue dissonance such that the person will exclude the counterrole from consciousness. In such an instance, the denied role will be repressed and may become, in the language of Jung, a shadow figure that exerts its power from a dark place in the psyche, just out of consciousness.

A role system exists on several planes at the same time. As roles are located within the person, between people, and even between people and the natural and supernatural worlds, they form intricate, magnificent webs. These webs are contained within a role system, which is a dynamic work in progress, responsive to stasis and change, to biology and psychology, to internal and external demands.

Role and Story

In theatrical terms, role is the most essential and indivisible aspect of the dramatic process. Other dramatic elements, such as text and subtext, spectacle and setting, sound and movement, are expendable. There are many theatrical plays and dramatic actions in everyday life that occur without words, without sound and movement, without text, subtext, and context. Certain theatrical, neurological, and psychological conditions might preclude all these elements, but as long as a person is conscious enough to imagine himself as other, in another space, there is drama and thus hope of change.

Generally speaking, then, for drama to occur, actors take on roles. In most instances, once they take on the roles, they express themselves by telling their role-bound stories. As role is the form of dramatic action, story is the content. Although role precedes story, it takes on a fuller meaning and fulfills its social function when it moves into story. Story is the narrative of an actor in role, whether the actor is a theatrical performer or simply a human being recounting aspects of daily life from the point of view of a particular role. The same person will tell many stories throughout a day based in her roles of, for example, mother, intellectual, wife, sister, person of faith, and artist. Like role, implying a separation from self and from counterroles, story implies a separation from real-time events. A story is told after an experience has taken place, as a means of making sense of the event. Or a story can be told in anticipation of an event that has not yet occurred, such as one's death, or may never occur, such as a wish to reconcile with a lost lover. A story is told generally to another, real or implied, who can provide a means of validating the story and the storyteller. While engaged in drama therapy as informed by role theory, clients identify roles and tell stories through and about their roles.

Therapeutic Goals

The purpose of working this way is to help clients move toward a balanced state, where problematic roles are integrated with appropriate counterroles by means of the transitional guide figure. Although the goal is reached as clients play out the role trinity, the therapeutic benefit is achieved when the process has an internal component and clients are able to tolerate the dissonance caused by living a paradoxical reality. This goal, applied to the role method of treatment is articulated by Landy (2005) in the film:

> The aim of Role Method is to help individuals, groups, and communities live a full and balanced life, accepting and working through the natural struggles with emptiness and imbalance. Wholeness springs from the ability to play many roles, to tell and enact many stories and, in the end, to discover value not only in one role or story that is most authentic, but in all.

Role of the Therapist

According to role theory, the therapist functions as a guide figure, leading clients toward stories and roles that need to be told and enacted. Further, the therapist helps clients discover ways to internalize the guide and eventually guide their own process.

In theatrical terms, the therapist is more director than actor, maintaining an empathetic stance while encouraging clients to play out all of the evoked roles themselves. Sometimes, however, the therapist will take on a complementary role in relationship to a client, especially when working individually. If, for example, a client in the role of son is working through an issue with his father, the therapist might take on the role of father and engage in the drama with the client as son. The therapist tends to do so when asked by the client or when the client appears to be unable to play the dual roles himself.

The interplay of therapist and client in role implies a mutual relationship, although one that is less intense than the mutual analysis innovated by Ferenczi. In engaging in role-play with the client, the therapist maintains a certain aesthetic distance and the awareness that he is not a mutual client, but a mutual player. By moving in and out of role, he is able to demonstrate this reality. While working in role with the client, the therapist needs to be

How to handle touch?

How is the trans- given to the group?

especially aware of countertransferential feelings so as to maintain focus upon the client's issues. Such feelings can be communicated to the client in role, through the body or through emotional expression, challenging the client to respond in kind.

As to the issues of transference, the therapist working with a group attempts to move the transference onto the group who holds the transferential figure for the client (for a full discussion of this process, see Eliaz 1988). In individual work, the therapist can view the transferential figure as a role and give it form by either taking it on himself, as in the example above of therapist as father, or by moving it outside, onto an empty chair, for example, tangible enough for engagement from the client.

As we shall see in the session with Derek, however, the therapist working from a role theory point of view tends to mostly encourage the client to enact all the roles himself. As such, the therapist maintains the status of a theatrical director, but one that is neither too distanced nor too enmeshed with the client. In applying the paradigm of distancing, it becomes incumbent upon the therapist to determine when to take on a more or less distanced stance to better serve the needs of the client. In an earlier paper, Landy (2000) states that the determination is based upon two primary factors:

1. The client's diagnosis and ability to handle closeness and/or separation; and
2. The therapist's ability to contain emotion and to deal effectively with his countertransferential reactions within a session (61).

Finally, within role theory, the director is not only a guide figure, helping clients integrate discrepant roles, but also a witness, one who uncritically stays with clients, validating all their struggles with roles and counterroles. Essentially, the witness is another way to conceptualize the guide, at least in a spiritual sense. The therapist as guide and witness is far removed from Freud's notion of the analyst, who remains separate from the incumbent client, encouraging transference and provoking resistance so as to analyze it for the benefit of the client. The classical distanced analyst has given way to models based in relational theories (see, for example, Mitchell and Greenberg 1983; Fonagy 2001) and existential ones (see, for example, Yalom 1980). These newer models of the therapist are more consonant with the earlier theories of Rank and Ferenczi, who argued for an active and human stance on the part of the therapist, more of a guide and witness than a god.

View of Wellness and Illness

From the point of view of role theory, the healthy human being is one who is able to take on and play out a variety of roles with some level of proficiency throughout the lifespan. Wellness is marked by one's ability to live within the contradictions of dissonant roles. It is also about the presence of well-developed guides, both mentors and inner figures, to help negotiate the difficult moments of imbalance. The healthy human being is one who is able to transform experiences into stories, to tell the stories to appropriate listeners, and to change the stories according to changing circumstances from within and from the outside world. Health is determined by the creation of a balanced, dynamic, and interactive role system as well as a capacity to tell and revise the stories of one's life within a group context. Balance as a goal is not an absolute, but rather a relative measure of intrapsychic and interpersonal stability.

Illness occurs when the role system is unbalanced. Lack of balance can mean too many free-floating roles existing separate from appropriate counterroles. Some people collect roles like they court people, taking on more professions and lovers and friends and beliefs and emotional experiences than they can effectively process. It can also mean a poor match between specific roles and their counterroles. For example, a son who has grownup with an abusive father might search for his counterpart in abusive friends. And finally, imbalance can mean the attachment to a single role or related cluster of roles to the exclusion of all other counterroles. Examples include those who have embraced a single belief or relationship in an extreme, uncritical way. Many, of course, do not choose their roles. Some are born with physical disabilities, mental or physical illnesses, or even superior gifts of mind and/or body. For these people, balance implies a capability to conceive of themselves beyond the limits of their disabilities or abilities, reaching out to other parts of themselves and to others who are similar and different from them. Imbalance, leading to a more limited existence, means the opposite—a definition of self and a view by others as a one-dimensional person, locked into a prison of one's own construction.

Assessment and Evaluation

Landy (2001a) developed two assessment instruments stemming from his theory of role and story. In the first, Tell-A-Story (TAS), subjects are given the following directions:

> I would like you to tell me a story. The story can be based upon something that happened to you or to somebody else in real life or it can be completely made up. The story must have at least one character.

Those who have difficulty expressing themselves verbally are encouraged to tell their stories nonverbally, through movement or puppetry. Following the storytelling, the subjects are asked to name the characters in the story. The assessor then asks a series of questions intended to assess the subject's ability to identity qualities, functions, and styles of each character, to specify the theme of the story, and the connection between the story and the everyday life of the storyteller.

The second role-based assessment, Role Profiles, was developed by Landy (2001b; Landy et al. 2003) to determine how people see themselves in terms of seventy role types, each one written upon an index card. The assessment begins with the following instructions:

> This experience is intended to explore your personality as if it were made-up of characters commonly found in plays, movies, and stories. You will be given a stack of cards. On each card is the name of a role, which is a type of character you have probably seen in movies and plays or read about in stories. Please shuffle the cards thoroughly. Place each card in one of four groups that best describes how you feel about yourself right now. Each group is labeled by a large card which says: I Am This, I Am Not This, I Am Not Sure If I Am This, and I Want To Be This. Try to group the cards as quickly as possible.

Once the subjects have sorted the cards, they are asked a number of questions to ascertain their ability to reflect upon their role choices. In assessing the subjects' responses, the assessor considers the form and content of the card sort to determine such issues as method of sorting cards, use of time and space, quantity of roles in each category, balance and imbalance among categories, emotional reactions to certain roles, and connections among roles.

Beyond Role Profiles, Landy developed a simpler instrument called Role Checklist, which lists fifty-six roles on a single page, with four columns that read: "Who I Am, Who I Want to Be, Who Is Blocking Me, and Who Can Help Me." These categories are consistent with Landy's understanding of narrative structure as concerning the journey of a hero (who I am) toward a destination (who I want to be). The hero's journey is difficult because there are obstacles along the way (who is blocking me). Due to the difficulties in traversing the obstacles, the hero needs a guide (who can help me) to help move the journey forward. The subject is asked to check the categories that best pertain to a selection of roles.

None of the three instruments have been rigorously tested as to reliability and validity. Only the most fully developed of the three, Role Profiles, has been subjected to a number of trials with various clinical and nonclinical populations (see Tangorra 1997; Landy 2001b; Landy et al. 2003).

THE ROLE METHOD OF DRAMA THERAPY

The role method of drama therapy extends naturally from role theory as clients create effective roles and stories within which to explore their dilemmas. Although role method does not necessarily proceed in a linear fashion,

Landy (1993, 2000) presents a basic roadmap through the following eight steps:

1. Invoking the role
2. Naming the role
3. Playing out/working through the role
4. Exploring relationships of role to counterrole and guide
5. Reflecting upon the role-play: discovering role qualities, functions, and styles inherent in the role
6. Relating the fictional role to everyday life
7. Integrating roles to create a functional role system
8. Social modeling: discovering ways that clients' behavior in role affects others in their social environments

The clinical process of drama therapy begins with a warm-up experience, encouraging the client or the group to invoke or summon roles. Having invoked the role, clients are asked to name it. The naming provides greater specificity to the role and opens up the possibilities of discovering its qualities and function. As a third step, the therapist helps move the client or the group into role and into the creation of a story. At times the storytelling will be sufficient in itself for a given client. Many times, however, the story is moved into some form of dramatic enactment through words and/or movement. In the work, the therapist, when appropriate, will encourage the client to discover a counterrole and a guide role. The full process is not necessarily realized within a single session.

The next part of the process, steps 5 and 6, involves reflection upon the role-play and story enactment. At this point, the client or the group de-roles, that is, moves from the fiction of the drama to the everyday reality of the present moment. De-roling points to the central paradox of the dramatic experience—that of the continuity of the actor and the role. In departing the fictional role, the actor resumes a life in a parallel universe that is less obviously stylized. Because work in and out of role can become complex and even confusing, it is important that the therapist aids the client to fully de-role each character. While too fully enrolled, the client can easily lose distance and thus have trouble reflecting upon the role-play.

Reflecting upon the experience is a cognitive part of the role method and places it closer to psychoanalysis and cognitive therapy. Reflection upon the dramatic work involves two parts. The first concerns a consideration of the roles as fictions, attempting to make sense of them in terms of their qualities, functions, and levels of emotion and distance. The second part seeks to connect the fictional roles to the everyday lives of the clients. As fictional roles have counterparts in reality, heroes and demons in a story represent the heroic and demonic parts of the person in everyday life.

Following the reflections, clients often engage in further dialogue with the therapist to work toward discovering integration between and among roles. Integration, however, is not necessarily a conscious process, to be discovered in conversation. It often occurs unconsciously, as clients trust the process (see McNiff 1998), allowing themselves to stay open to unconscious experience (see Ormont 1992).

The final stage, that of social modeling, concerns the effects of a positive, integrative therapeutic experience. Given a change of role or a new configuration of role-CR-guide, clients enter old relationships in new ways. In modeling new sets of role behaviors, clients serve as positive role models for others within their social spheres. As mentioned earlier, these steps are not necessarily linear. Some clients begin by reflecting upon ineffective roles in their lives and then move into dramatic action. Others jump right into the action but do not name the roles until a later point. Some have difficulty abstracting their experiences and resist moving into the fictional frame. The importance in role method is to meet clients wherever they are and to move them through the steps as they are ready and willing.

Some drama therapists, such as those who practice developmental transformations, believe that healing occurs fully through the play and drama and that cognitive reflection outside of play is not necessary to affect change. From the point of view of role method, reflective verbal processing occurring following the enactment is an important step along the way to fully working through an embedded issue. This point of view is consistent with current research in neuroscience that provides a neurobiological rationale for integrating mind, body, and emotions through the process of psychotherapy (see, for example, Demasio 1999; Cozolino 2002).

Role Method with Derek

The following is a transcript of the filmed session in role method, edited minimally for redundancy. It features Derek as client and Robert Landy as therapist. The session will be followed by several reflections of Derek and Landy and then will be examined according to the several polarities of emotion and distance, fiction and reality, verbal and nonverbal expression, action and reflection, directive and nondirective action, transference and countertransference.

ROBERT: Hey Derek. How are you doing?

DEREK: Fine.

ROBERT: So we're going to work for forty minutes and we'll see where we go. This will be about working in role method of drama therapy. And you know this might be fairly intimate work that we do. But outside of us we have a group of students who are watching who will be asking questions later. And we have a cameraman and a camera. So I'm wondering what your thoughts or feelings are about that.

DEREK: I'm a little bit nervous. . . .

ROBERT: Are you more nervous about the camera or the students?

DEREK: The camera.

ROBERT: What are your feelings about the camera?

DEREK: I don't turn out very well with cameras.

ROBERT: Oh, you don't like the way that you look on camera?

DEREK: To be perfectly honest, I'll come out so dark all you can see is my teeth.

ROBERT: OK. So it has to do with the color of your skin.

DEREK: Yeah.

ROBERT: Ah. If you were to take on a role and say: "I am a camera, and I am filming Derek, and this is what I'm going to pick up," let's see where you go.

DEREK: I am a camera. I am here to shoot Derek. Literally, figuratively. Shoot Derek.

ROBERT: Shoot Derek.

DEREK: Yeah. And my job is to make him look as unflattering as possible.

ROBERT: So you're a pretty rough camera.

DEREK: Yeah.

ROBERT: Why would you want to make him look as bad as possible?

DEREK: Because that's the way he already feels and I know that.

ROBERT: So you're going to shoot him the way he feels . . .

DEREK: I'm like his . . . I'm his mind reader. I'm a mind reader camera.

ROBERT: He's concerned that you, mind reader camera, are going to make him look very dark except for his teeth. Is that what you'd like to do, to make him look dark?

DEREK: I think I want to make him look dark, but yet I want him to feel comfortable.

ROBERT: So what can you tell him, camera, to make him feel more at ease?

DEREK: Be yourself.

ROBERT: Let's get another chair. Let's say for a moment this is Derek sitting over there, and you're going to put him more at ease. Tell him something that you think might help him.

DEREK: Relax, Derek, you're not so bad. You're working through most of your shit anyway. So you might as well just relax.

ROBERT: What about his concern about the darkness of his skin and the brightness of his teeth? What can you tell him about that?

DEREK: You should take pride in your teeth. They can be as white and shiny as possible. Take pride in the sheen that comes off your skin. Chill. Relax. I'm gonna make you look good.

[Both take a deep breath and sigh.]

ROBERT: I like that.

DEREK: You like that?

ROBERT: Yeah. You think you've told him enough? You think you've helped him relax a little bit more after this?

DEREK: Just chill. I think that's enough.

ROBERT: OK, good. So let the role of camera go for now. Come back to Derek. Put the chair back. How did that work?

DEREK: At first it was a little nerve wracking, but the more the camera told me to chill the more I was like, alright, relax.

ROBERT: Do you think you can tell yourself that message today as we proceed in our work?

DEREK: Should I tell myself that now?

ROBERT: Yeah, tell yourself that now.

DEREK: Derek, chill.

ROBERT: Alright, good.

[Both take a deep breath and sigh.]

ROBERT: How are you feeling in your body?

DEREK: I'm a little tight around here. [Derek gestures to his shoulders.]

ROBERT: Do you want to loosen up a little bit?

DEREK: Yeah, can I warm up a little?

ROBERT: I tell you what—push that chair back. I'm a little nervous, too in front of the camera. You know, I might look a little too white. I don't want to look too white. Who knows? Can you help us both warm up a little bit?

DEREK: [Raising his arms.] I'm a little stinky here so . . .

[Both stretch out their bodies.]

ROBERT: Is that good?

DEREK: Better.

ROBERT: Better. Can we sit down again? So . . . there are a couple of things that you said about yourself already. . . . One is in terms of the camera picking up the darkness in your face or the brightness of your teeth, and you also mentioned something about being stinky. Let's just keep that in mind and see . . . if that stays the same or changes. Remember the idea that you can talk to yourself. The voice that says: "chill," the voice that says: "let go," maybe it will happen again. So, I asked you to bring an issue with you today, and I know you'll work on a common issue with the other two therapists. Rather than tell me the issue, could you think of it as a story and give the story a title?

DEREK: The struggle of a man and his father.

ROBERT: The struggle of a man and his father. Great. Now if you were to tell a story with that title and think of the story as occurring among three characters, who would the three characters be?

DEREK: Father, Son, and Pain.

ROBERT: The Father, the Son, and Pain. Great. Can I ask you to make up a story now? You can go wherever you want to with it, but make it somewhat of a fairy tale. Would you start: "Once upon a time there was . . ."

DEREK: Once upon a time there lived a father and a son in a little house. There was always stuff to do. The son tried to do every possible thing to make the father happy. Father was too busy hanging around with Pain. See, Pain was the bad guy from the neighborhood. All Pain did to the father was to hurt him and curse out the father and beat the father and that's what the father was doing all the time—hanging out with Pain. Even though he didn't like hanging out with Pain, he needed someone to hold onto. So there was the son in the house, always trying to be the best son, the good son. He stumbled along the way. He wasn't always very good, but he tried to please the father. So there be one particular day the father came home. The father was angry about something. Came home. Son was there. Father started bringing Pain home with him. All Pain would do is curse out the son and tell him that he was no good and that he should probably just drift off and go to the local military, because he was gonna be a pain in the ass. So the son just would try to hide inside the house, find any kind of refuge inside the house, mostly by the radiator trying to keep warm and hoping that his father wouldn't come and find him. But the father always found him, and he always was hanging out with Pain. Pain was that hard ass son of a bitch who always followed the father. So they found the son and laid into him pretty good and told him that he was shit and confronted him and went up to the son for no apparent reason and put his hand in the son's face and pointed in his face and all the son could hear was the screeching of the radiator. This whistling. I don't know if you've ever heard that but the whistling of the radiator was like shhhhh.

ROBERT: Oh yeah.

DEREK: So all he tried to pay attention to was hearing the father, and Pain talked shit about him. So that's all he could possibly remember was shhhhh. And it came time when the son was growing and growing, and he took years of the same shit with Pain and the father. You're this, you're that, you're a black son of a bitch. So the son had to learn how to do a lot of things on his own, learn how to go outside and chop wood on his own. He had to learn how to be a father or at least an image of being a man. He was never taught that by Pain or his father. . . . One day, the son just looked at a mountain and he said one day when he was a little boy he was gonna climb that mountain. And so that day came. The son had almost become a father himself or a man himself and he started climbing and climbing and climbing. And he came stumbling down every now and then because Pain was always after him, whispering stuff to him. "You're no good, you're a piece of shit, get out of the house, you can't chop wood right. You don't do errands right. You can't do anything right." Son finally got on top of the mountain and all he could hear was the whistling of the radiator. It was going shhhh. . . . Even though he was dead tired, he couldn't feel anything, his legs or his hands, but he had to just keep moving up that mountain. Came the day when the Father had to clean up himself, stop hanging around Pain, because he realized Pain wasn't doing anything to him. And he just looked at his son and was just happy one day. Keep going up that mountain son, keep going up that mountain. All the son had to do was keep climbing. He was waiting for those couple of words. All he needed was two words from the father. He never got them, so the son keeps climbing up that mountain and falling down, but he keeps getting back up. And that's the end of the story.

ROBERT: What were the two words?

DEREK: I'm sorry.

ROBERT: So in the story you named three characters—the Father, the Son and Pain. Where is Pain at the end of the story?

DEREK: Pain is broken into pieces. Pain isn't actually standing up next to the father now; he's just in little dabs trying to get up the mountain with the son.

ROBERT: Was there some kind of a separation between Pain and the father?

DEREK: Yeah, they separated. The father decided he wasn't hanging around Pain anymore.

ROBERT: What made the change?

DEREK: Because Pain was toxic.

ROBERT: But he had been around Pain for such a long time. What made him decide he was too toxic to hang out with?

DEREK: A higher being . . . and looking at that son climb up that mountain. So that's when the father decided I can't hang around this clown anymore, because he's messing around with my head too much and messing around with my son too much.

ROBERT: But even though Pain is in pieces, he's still following the son up the mountain.

DEREK: Yeah, he tried to go up the mountain. That's why he's in little pieces. One piece I didn't tell you. He tried to go up the mountain as well.

ROBERT: Who tried to go up the mountain?

DEREK: Pain. But the son, it wasn't accidental. The son kicked Pain down. See, he tried to commit homicide. Part of Pain died. Was one of the most satisfying . . .

ROBERT: Satisfying to whom? The son? Ok, so I'm going to interrupt the story. I want to hear from the son. You're going to give a monologue from the son as Pain begins to break. Imagine for a moment where you'd be as the son—on the mountain?

DEREK: I'd be almost at the top.

ROBERT: Can we do it now with you as the son? Do you want to stand on top of something? How do you want to do it?

[Derek kneels on chair.]

ROBERT: And where is Pain?

DEREK: [Points behind himself.] He's right here, almost right behind me.

ROBERT: Can we use a chair?

DEREK: Yeah. Put it right there.

ROBERT: You are the son, and you are watching this thing happen in the moment. I'm gonna listen to you as you watch it. Tell me what you see.

DEREK: Get off me, motherfucker! [Kicking] He's got a strong grip. [Pushes chair away. Laughing.] He busted his ass. That would be the story. He busted his ass. But see, if I cut that chair in half, I would divide it into little pieces.

ROBERT: Now we can't easily break the chair into pieces, but we have a couple of different chairs so I'd like you to show me how you do that. Here, let's say these chairs are the pieces.

DEREK: [Arranges chairs.] There, that's it.

ROBERT: OK, so continue as the son. What's going on? What are you seeing? What are you thinking about? What are you feeling?

DEREK: I'm thinking I want to get more distance from Pain. That's what I'm feeling. I'm thinking that a little bit of Pain helps me climb the mountain, so I'm actually going to move this if I can. [Moves chairs.] Not exactly touching, but it's close, because it's helping me climb the mountain.

ROBERT: Alright, can you speak to that piece of Pain and tell it what you think.

DEREK: I hate you for what you did for messing up my father and messing up me. But I need you to keep moving. No, I don't need you to keep moving, 'cause I can move on my own, but seeing you sometimes will help me keep moving, because I wouldn't be sad if he fell apart and I never see him again.

ROBERT: Sit on that chair and take on that role of Pain. Now having heard that speech from the son, how does Pain respond?

DEREK: How do you think you actually got that far? You think you would've gotten that far because of love? He needed some of me in him to drive him this far.

ROBERT: You need some of me . . .

DEREK: You need some part of me to get this far in life. You need me to keep kicking you in your butt to remind you of what you can be. Even though you keep trying to run away from me, I'm a part of you. Accept me and we'll be all good. But remember the moment that you think everything is hunky dory, I'll just whisper a couple of words.

ROBERT: Great. OK, let that role go.

DEREK: Thank the Lord.

ROBERT: Shake it out of your body. Now one piece is missing in this enactment, and that is the father. Those words that you told me were really important—what were they?

DEREK: I'm sorry.

ROBERT: Two words. Alright, if I gave you a choice to either be the father saying those words or the son hearing those words, which role would you rather play?

DEREK: I can't be the son.

ROBERT: You can't be the son hearing those words?

DEREK: Uh-uh. I want to be the father.

ROBERT: You want to be the father. Alright. Let's put the son someplace. Take a chair to represent the son. Put the son someplace in the space that feels right. We'll let go of Pain for now. You might want to bring him back.

DEREK: No, put him here.

ROBERT: Yeah. You want a piece of Pain or whole Pain?

DEREK: Just a piece.

ROBERT: Alright, a piece of Pain. [Referring to three chairs.] So, that's the son, that's a piece of Pain, and that's the father. Is the son on or off the mountain?

DEREK: Preferably he'd be off, but he can't get off right now so I think he's on there.

ROBERT: He's on there. Is he moving or . . .

DEREK: He's gotta keep moving.

ROBERT: So he's on the move. And Pain is just staying with him as he's moving—the part of Pain, that is.

DEREK: Yeah.

ROBERT: And where's the father?

DEREK: [Laughing.] That's a good question. Umm. Back here.

ROBERT: Alright. Do you mind if I hang out with you a little bit back here?

DEREK: Why not?

ROBERT: I don't know. Maybe because it's not easy to play the father. Or maybe it is.

DEREK: It's a little bit easier than playing the son.

ROBERT: Alright, then maybe I should hang out over here. [Walking toward the chair that represents the son.] Maybe this one needs a bit more support. Is that better? Or do you want me to be with you?

DEREK: Come back.

ROBERT: OK, so basically what I want you to do is, as the father, give the son what he needs. Those two words, but maybe they need to be prepared instead of just blurted out.

DEREK: Yeah, then it'd sound phony.

ROBERT: So you have to do it in a way that sounds authentic. How are you gonna do that?

DEREK: I can always write him a letter.

ROBERT: You can do that. I have a blackboard here, and I can get you some chalk.

DEREK: Yeah.

ROBERT: You want to do that?

DEREK: Absolutely.

ROBERT: Alright, here's the chalk.

[Derek writes on board:]
I'm SORRY, My son
for ALL bringing Pain in our home.
P.S. I'm proud of you.
And you're a good man.
[Man is underlined several times.]

ROBERT: OK.

DEREK: You're breathing. You're not supposed to be breathing.

ROBERT: I'm not supposed to be breathing? Should I stop breathing?

DEREK: No, I want you around.

ROBERT: Alright, I'll stay around. I'll stay alive with you. So you've written it out.

DEREK: I'm sorry, can I . . .

ROBERT: Absolutely, do whatever you want.

DEREK: [Erases the word "ALL."] Geezz, I need to go back to school.

ROBERT: So the ALL is very big. I guess I was thinking: "I'm sorry my son for ALL, for everything. Did you mean everything?

DEREK: Yeah. [Writes ALL again on board with a circle around it.]

ROBERT: So there's one more thing—I'm going to ask you as father to deliver the message to the son.

DEREK: I thought I was gonna read it.

ROBERT: Well you can do that. How do you want to read it? Do you want to read it in a deeply feeling way or cool, removed?

DEREK: Cool.

ROBERT: Cool, calm, and collected. Alright.

DEREK: I'm sorry my son for bringing Pain into the home. All of it. P.S., I'm proud of you, and you're a good man. And I mean it.

ROBERT: And what?

DEREK: I mean it.

ROBERT: You'd better write that down.

DEREK: [He writes: "I mean it." Then writes: "Please forgive me."] Sorry, everything's just coming out.

ROBERT: OK, great. There's more that came out that time. Can you try again and now do the whole thing. If you want to change the tone of it and go more into the feeling, that's OK, but you don't have to . . .

DEREK: [Calm and cool.] I'm sorry my son for bringing Pain in our home. All of it. P.S., I'm proud of you and you're a good man. I mean it. Please forgive me.

ROBERT: Can you do it one more time, but this time, here's the son. And here's Pain. Part of Pain, the Pain that hangs out with the son. Is this right?

DEREK: Yeah.

ROBERT: Now take it one step further.

DEREK: In terms of reading?

ROBERT: Yeah, in terms of an actor who's more in touch with his feelings.

DEREK: I'm sorry my son for bringing Pain in our home. All of it. I'm proud of you and you're such a good man and I mean it. Please forgive me. . . . It kind of frees you up.

ROBERT: Yeah. Do you want to take it one little step further? You want to try one more thing?

DEREK: What, you want me to sing it?

ROBERT: You want to sing it? You know, I thought about singing it.

DEREK: You did? [Singing in a jokey way.] "I'm sorry my son for bringing Pain in our home. All of it. I'm proud of you and you're such a good man and I mean it. Please forgive me." An old Negro spiritual. I think there's something in there.

ROBERT: It took you a different way, but I want to bring you back. Could you sit down in that chair, so you're facing Pain and the father over here. Now this time you're the son. You don't say a word. Is it OK if I read it to you and you listen?

DEREK: Yeah.

ROBERT: [Reading slowly, with feeling.] I'm sorry my son for bringing Pain in our home. All of it. P.S., I'm proud of you and you're a good man and I mean it. I mean it. Please forgive me.

DEREK: [Derek is visibly moved.] You ain't getting me to cry here.

ROBERT: Alright, fine. I'll tell you what I want you to do. I want you to take a nice deep breath. You're no longer the son. Let it go. Get out of the chair. Move that chair away. Make it into just a chair again. That's not Pain anymore. We're going to sit together. We only have a couple minutes. First of all, are you OK? Where did that work go for you?

DEREK: It went between my shoulder blades.

ROBERT: Is it there right now?

DEREK: Uh-huh. It's still trying to ease its way through.

ROBERT: I urge you to keep breathing. . . . Don't hold onto it. Let it pass through. This story felt very thinly disguised from reality, even though it felt like a fairy tale. How is it connected to your everyday life?

DEREK: As me Derek?

ROBERT: Yeah.

DEREK: Well, just the same sort of story. . . . I did the same thing.

ROBERT: Climb the mountain, you mean?

DEREK: I'm trying to climb a mountain. I hid by the radiator. Still hear the whistling.

ROBERT: That was a beautiful character in the story, the radiator.

DEREK: Yeah, it was comforting. Somedays, it'd be warm.

ROBERT: Was the whistling comforting, too?

DEREK: The whistling was comforting. Certain noises make me fall asleep such as garbage trucks and whistling radiators.

ROBERT: So they're soothing.

DEREK: Yeah. And rain. Whenever I hear rain, I'm comforted. Same sorta stuff.

ROBERT: It's almost like the radiator is kind of a guide figure that holds together some of that pain that's attached to the father and the son.

DEREK: Yeah, the son now has to hold on to all that pain that the father brought that he never got rid of. . . . So now the son is gonna have a hard time trying to grow up to be a man and trying to climb the mountain.

ROBERT: Maybe that's a good place to end, a clear way of thinking of the whole thing. It was good working with you.

DEREK: It was good hanging out with you too.

Reflections on the Session

Before discussing the polarities, let us look at some of Landy's and Derek's reflections just after the session. Landy stated that he first wondered how Derek would deal with his initial self-deprecating images and how he could guide him toward a more balanced place. Conceptualizing the problem in terms of role theory, Landy (2005) said:

> When he identified the problem as a father and son issue and even came up with the third role as Pain, I was able to think about this work in terms of role, counterrole and guide. I thought of the son as the primary role of the hero going on a journey. . . . In the story Derek, as son, goes on a journey up the mountain. The counterrole I saw as the father, and Pain in some ways I saw as the guide. Sometimes the guide is a negative figure.

Landy noted that his task as therapist was to remain a consistent, positive guide figure for Derek, even to the point of asking Derek if he wanted him to remain physically close in the dramatization. He thought that by doing so, Derek was better able to proceed on his difficult journey up the symbolic mountain. As a guide figure, Landy needed to be a stand-in for a more positive, transformed father. Derek provided that image in the story as the father let go of pain and supported the son's journey up the mountain. After internalizing the words of forgiveness uttered by the fictional father, Derek was able to acknowledge the spiritual transformation of his real father.

Landy also noted that the story structure and the writing and then singing of the difficult words of forgiveness provided the optimal distance for Derek to eventually take on the role of the son and accept the words he had never before received from his father.

Reflecting upon the goal of role method, that of balance, Landy (2005) noted:

> I was hoping that the balance would come if he could, as the father, say those words to the son, and if the son could take in those words, and if Pain could be transformed in such a way as to stand between father and son. It was interesting because Derek didn't banish Pain forever from the mountain, but he broke it into pieces and he kept on holding a piece of it as if it had a certain guiding energy. . . . I think at the end I did feel a certain balance and integration among . . . father and son through the mediation of Pain, which follows the model of working toward the balance of role and counterrole mediated by the guide.

For Landy, the image of the radiator and its comforting hissing sound was another form of guide figure for Derek. Although born of pain and abuse and functioning to numb these feared experiences, the radiator "seemed transformed and transforming as it became a signal of calm, a way of working through some of the Pain, and making peace with the knowledge that Pain is part of him . . . as a legacy from the father" (Landy 2005).

In the end, when asked by the panel of graduate students further about the guide figure, Landy referred back to the camera as a critical eye. He noted that at the beginning of the session Derek was concerned that he would be judged harshly by the camera as too black, as he had been judged in the eyes of his peers when growing up. But Derek was able to turn around the negative image and view the camera as positive, just as he was able to see himself finally in a positive way through the eyes of his father. As a final reflection upon the guide, Landy (2005) said:

> The negative guide became a positive guide. If the camera's a guide . . . it is a representation of how others see us and how we see ourselves . . . A guide is a figure that helps us see ourselves as we really are. Are we really beautiful? Are we really not beautiful? Maybe we're a little of both. And if we can . . . love the way we look, then the guide has done its work.

As Derek (in Landy 2005) reflected upon the experience, he noted that the experience of hearing the words of forgiveness and love from his father were powerful: "Like oxygen couldn't get through to my heart because I couldn't believe what I was actually hearing." In making the connection from the fiction of the drama to his actual life, Derek expressed sadness that he might never hear these words from his father, but that "there's a large part of me that's made peace with it."

One year after the filming, Derek further reflected upon the process. He said that he actually arrived at a point of compassion for his father that was completely unexpected. He realized "that my father was in need of a father himself" (Derek 2006). Further, reflecting on the role of son, Derek said:

When the male therapist switched roles with me and spoke my actual words I had written on the board as the father, it evoked an emotion I had never felt before. It was a feeling of affirmation I was deprived of having as a child, teenager and young man. These words I prayed I would hear from my father, that could heal a thousand wounds if they were ever spoken, and it felt good hearing them.

At the conclusion of the session, Derek did make peace at least with his fictional roles and story. He split Pain up into a manageable size. He took in the words of the father that he always longed for. He climbed the mountain and identified a soothing guide figure. In reality, he made a positive connection with Robert, a stand-in for the father. He viewed himself as strong and beautiful. He recognized that there was much more work to do not only on the relationship of father to son, but also on his identification as a black man in a white society. He (Derek in Landy 2005) said: "The color complex is still there, and that is to me almost directly related to the father/son issue." More work on both issues was to come in the next two sessions.

In a final reflection one year after making the film, Derek realized that he had become a role model for his father, echoing Landy's final stage of social modeling in the role method. Derek (2006) noted: "My father in the story saw me climbing the mountain and achieving so much with my life, and so I became a role model to him, showing him how to break free of Pain and work on self-improvement."

THE POLARITIES

Emotion and Distance

Role method is an indirect dramatic approach that depends upon the safety of role and story to contain strong emotion. Among the three featured drama-therapy approaches, it is the most distanced and most containing. It is well indicated for clients who have experienced trauma, as it allows them to project aspects of their actual dilemmas upon created fictions and then to reflect upon the connection between the fiction and the reality. Derek is a case in point as he has experienced a traumatic childhood and required a degree of safety to contain his strong feelings toward the object of his abuse—his father.

When working through role method, clients often experience catharsis, especially when they become aware of the connection between the fiction and the reality. This awareness can occur unconsciously in the enactment, or more consciously in the reflection. However, the form of catharsis is unique in that it integrates both affect and cognition. The feeling evoked in the playing is balanced by the reflection upon the playing. The actor is aware that he is acting and thus is able to take on the dual roles of actor and observer. Generally speaking, the therapist who employs role method works toward facilitating a balanced state of feeling and thought, neither too emotionally overwhelming nor too intellectually isolating.

Derek experienced this form of balance when he took on the role of son and listened to the words of forgiveness spoken to him by Robert as the father. And yet, in pulling back from the role of son, he told his therapist: "You ain't getting me to cry here." Derek's choice to distance himself from a deeper expression of emotion can be explained in several ways. For one, this was Derek's first filmed session before a group of his peers, and he was not fully warmed up to the process, despite his working with the image of the camera. Further, he was working with a man, and although he had previously experienced Robert as validating and containing, he might have transferred his past fear of his actual father onto Robert in the present. And finally, the method of working through role and story supported Derek's need for containment. He accepted the safety of the distance, aware that there were two more sessions to come.

Fiction and Reality

Extending from the previous discussion, role method requires the client to work imaginatively, that is, to create a fictional world and then attempt to inhabit it. It could be argued that most traditional and psychodynamic forms of therapy do the same. When one works through shamanism, the boundaries of reality are transcended as participants reach for the healing power of the gods. And even in classical psychoanalysis, the method of free association leads clients away from the everyday and into the realm of unconscious imagery. Those, like Jung and Rank, who embraced the mythological powers of the hero, the child and the artist, encouraged clients to work imaginatively.

But role method departs from the earlier approaches in its conscious use of role and story as the form and content of the therapeutic experience. The work remains entrenched in the dramatic experience of the hero on a journey toward some unknown destination, passing through obstacles and requiring the help of a guide. Role method, at best, functions as classical theater, which invites an audience into a fictional world that is not so different from reality as it first appears. If the play is successful not only as entertainment but also as enlightenment, it offers a heightened sense of reality.

Unlike some forms of creative arts therapy that suggest that the healing occurs fully in the action, role method seeks to help clients discover a conscious link between the fiction of the drama and the reality of everyday life. In role method, role and self, stage and world not only reflect one another, but seek integration with the other in order to be more complete. Derek's story of the legacy of pain and the journey up the mountain is more than a metaphor. It is, in the language of James Hillman (1983b), a healing fiction, a link to a transformed reality.

Verbal and Nonverbal Expression

As theatrical texts are written in the form of dialogue, it is expected that most forms of improvised drama therapy will be verbal. Role method is verbal not only in the enactment, but also in the preparation of the roles and the story. The quantity and quality of verbal expression is dependent upon the needs of the client in relation to the therapist. In Derek's case, there was much verbal exchange preceding and following the story. In telling, enacting, and then reflecting upon his story, there was also considerable verbal expression.

Following the storytelling, Derek took on several roles and played them out in words and action. He began as the son first contemplating Pain, then fighting off Pain in a highly physical way, and finally speaking directly to Pain. By engaging with the image of Pain in thought, action, and language, he allowed it to change from a large mass to a smaller piece of the whole. As such, he engaged in an experience of active imagination, similar to that described by Jung.

Then Derek took on the role of Pain, both verbally and nonverbally, leading him to the insight of Pain as a guide: "He needed some of me in him to drive him this far." Next, Derek took on the role of the father, but because he could not speak the charged words of forgiveness to the son, he wrote them on the board and then spoke them aloud, encouraged by Robert to find more emotional, nonverbal means of expression. When pushed to go even further into his feelings as father, he chose another nonverbal, expressive route, singing the words in a joking way, distancing himself further from the difficult emotions that lay just beneath the surface.

When Robert finally asked Derek to play the role of the son listening to the words, he became very quiet and focused, taking in the feelings behind the words, the possibility of reconciliation and forgiveness. At that moment the work was most heightened and Derek, despite his ironic statement, "You ain't getting me to cry here," was fully present.

Role method, then, can be highly verbal, but also moves easily into nonverbal action as clients enter more deeply into their roles and the emerging feelings they elicit. Role method can also be effective with nonverbal populations, such as autistic and selectively mute children and catatonic schizophrenic adults. In such cases, the roles can be invoked and the stories enacted through movement and play. Specific techniques mentioned in previous chapters, such as world technique, sandplay, puppetry, and Erikson-based dramatic productions, are projective forms of expression through role method.

Action and Reflection

Dramatic action can be verbal and nonverbal. We see it at its most non-verbal when Derek breathes and stretches at the beginning of the session. Likewise, when Derek, struggling with his tears, verbalizes, "You ain't getting me to cry here," he is fully engaged in dramatic action. As noted above, it is characterized by a degree of distance from an initial stimulus and the presence of role. It occurs spontaneously, in present time, an aspect that distinguishes it from analysis, interpretation, and reflection. In the later work of Wilhelm Reich and his followers in biophysical therapies, we see a movement away from analysis that fully embraces action. For some who practice highly primal, cathartic forms of therapy (see, for example, Janov 1970), action is all that is required to effect therapeutic change.

Role method embraces both action and reflection. Throughout Derek's session, as he proceeds through the steps of the role method, he begins in action, invoking and naming the three primary roles, then working them through in the story and subsequent enactment. Toward the end of the session, as he de-roles from the part of the son, Derek reflects upon his dramatic action. His first reflection is physical. He tells Robert that the experience of the drama "went between my shoulder blades." And after recognizing the fictional story as an "abbreviated version" of his own life, Derek (in Landy 2005) returns to the story and offers this final, sobering reflection: "The son now has to hold on to all that pain that the father brought that he never got rid of. . . . So now that son is gonna have a hard time trying to grow up to be a man and trying to climb the mountain." Reflection is different from resolution. It simply provides a moment for the client to look back on his action in a thoughtful way and bring it into the present moment. Doing so can lead to further balance.

Directive and Nondirective
Action/Transference and Countertransference

Therapists in role method are somewhat equivalent to theatrical directors. They guide the action and provide a clear structure for the taking on and playing out of roles, for the telling and enactment of stories and for the reflection upon the role-playing and storymaking. In some cases, therapists will engage in the role-play with their clients and direct the action from within, even as they are guided by the needs of the clients. For example, when Landy made the choice to read the words of forgiveness to Derek, he did so in the role of the father. Derek took on the counterrole of son as he listened to the words.

The early model of the distant, detached analyst is rarely found in any form of drama therapy. Neither role method nor the other dramatic therapies work from a purely psychoanalytical view of transference and countertransference. In that therapists are often actors in the drama of the client, their objectivity is somewhat compromised. In the major research study on transference in drama therapy, Eliaz (1988), in fact, advises drama therapists working in a group to help shift the transference from themselves to the group, so that the group both holds and works through the transference on their own.

In theory, the more directive the therapist, the less transference he will engender. Role method falls somewhat in-between the highly directive approach of psychodrama and the seemingly nondirective one of developmental transformations. In the session with Derek, Landy was certainly directive in implementing the steps of the role method, but less so as Derek wrote the words of forgiveness, sang them, and then took the journey up the mountain. At these times, Landy served as empathic witness.

During the session, Landy was well aware of taking on the transferential role of father. And yet he chose to move the transference from himself onto the fictional role of father. Thus he did not become Derek's actual father, but the father Derek created through his drama. As such, he transformed the abusive father to the compassionate and accepting father, providing a corrective experience for Derek. Unlike many of the early psychoanalysts, he did not seek to frustrate Derek in order to further enhance the transference, but rather to guide him along his journey up the mountain.

Transference in psychoanalysis can be seen as a dramatic moment of replaying a past experience which, once enacted, becomes the content of analysis. A recent theoretical development in psychoanalysis is actually called enactment, a relational approach involving the working through of heightened moments of transference and countertransference (see, for example, Johan 1992; Field 2006). Transference through role method, unlike psychoanalysis, offers three forms for enacting an unresolved past relationship in a client's life: the actual form, as in the real father; the transferential form, as in the projection of father onto the therapist; and the fictional form, as in the father who appears in the story. Given this third fictional form, the therapist has more leeway in working with the client's need for encounter and containment.

As for countertransference, it is inevitable that once a therapist engages in role-play with a client, some personal issues will emerge. For Landy, the personal issues concerned his relationship to his own father which, though nonabusive, was also full of regret and missed opportunities to express forgiveness and love. Also, Landy held positive feelings as a father toward his own son, a stronger tie in his life than that of son to his father. Thus, when taking on the role of father, he drew on his actual experience of being a good enough father and used those feelings to father Derek.

Landy occasionally directed the action from the inside in the role of father, but most often from the outside, as a more empathetic, uncritical figure. As such, Landy recapitulated Carl Rogers's (1951) humanistic stance as a nondirective therapist, unconditionally accepting and prizing his client, mirroring back his words in such a way that he is empowered to take his own journey. Whether directing from the inside or taking a more nondirective posture from the outside, Landy attempted in the session to embody a good enough guide, one who seeks to help the client integrate his discrepant roles, one who seeks to offer an alternative to past relationships with caretakers who did not have the ability to effectively guide their children.

5

Psychodrama
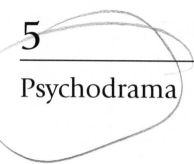

Derek's second session was in psychodrama. The therapist was Nina Garcia, a certified trainer, educator, and practitioner of psychodrama and a noted expert in the field. Garcia is a second generation practitioner, trained by a prominent student of J. L. Moreno. She has coauthored a major text on sociodrama (Sternberg and Garcia 2000b) and written many articles and book chapters on psychodrama. Before discussing Garcia's work with Derek, let us look at some of the specific aspects of psychodrama.

HISTORICAL OVERVIEW

A historical overview of Moreno's work in psychodrama, sociometry, and sociodrama is given in chapters 2 and 3. From these chapters, it becomes clear that Moreno was the foremost figure to define and develop modern approaches to action psychotherapy. Although aware of the productivity of his Viennese contemporaries in psychoanalysis, he was not one to imitate or identify with the work of others. Moreno was, at his most immodest, a fully innovative, larger than life character, who played the role of God, the creator, as much as that of mere mortal, content to write books with such prophetic titles as *Words of the Father* (1920) and *Who Shall Survive?* (1934/1978)

Without repeating the apocryphal stories defining Moreno's life and career, let us look at some of his own historical speculations. Placing his work fully into the context of action psychotherapy, Moreno (1946/1994) wrote:

There were in 1914 in Vienna two antitheses to psychoanalysis: the one was the rebellion of the suppressed group versus the individual; it was the first step beyond psychoanalysis, "group psychotherapy." . . . The other was the rebellion of the suppressed actor against the word. This was the second step beyond psychoanalysis, the "psychodrama." In the beginning was existence. In the beginning was the act (1).

Moreno's emphasis upon the act, the moment of dramatic action as a form of healing, was his most significant contribution to the history of action psychotherapy. As a psychiatrist with a great knowledge of theater, Moreno also spoke about therapeutic processes from a theatrical point of view. He noted that Aristotle defined catharsis as an imitation of an action and life. Not content to accept Aristotle's point of view, Moreno (1946/1994) offered the following:

> Psychodrama defines the drama as an extension of life and action rather than its imitation, but where there is imitation the emphasis is not on what it imitates, but upon the opportunity of recapitulation of unresolved problems within a . . . more flexible social setting (15).

Psychoanalysis was also about recapitulating unresolved problems in the transference. But its method of free association, as viewed by Moreno, was "a battle of words" (1946/1994, 11). Unlike Freud who saw his technique as a freedom of thought, Moreno viewed psychodrama as a freedom of expression through the body and the emotions. Many early psychoanalysts, as we have seen, were quick to label too much somatic and emotional action as acting out, a form of resistance. Moreno (1946/1994) ventured an explanation as to why: "Action seemed dangerous, it could easily lead to excesses and anarchism" (11).

In between Freud and Moreno stood Jung, Rank, and Ferenczi, who recognized the curative possibilities of play, imagery, and emotional expression. And in the work of Reich, Lowen, and Perls lay the possibilities of healing through the body. But it took the sustained effort of Moreno over more than half a century to promote and demonstrate the idea that action precedes and supercedes words, that as a method of healing actions speak louder than words.

BASIC ASSUMPTIONS OF PSYCHODRAMA

Moreno's image of humanity is broad and spacious, encompassing personal, interpersonal, and transpersonal aspects of life. Further, the psychodramatic worldview is noted by its insistence that survival depends upon the interplay of spontaneity, creativity, and the cultural conserve. Moreno used the term "cultural conserve" to refer to the artifacts and conventional structures of any given culture, including its art and technology, its social, political, and economic institutions.

Moreno's (1946/1994) vision begins with God in the role of artist, actively creating the universe: "that is the status of God before the Sabbath, from the moment of conception, during the process of creating and evolving the worlds and Himself" (32). God, the Creator, becomes a central metaphor of the possibilities of human creation. For Moreno, the liberation of the creative potential occurs through psychodrama.

In psychodrama, creation occurs in present time. It is qualitatively different from the things created, just as improvisational theater is different from the performance of scripted plays. Moreno (1946/1994) spoke of the act of creation in terms of a vivid metaphor: "A creator is like a runner for whom in the act of running the part of the road he has already passed and the part before him are qualitatively one" (35). The assumption is that the past and the future all meet in the present moment of experiencing.

Alongside the dimensions of time, Moreno's philosophical system included an understanding of space as the location of a dramatized act. For Moreno, the image of the couch gave way to that of the stage. He referred to the location of the psychodrama as the *locus nascendi,* literally the place of birth. In this metaphorical space any role could be played and any action could be dramatized safely within the confines of the fiction. The actual place of action could be a psychodramatic stage designed to Moreno's specifications or a natural location on a street corner, a park, a classroom, or an institution, where Moreno treated groups of people.

A third dimension of Moreno's philosophical system is that of surplus reality, a term denoting experiences in imagination, beyond the scope of the five senses. Moreno based the phrase upon Karl Marx's concept of surplus value, referring to the capitalistic practice of exploiting extra income from workers. Moreno assumed that human beings in the course of their lives shun many opportunities to be fully expressive. While engaging in surplus reality through the techniques of psychodrama, they are encouraged to express themselves, trying out new actions that might change the direction of their lives. The fiction of the drama adds a surplus dimension to reality and serves not only to heighten the reality of the moment, but potentially to alter it.

The final dimension is that of the cosmos. Moreno spoke of the cosmic dimension as situated somewhere between Freud, who conceived of the primacy of the individual, and Marx, who conceived of the primacy of social and economic factors in determining the fate of the individual. Moreno's cosmic person was one who can imagine all possibilities and all personal, social, and spiritual roles. Moreno (in Fox 1987) characteristically ends his discussion of the cosmic by returning to God, not as a religious figure, but as a theatrical one:

The image of God can take form and embodiment through every man—the epileptic, the schizophrenic, the prostitute, the poor and rejected. They all can at any time step upon the stage, when the moment of inspiration comes, and give their version of the meaning which the universe has for them. God is always within and among us, as he is for children. Instead of coming down from the skies, he comes in by way of the stage door (12).

In Moreno's (1946/1994) worldview, the artist and the creator are the supreme beings, the ones who in a Darwinian sense are destined to survive:

Races of man adhering to conserved production will die out. Thus Darwin's "survival of the fittest" will be found to be too narrow. It will be replaced by the survival of the creator (46).

BASIC CONCEPTS OF PSYCHODRAMA

On the surface psychodrama appears to be less theatrical than drama therapy. And yet Moreno often thought and spoke in theatrical terms. Thus his conceptual framework contained many drama-based ideas. In 1940, while considering the theatrical basis of psychodrama, Moreno (in Fox 1987) wrote:

The therapeutic aspect of psychodrama cannot be divorced from the aesthetic. . . . In the therapeutic theatre, an anonymous, average man becomes something approaching a work of art. . . . Here his ego becomes an aesthetic prototype—he becomes a representation of mankind. On the psychodramatic stage he is put into a state of inspiration—he is the dramatist himself (59).

The following are several of the major concepts informing Moreno's therapeutic theater. Preceding drama therapy–based role theory by half a century, they provide conceptual models for the action approaches to come.

Role

Moreno's (1946/1994) best-known definition of role is a psychological one: "the actual and tangible forms the self takes" (153). And yet when he first defined role he referred to its theatrical origins in Latin and Greek as the ancient scrolls upon which were written the text of a play. Moreno offered several theatrical examples, speaking of roles as imaginary characters in plays, like Hamlet or Faust. Given his interest in group dynamics, Moreno also referred to various social roles. Summing up his several views of role, Moreno (1946/1994) provided these two related definitions of role as: "the functioning form the individual assumes in the specific moment he reacts to a specific situation in which other persons or objects are involved" (iv), and "a final crystallization of all the situations in a special area of operations through which the individual has passed" (153).

In creating his role theory, Moreno made reference to three kinds of roles: social roles, psychosomatic roles, involving the body, and psychodramatic roles, involving the psychological aspects of the individual. These three categories relate to the social, somatic, and affective domains in Landy's Taxonomy of Roles. Moreno does not attempt to systematically categorize specific role types. He does, however, speak about the general function of the role as such: "The function of the role is to enter the unconscious from the social world and bring shape and order to it" (Moreno 1946/1994, v). In Landy's case, each role type serves a specific function.

Moreno also referred to counterroles, from which people see others in their social world. Again, the concept is different from Landy's, which concerns self-perceptions noted in a polarity between roles. For Moreno, the concept of ego represents the totality of one's roles and the patterns of one's role relationships.

It is noteworthy to mention that one of the first publications on the psychodramatic conception of role was written by Zerka T. Moreno (1944) originally in 1942, based upon her work with soldiers during the war. Although she does not define role at this time, she creates a structure of analyzing one's presentation of role within a psychodramatic context.

Tele

Moreno distinguishes between psychoanalytic transference, the temporary projection of past fantasies onto the therapist in the present, and "tele," a more positive and permanent marker of the relationship of client and therapist. He (1946/1994) defines "tele" as: "feelings of individuals into one another, the cement which holds groups together" (xi). Through observing telic factors, one can gauge the degree of affiliation and separation between both therapist and client and among all group members.

Spontaneity

Moreno (1946/1994) defined spontaneity as an ability "to respond with some degree of adequacy to a new situation or with some degree of novelty to an old situation" (xii). Spontaneity is a readiness of a person to act and is thus modified by training in action methods, particularly psychodrama. For Moreno, spontaneity was linked with creativity. In his model describing this relationship, the Canon of Creativity, Moreno related the two concepts to that of the cultural conserve. In his book, *Who Shall Survive?* Moreno speculated that the future of civilization belongs to those who can respond to the cultural conserve with an adequate degree of spontaneity and creativity.

Catharsis

Moreno described Aristotle's concept of catharsis as a moment of emotional release on the part of the spectators who identify with the dilemma of the actors on stage. For Moreno, Aristotelian catharsis was based upon an experience of witnessing a drama for the first time. It was the novelty and surprise of the dramatic actions that fueled the release of feelings. Moreno postulated that the more familiar the spectator was with the play, the less poignant the catharsis. As such, Moreno understood the concept of catharsis as related to that of spontaneity. The more novel the dramatic action, the more spontaneous the cathartic reaction.

Moreno redefined Aristotle's concept from audience-centered to actor-centered, noting that psychodramatic actors engage in direct, spontaneous reenactments of their life experiences. He contrasted the theatrical performer with the psychodramatic performer in terms of a metaphor of a volcano—the former watches a film of a volcano erupting, and the latter watches it from the foot of the mountain. As his notion of catharsis broadened, Moreno came to recognize cathartic reactions not only on the part of the protagonist but also on the supporting auxiliary egos and audience members who identify with the dilemma of the protagonist.

Finally, Moreno distinguished between two types of catharsis, that of abreaction and that of integration. Catharsis of abreaction is a moment of purgation in an Aristotelian sense, when emotion is released in relationship to a strong dramatic stimulus. Psychodrama can easily become highly cathartic as a protagonist revisits a painful experience and discharges anger, for example, through dramatic action. Heightened expression of emotion, especially when underdistanced, can provide a release without a connection to the inner life of the protagonist or relationships within the group. Catharsis of integration provides that connection to self and group. It is a moment of insight, closer to Scheff's and Landy's understanding of aesthetic distance. It is a point when a protagonist is able to express an intense feeling in the drama and then relate it back to both the group process and to everyday life. For Moreno, a successful moment of catharsis, whether as a release of feeling or as an integration of thought and feeling, is marked by one's ability to act spontaneously.

Act Hunger

Act hunger is the biologically based need to seek expression through action. For Moreno, act hungers begin in disequilibrium and are motivated by the need to complete unfinished business. According to Garcia and Buchanan (2000): "The act hungers are strong urges or desires for expression, for understanding, for mastery in a situation or for connection" (177).

Dayton (2005) makes the point that act hunger is different from a psychoanalytic understanding of the repetition compulsion. In repeating a traumatic experience over and over in psychoanalytic treatment, a client remains unaware of a compulsive need. In dramatizing an act hunger, the client is given the opportunity to consciously experience and in fact satisfy the need in relationship to auxiliaries in the group.

Auxiliary Ego

The primary ego, or client within a psychodrama session, is known as the protagonist. Moreno noted that this person is often unable to solve a dilemma between himself and significant others in his life. Rather than talking about the other, the primary ego works with an auxiliary ego, a member of the psychodramatic group who stands in for the other. Moreno (in Fox 1987) referred to the auxiliary ego as "the representation of absentee individuals, delusions, hallucinations, symbols, ideals, animals and objects. They make the protagonist's world real, concrete and tangible" (9).

Because of the dramatic nature of the relationship between the protagonist and the auxiliary ego, Moreno noted that often bodily contact is involved. He distanced himself once again from the psychoanalysts by underscoring the importance of nonabusive touch to the dramatic therapeutic process.

Sociometry

Moreno developed sociometry as a means of understanding the dynamic interactions within and among groups. According to Zerka T. Moreno (2006b), Moreno considered sociometry to be "the umbrella under which all his other work fell. His idea was to reconstruct society at large through action sociometry." Moreno formulated many of his early plans for doing so in *Who Shall Survive?*, published in 1934, twelve years before the appearance of the first volume of *Psychodrama*.

For Moreno, sociometry was a science that was predicated upon an understanding of mutually valid criteria within a given real-life social situation. In determining the sociometric dynamics of, for example, a residential treatment center, Moreno asked all involved such questions as: Who would you like as your roommate? Who do you want to sit next to in the dining room? Who do you want to work with in the kitchen? In tabulating mutual responses, Moreno suggested optimal ways of reorganizing the social dynamics.

Moreno also invented several instruments to measure social relationships within groups. Some of his sociometric tests will be discussed below in the section on assessment. In this section, we will look at several self-assignments that are used more as techniques of clinical practice than as research-based assessment instruments. For all forms of sociometry, there needs to be sufficient interactions in role to clarify the social relationships.

One instrument is the social atom, which Moreno viewed as the smallest sociometric unit as it entails a single person in relationship to significant others. A social atom is executed as a diagram, using circles and triangles to represent people, and arrows to represent relationships between self and other in a family or workplace. The purpose of such diagrams, according to Garcia and Buchanan (2000), is "to gather information, assess functioning level, set treatment goals with the client, and make interventions" (167).

Another sociometric technique is the role diagram, in which people depict the roles that they play in their everyday lives, again in the form of a diagram. A third, the spectrogram, is a more active technique in that members of a group are asked to place themselves along a continuum in response to a question, such as: How comfortable are you disclosing details about your life? The continuum takes the form of an imaginary line traversing the room, with one pole representing very comfortable, and the other very uncomfortable. A similar technique, the locogram, asks individuals to group themselves in given areas of the room, again in response to a question, such as: Which developmental stage do you feel closest to—child, adolescent, adult, elder? Once individuals in the group find their places in a spectrogram or locogram, they are encouraged to share the reasons for their choices.

Stages in Child Development

Before leaving Moreno's basic concepts, let us look at three psychodramatic techniques that have an important conceptual basis in his theory of child development. Moreno (in Fox 1987) referred to three developmental stages: identity, recognition of the self, and recognition of the other. The first stage of identity is marked by the notion of the double. Moreno (in Fox 1987), in a playful mode, refers to the spiritual underpinnings of the double: "It has always been my idea that God created us twice. One time for us to live in this world and the other time for himself" (130). Zerka T. Moreno (2006b) mentioned that Moreno based his understanding of the double on his reading of literature rather than psychology, with Dostoyevsky and de Maupassant as major sources. He was particularly impressed by de Maupassant's anecdote of seeing himself sitting at his desk writing as he entered the room.

After describing the double in psychodrama as a person who represents the inner life of the protagonist, Moreno spoke of the double relationship of mother and infant. He refers to this as the matrix of identity, a time when the two entities are one, undifferentiated. Garcia and Buchanan (2000) describe the significance of the mother as double for the child at this stage: "In order to develop functionally, Moreno believed that each of us must first be doubled when we are newborns" (174). The mother doubles the child's sounds and movements, providing the child with a clear and safe sense of identity.

The second stage, recognition of the self, occurs as the two entities separate and the mother mirrors the child, that is, plays back the child's action accurately, as if to say: "I see you as yourself, separate from me." As a technique, the mirror is an auxiliary ego who models actions for protagonists so that they can see themselves more clearly.

The third stage, recognition of the other, concerns a role reversal of mother and child, and marks the ability of the child to take on the role of the other, leading to a further differentiation of the self. In psychodramatic role reversal, the protagonist and auxiliary reverse roles in order for one to internalize the situation of the other and thus develop a more expansive sense of self.

Through the three stages, the child moves from a state of dependence and connection, marked by the presence of a double, to one of independence and separation, marked by the stage of the mirror, to one of interdependence, marked by the stage of role reversal. In good enough doubling, mirroring, and role reversal, the child develops a strong enough sense of self in order to create clear boundaries with actual and representational mothers.

THERAPEUTIC GOALS

Moreno's overriding therapeutic goal was to facilitate the growth of spontaneity within individuals, groups, and societies, perpetuating the survival of all. Likening his creative output to that of God, Moreno (1920) wrote: "God is spontaneity. Hence the commandment is: 'Be spontaneous!'" (xviii).

Moreno conceptualized four categories of goals within the domains of affect, behavior, cognition, and spirituality. This was his therapeutic primer, his notion of the ABCs. The goal within affect was the expression of feeling through catharsis, both of abreaction and integration. Garcia and Buchanan (2000) remind the reader that catharsis can be expressed through both tears and laughter.

The goal of behavior, according to Garcia and Buchanan (2000) was for "people to practice new and more satisfying ways of handling situations" (176). This goal is similar to that of behavior rehearsal specified by Wolpe and Lazarus (1966) and later by Kipper (1996) in psychodrama. The goal within cognition was insight, a moment of understanding a dilemma through engaging in the action of psychodrama.

The final goal of spirituality concerned the expression of a common humanity, a deep connection among people on an intrapersonal, personal, group, and cosmic level. This spiritual goal well recapitulates that of Moreno's contemporary, Martin Buber, who applied his philosophy of I and Thou, the relationship of persons and God, to the relationship among human beings. Both men knew one another as Buber published articles in Moreno's literary magazine, *Daimon*, in the 1920s. Zerka T. Moreno (2006b) claims that Buber was directly influenced by Moreno, even using Moreno's language in his writing on the meaning of the human encounter (*Begegnung*). Moreno published a series of articles called *Einladung zu einer Begegnung* (*Invitation to an Encounter*), beginning in 1915, nine years before Buber's *Ich und Du* (*I and Thou*) was published.

ROLE OF THE THERAPIST

As in role method, the therapist is primarily a director, a term used often by Moreno. Moreno noted that there may well be resistance on the part of the protagonist and that the struggle for power between the protagonist and the director can be intense. Moreno (in Fox 1987) wrote:

> Both of them have to draw spontaneity and cunning from their resources. Positive factors which shape the relationship and interaction in the reality of life itself exist: spontaneity, productivity, the warming up process, tele and role processes (16).

For Moreno, the therapist, like the protagonist, goes through a parallel process of warming up to the action and moving toward a state of spontaneity. Once warmed up, the director steps back somewhat, allowing the drama to proceed between the protagonist and the appropriate auxiliaries. Generally speaking, the director does not take on a role in the drama, although many directors double and mirror the protagonist. The presence of the director, however, can be very powerful in setting up the scenes, inviting the auxiliaries to the stage, moving the protagonist into and out of roles and toward moments of catharsis and insight, engaging the full group in the creation of the drama and its subsequent reflection, and providing a commentary in action and words. Moreno (in Fox 1987) put it this way:

> The director is not satisfied, like the analyst, to observe the subject and translate symbolic behavior into understandable, scientific language. He enters as a participant-actor, armed with as many hypothetical insights as possible . . . to talk to [the subject] in the spontaneous languages of signs and gestures, words and actions, which the subject has developed (17).

The director shares personal insight throughout the full process of warm-up, action, and closure. As to matters of transference and countertransference, Moreno preferred to use the term "tele." As noted above, tele concerns the dynamics of the relationship between client and therapist and is a more permanent structure than that of transference. Therapeutic progress in psychodrama is a measure of the clear and positive tele among the director, the protagonist, and the group.

VIEW OF WELLNESS AND ILLNESS

Wellness from the point of view of psychodrama can be defined by the degree of spontaneity demonstrated by an individual, group, and society. As noted above, Moreno's vision of a positive future concerned a dynamic relationship among spontaneity, creativity, and the given ideas and artifacts of any culture. Healthy individuals are, by nature, integrated, not only in mind and body and spirit, but also in their ability to double (and to be doubled), to mirror (and to be mirrored), and to reverse roles with another. The healthy group and society are similar in their capacities to facilitate the same integrations among their members.

Illness is a break from the canon of creativity, an inability to act with some measure of spontaneity in the face of the cultural conserve. It can also be seen as a misuse of creativity. Garcia and Buchanan (2000) refer to three forms of pathological creativity. The first is an overwhelming compulsion to search for the new at the expense of the demands of reality. The second is a form of blocked creativity caused by an inability to seek new roles and relationships. And the third is a retreat from creativity due to a fear of taking on the responsibility of the creator. This third form leads people to play passive roles and abrogate their control to a perceived authority.

Moreno, who as a physician worked with a range of clinical disorders, certainly accepted psychiatric classifications of mental illness. However, as a psychodramatic theorist, he held a broader conception of illness, not too dissimilar from the role theories of others. One might well have a mental illness or a physical disability, but that alone does not limit one's capacity to create new roles or to play any given role with an adequate degree of spontaneity. Illness is an imbalance between the person and the role. Healthy human beings are able to play many psychosomatic, psychodramatic, and social roles throughout their lifetimes and are able to accurately perceive and reverse roles with others. Unhealthy people, despite their physiological make-up, choose to limit their role choices and role perceptions. By embracing the cultural conserve or the chaos of unlimited choice uncritically, by behaving with hubris or with self-effacing humility, they limit the possibility of living the spontaneous life.

ASSESSMENT AND EVALUATION

Throughout his lifetime, Moreno devised a number of tests assessing and evaluating spontaneity and sociometry. Many have been described within his books and articles, and some have been used by others. For example, Tian Dayton (2005) regularly applies sociometric tests to the assessment and treatment of people facing trauma and addiction.

An early test devised by Moreno (1946/1994, 93–101) attempted to measure spontaneity. The test concerned a series of emergency situations given by a psychodramatic director to more than 300 subjects. The subjects, sometimes singly, sometimes in groups, were asked to respond to the situations in action, using given props and auxiliary egos. Props included a telephone, water, book, radio, and broom. The director began by setting the scene and then introducing the emergency situation. The subjects responded, and their actions were scored by a jury of three. Criteria included timing of a response, adequacy of motion and role perceptions, endurance, and appropriateness of actions and roles.

In a later, more formal version, called the spontaneity test (Moreno 1946/1994, 123–29), a prepared auxiliary administers the test to given subjects, one at a time. The auxiliary is trained in playing out one or more given roles and a given scenario. Moreno gives an example of the auxiliary in the role of a husband who comes home and informs his wife that he has a new lover and wants a divorce. Each subject, in the role of the wife, is asked to respond to the situation and is then rated by two recorders according to set criteria, similar to those given in the previous example.

Moreno was fond of drawing scales and diagrams to provide evidence of the validity of these and other sociometric tests. However, the scientific veracity of his sociometric instruments has not been sufficiently validated. Those who use his tests of spontaneity and sociometry tend to apply them to clinical rather than research situations. As an example, Dayton (2005) speaks of applying sociometric tests for several purposes: to reveal affiliations among members in a group, to process dyadic relationships in a group, and to foster group cohesiveness (106). For Dayton, the test focuses upon specific questions of concern to the group, such as: Who in the group are you drawn to? The questions are explored in action as group members place their hands on the shoulders of those to whom they are attracted. And finally, the experience is processed as group members share their feelings concerning the choices made.

Moreno used similar approaches to evaluation, that is, measuring the outcome of a psychodramatic task through action. The paper and pencil tests such as the social atom and role diagram, like the action tests based in the sociometry of the group, served to reflect upon the process more than to provide research data measuring outcomes of the work. As research, these approaches are useful in their descriptive qualities, as is the case for the assessments surveyed in the role method of drama therapy.

THE METHOD OF PSYCHODRAMA

Early on, Moreno (1946/1994) described five instruments of psychodrama—the stage, the subject or protagonist, the director, the auxiliary egos, and the audience. Most of these instruments have been discussed earlier, with the exception of the audience. Moreno (in Fox 1987) referred to the function of the audience as twofold. First, the audience members serve the protagonists, responding to their dilemmas and providing significant feedback, support, and validation. Secondly, the audience members are, in turn, helped by the protagonist as they identify with the dramatized dilemmas, experience their own catharsis, and view their own problems in a more lucid way.

The process of the psychodrama proceeds in several steps and through several techniques. Abstracting many of Moreno's descriptions of the therapeutic process, Garcia and Buchanan (2000) list a number, beginning with the warm-up. Thousands of psychodramatic warm-ups exist, all serving the purpose of moving the group into a state of readiness to engage in dramatic action. Emerging from the warm-up, the group chooses a protagonist. Garcia and Buchanan note that there are four ways to make this choice, based either upon a prior plan, the director, the group as a whole, or a self-selection process in the moment.

Following the choice of protagonist, the group moves into the action phase, the dramatization proper, which involves several steps. Garcia and Buchanan begin with the walk and talk, a moment when the director and protagonist walk side by side around the group and discuss strategies for enactment. The walk and talk deepens the tele between director and protagonist and sets the therapeutic contract.

The next step, according to Garcia and Buchanan, is casting and role training the auxiliary egos. At this point, the protagonist chooses people in the group to represent the figures in the drama. At times, directors will make a choice if they feel a particular need for doing so. Role training involves preparing each auxiliary for the demands of the role. Often the protagonist will reverse roles with the auxiliary to demonstrate some of the required qualities in movement, affect, and/or words.

Garcia and Buchanan refer to the next step as scene setting. The director encourages the protagonist to describe the place of action and to be specific as to the time. The protagonist chooses objects to place within the scene that represent certain figures or even feelings. Chairs, colorful scarves, books, keys, objects of clothing are all commonly used in scene setting. Once the scene is set, the action begins, led by the director. The director uses a wide variety of production techniques in facilitating the action (see Z. T. Moreno 1965, for a full description of techniques). Garcia and Buchanan (2000) refer to the five most basic ones as soliloquy, double, aside, role reversal, and mirror.

Soliloquy, as in classical drama, is a moment when the protagonist removes himself from the flow of the action and verbalizes internal thoughts and feelings. It is often used at the beginning or end of a scene to prepare the protagonist for the specific action or to reflect upon the action that just occurred. The aside, again derived from theater, is a moment when protagonists are asked to comment on their action by literally moving their heads to the side and articulating unspoken thoughts or feelings, supposedly out of the range of the auxiliaries. Both methods are intended to deepen the enactment and/or reflection.

The double, referred to above, is an auxiliary who stands beside the protagonist, taking on his posture and emotional tone, and externalizes unexpressed thoughts and feelings of the protagonist. The double, like the good enough parent, both supports and challenges the protagonist to explore a dilemma in a full and complete manner. The words of the double are only to be heard by the protagonist, who repeats or revises those words within the drama, in relationship to the other auxiliaries. In the case of a session with a single client, as we shall see with Derek, the director often doubles for the protagonist.

Role reversal is a moment when a protagonist and auxiliary exchange roles and positions in space. It is intended to provide an empathetic experience of the other. Garcia and Buchanan (2000) note several reasons for reversing roles: to share information with the other and verify its accuracy, to view oneself as the other, to avoid physical harm, and to enhance empathy, spontaneity, and affect.

The mirror technique is another way to allow protagonists to create a degree of distance in order to better see themselves. In mirroring, protagonists choose another to play themselves. From this removed position, they observe the other play out a scene, helping them to view themselves in a more accurate fashion or to provide an alternative way to play out a situation within which they have become stuck.

Another common psychodramatic technique is the use of the empty chair, representing a figure in the protagonist's life with whom he has unfinished business. As we have seen above, this technique, borrowed by Perls from Moreno, is a mainstay of Gestalt therapy. Future projection is another common technique, involving a scene where the protagonist images a moment in the future where a desired or undesired action has occurred. In future projection, auxiliaries represent figures within this imagined scene. A final technique that is used with Derek is that of *psychodrama à deux* or psychodrama for two. In this form, a director works one-on-one with a protagonist, without an audience present. The two make use of many empty chairs to represent needed auxiliaries, as well as a host of techniques mentioned above.

Finally, following the action of the psychodrama, a closure occurs wherein the group interacts with the protagonist, reincorporating him within the group and revealing many of their own feelings stimulated by the enactment. As a transition to the closure, protagonists are asked by the director to de-role themselves and the setting they have created. Group members then reflect upon the experience, sharing feelings of their own, based in an identification with the protagonist. They are cautioned against interpreting and criticizing as this is a time for community building. During the sharing, the director helps all to clarify their feelings and thoughts and points out the sociometric connections between the protagonist and auxiliaries, the protagonist and the group, one group member and the others. In reflecting upon the drama, the director, as well as the protagonist and group members, take a moment to ground the fiction of the drama in the reality of their lives. As such, this process in similar to reflection in role method.

PSYCHODRAMA WITH DEREK

As before, we will now look at a psychodrama session, minimally edited, between Derek and Nina Garcia. Garcia and Derek will briefly reflect upon their work and then the session will be analyzed according to the given polarities.

NINA: It's good to see you.

DEREK: Good to be seen by you.

NINA: What's been going on?

DEREK: Basically the same reoccurring theme of the relationship with my father and even though we get along ok presently, I still have recurring dreams at times. Especially when things get stressful in my life. He's usually a part of it.

NINA: Have you had some dreams recently?

DEREK: About two weeks ago.

NINA: Hmm. Do you remember the dream?

DEREK: Basically, yeah. I just remember getting up and having to use the bathroom immediately to go and pee. I knew where that was coming from though.

NINA: Where was it coming from?

DEREK: I was a constant bed-wetter until I was about 15 or 16. Not something a grown man wants to say, but it's true.

NINA: Yeah, but it sounds like you were saying something in your dream life was like something in your waking life when you got up. Say a bit more about the dream. Have you worked with this dream already?

DEREK: No. I don't usually tell people about my life too much. Just enough, but not everything.

NINA: Today you will tell me whatever you want to tell me, and you won't tell me whatever you don't want to tell me. Is that OK?

DEREK: Yeah.

NINA: Is it OK to talk about this dream?

DEREK: Yeah. It came out of real life.

NINA: Good.

DEREK: I remember my father right near the kitchen, and he's looking at me and pointing and. . . .

NINA: Is this real life recently or in the past?

DEREK: Real life in the past.

NINA: OK.

DEREK: He's pointing at me and at the time he had two gold teeth, which he used to brag about. I thought they were ugly. But all I can remember is him pointing at me and seeing his teeth with a scowling look on his face.

NINA: And pointing at you.

DEREK: Yeah. Then he turns to my mother and he actually spits in her face.

NINA: Hmm.

DEREK: And all I remember after that . . . [Smiles.]

NINA: What has just happened to you just then? That smile? Something else about the mom?

DEREK: Yeah.

NINA: Do you want to say?

DEREK: My mom. She was the man in the family. She was the father, the mother, the butcher, the candlestick maker.

NINA: She did it all.

DEREK: Yeah. But she couldn't quite teach me how to become a man. She told me how to be a good boy, but not how to be a man. I always tried to look to my father to do that but that wasn't going to happen.

NINA: Yeah.

DEREK: I just remember a lot of slamming doors. Hearing the slam and then hearing the lock swing.

NINA: The chain lock?

DEREK: Yeah, the chain lock. After the argument, they'd go into another room.

NINA: But the chain lock?

DEREK: That was always when . . . I'd always put pillows near my ears. I slept like that and kind of prayed that I wouldn't wet my bed. Or at least let my brother know or anybody else know. I knew it'd be safe after he'd go to work at like 5:45 exactly. Slam the door. The chain. I'd take the pillow off and, surprise, big old yellow mark.

NINA: But then it would also be safe. Safe and unsafe at the same time.

DEREK: Yeah safe because . . .

NINA: Because he was gone.

DEREK: Yeah.

NINA: And so the dream that you had . . .

DEREK: So he spit in my mother's face.

NINA: In the dream?

DEREK: Uh huh. And I just remember her crying. But then I'd wake up from the dream, I'd go back into the dream, and I always remember her spitting back into his face.

NINA: Uh huh.

DEREK: And that's the time when I think I smiled, because I remember when she fought back and spit back into his face and he had a look like, of course he didn't hit her because then he'd have me on his case. . . . You know, I'd grab his ankle or something. But he looked shocked. But the one when my mother actually fights back, that's very real.

NINA: So it's that first part of the dream, not that second part. So when you had this dream last, which was two weeks ago, which version of the dream was it?

DEREK: The first part where he spits in my mother's face, and I remember her crying and feeling helpless.

NINA: So we're talking a lot about this dream. Is this dream the one you want to work with today, or was there something else that was compelling to you?

DEREK: It was that dream and then there was something else that I knew I became kind of like my father.

NINA: In what way?

DEREK: Fifth grade.

NINA: OK. In fifth grade. What happened in fifth grade?

DEREK: I terrorized a girl. Terrorized her. I punched her shoulder, kicked her. Spit at her. Cussed her out. I was actually, like, becoming my father.

NINA: And from what I know of you, you don't seem much like your dad today.

DEREK: No, thank God.

NINA: So what did you do to become a different kind of man than your dad?

DEREK: I looked for other male role models. That was unsuccessful for a long period of time. There was one or two along the way.

NINA: So it's been a struggle to find the male role models in your life?

DEREK: Yeah. Presently there's like four or five that I can actually speak very positively about and say that's what a man's supposed to be like. He's supposed to be gentle, he's supposed to be, you know, certain things.

NINA: So, Derek, what do you think? Would it be useful for us to work with this dream in action?

DEREK: Yeah. I'm tired of having it.

NINA: So you're ready to be done with this dream?

DEREK: Yeah. I'm tired.

NINA: That's terrific. So I want to ask you a couple more questions and then we're going to move right into the action of this dream. One is what was happening two weeks ago? Do you remember the evening or day that you had the dream?

DEREK: I think it was Monday night.

NINA: Monday night two weeks ago.

DEREK: Yeah, I was trying to get four or five things done at the same time, which is a problem.

NINA: So tell me what was going on. You were trying to get four or five things done. Tell me anything else that was gong on in your waking life. Had you been in contact with your parents?

DEREK: No. Actually, I called my mother Sunday night. Said everything's good.

NINA: And are she and your dad still together?

DEREK: Yeah, my mother's a faithful woman. Very faithful.

NINA: And she said things are OK.

DEREK: Yeah. You know she said everything's fine. . . . Your father's reading the Bible. . . .

NINA: Has your father changed a bit?

DEREK: Uh huh. He has.

NINA: Has the relationship changed or anything?

DEREK: Yeah. . . . We're on better terms.

NINA: Good. OK. Better terms, but it sounds like it's not so easy.

DEREK: It's not so easy because he never said I'm sorry. And I had to learn to forgive him through my faith.

NINA: Can I just double for you for a moment? May I touch your shoulder? [As Derek.] I learned to forgive him because of my faith, but it shouldn't have been this hard. [To Derek.] If that's right, repeat it.

DEREK: I learned to forgive him through my faith, but it shouldn't have been that damn hard.

NINA: And it would've been nice if he had met me halfway or even a quarter of the way.

DEREK: It would've been nice if he even met me just a half step just by acknowledging what had happened.

NINA: So forgiveness is a long road. So anything else that happened that Sunday or Monday? You talked to your mom; she said things were well. Your dad was reading the Bible.

DEREK: Uh huh.

NINA: And you said you had four or five things to do.

DEREK: I was stressed out. I was trying to prepare for my job, and I was trying to do laundry, and I was trying to clean the apartment, and trying to clean the darn litter box of this cat. And trying to get the recycling taken care of and washing the dishes. I was trying to do it like that. [Snaps fingers.]

NINA: Uh huh. Anything else going on in your emotional life in addition to that?

DEREK: In my job I'm always trying to. . . . My worst critic is myself, so I put a whole lot of pressure on myself.

NINA: As far as your job is concerned. OK, so that was in the mix.

DEREK: Uh huh, trying to come up with something better.

NINA: What we'll do is to enact your dream. Would that be OK?

DEREK: Yeah. I'm just always remembering.

NINA: Since we're in an individual session, you'll play all the parts. OK?

DEREK: Alright.

NINA: And I'll act as your double in whatever role that you're in. You say that the scene of the drama takes place in a house of your childhood, is that right?

DEREK: In an apartment.

NINA: An apartment. Where does the scene take place?

DEREK: Takes place in the hallway.

NINA: In the hallway, terrific. What I'm going to ask you to do is to try to set the scene as well as you can with the chairs and things we have available and also to pick a color to represent your dad and a color to represent mom with the scarves. You can use the scarves to delineate spaces if you want to also. You know that sometimes when we work with dreams we start with working with you being the dreamer first, but with the time that we have we're going to move away from that part, and concentrate on the dream itself, is that OK?

DEREK: Yeah, that's OK.

NINA: And what you told me you want from our work today is that you can work through this dream enough so that you don't need to keep having it. Did I get that right?

DEREK: Yeah.

NINA: OK, that's what we'll do. Say what you have as you set it up.

DEREK: [Laying down brown scarf.] This is the hallway. It's very narrow. It's claustrophobic.

NINA: Is this night or daytime?

DEREK: Night.

NINA: This is nighttime. It's claustrophobic and it's dark.

DEREK: This would be me. [Holding black scarf.]

NINA: That's you. And are you sitting in the hallway in the dream?

DEREK: I'm actually standing.

NINA: This will represent you standing in the hallway. How old are you in the dream?

DEREK: Eight.

NINA: Eight years old. Are you eight every time you have the dream or just this time?

DEREK: No, I get a little bit older, but this time I'm definitely eight.

NINA: Alright, I'll ask you about that in a minute. Let's set up the whole scene and we'll go back.

DEREK: This here is my father. [Holding gold scarf.]

NINA: It's his gold tooth.

DEREK: Yeah. And I'll use this one because it had a blue cap on it. [Pulling out blue scarf.] My mother was actually behind him trying to redirect the anger. . . .

NINA: OK. . . .

DEREK: I just remember her behind him trying to redirect the anger toward her and me.

NINA: How did she do that in the dream?

DEREK: She's tugging on his arm. She's tugging on his left arm.

NINA: She's tugging on his left arm. [Derek takes light blue scarf and lays it out close to the father scarf.]

DEREK: Uh huh. Do we need these or should we move them out of the way?

NINA: We can move them out of the way.

DEREK: Yeah, that's fine. Can I add something, too?

NINA: Yes. Of course.

DEREK: We have a lot of roaches running around our apartment, and so can I just lay this brown scarf here.

NINA: Ok, so these are roaches that are running all over the place. Do they run across Derek's feet, or do they run from him? What do they do?

DEREK: They're hanging out.

NINA: They're hanging out. OK. No place to go.

DEREK: Where's the food?

NINA: Where's the food? OK, so that's their comment. Good. Should we talk about mom? Start with mom's role, how she is. So here you are, and I'm going to speak to you as Mom. So Mom, what's happening now?

DEREK: [As mother.] I'm to get my hard-headed husband away from Derek. He acts like this whenever he doesn't have money. He acts like everything is Derek's fault and the rest of the family's.

NINA: And what are you going to do to get his attention away from Derek?

DEREK: [As mother.] I'm going to try and grab his arm.

NINA: What are you concerned he'll do to Derek? Does he holler at him?

DEREK: [As mother.] He hollers at him. He calls him awful names, so I don't even want him to get close to him.

NINA: I see it hurts you when he does that. You love your boy.

DEREK: [As mother.] Yeah.

NINA: And when he turns to you, do you get frightened?

DEREK: [As mother.] Him? You know he's hit me before.

NINA: That doesn't make it easy, though, does it?

DEREK: [As mother.] No. He knocked me out in a train station before.

NINA: So public on top of everything else. At least this is in the house, though.

DEREK: [As mother.] Yeah.

NINA: Ok, so can you take a step out of mom's role and take a step into dad's role. It's not so easy, is it? That's the least favorite. Is that OK? Do you want to do less?

DEREK: No, I want to do it now.

NINA: OK. So say how you're feeling before you step into the father.

DEREK: Right now, I'm feeling quite desperate.

NINA: You as Derek are feeling desperate?

DEREK: Yeah.

NINA: Desperate how?

DEREK: And sad really.

NINA: Sad, yes.

DEREK: I'll try my best not to cry.

NINA: What's bad about crying? Tears are the seeds of the soul, you know.

DEREK: The last person I cried in front of was my wife so . . .

NINA: What would you like to do now? You want to take a minute?

DEREK: [Derek cries for several minutes, a deep, penetrating cry.]

NINA: It's been so hard to hold this in. So I'm going to ask you to step over here. Is that OK? Can you say something about those feelings? What a relief, huh? Say some of these things. Do you want to talk to him on behalf of the feeling self? What were you going to tell the father?

DEREK: Stop.

NINA: Keep breathing. Can I double for you? [Doubling for Derek.] I hate what you did to me.

DEREK: [Banging wall as he continues to cry.]

NINA: If that's right, you can give it some voice.

DEREK: He really fucked me up! [Releasing anger and crying.]

NINA: [Doubling.] He really fucked me up. You have made it so hard for me to become a man. Give it a voice. If it's not right change it, but give it a voice. I know this is hard. [Doubling.] You sapped my strength. If this is right, repeat it.

DEREK: You sapped the shit out of me. I'm almost thirty years old and. . . . It's not right. I've been dealing with this my whole entire life.

NINA: [Doubling.] That was horrible what you did to me to make me fearful of you. . . . What's the nodding your head saying? Make it speak. Give it a voice.

DEREK: He shouldn't have done that shit. He had no right to do that shit. Other boys had fathers, and they would go out to the park and they would go to the White Castle for a couple of burgers. We couldn't even afford a couple dollars for the burgers 'cause the dumb ass kept . . .

NINA: [Doubling.] You were a lousy father.

DEREK: [Laughing and crying.]

NINA: Breathe. You want to say something?

DEREK: He just needs to see me cry, that's all.

NINA: He does. You think it would soften his heart, to see his son a man? So you think you can reverse roles as your dad?

DEREK: [Nodding head.]

NINA: So, let me ask you something. Should this be the dad in the train station or the dad who's reading the Bible? Which dad do we need?

DEREK: The dad that's reading the Bible. That's what we need.

NINA: OK, we're going to keep this scene here, because we're going to get back to it. . . . I'm going to have you be the dad who's reading the Bible. He can hear what he's done. And you know what? I'd like to have somebody to accompany you. How about one or two men who helped you be a good role model? Would that be OK? Can you name one of them? Just a first name.

DEREK: David.

NINA: OK, David. David will help you to talk if I can't. So just make one statement to dad today. And let's imagine that dad has observed your tears. Would he leave you or would he respond to it?

DEREK: I think he'd respond.

NINA: OK great, so let's reverse roles. Uh, Dad, do you stand or do you sit when you talk to Derek?

DEREK: I sit.

NINA: OK, great. Dad, you've seen your son today. What do you want to say to him?

DEREK: That I'm sorry.

NINA: And I don't want you to say anything that's not really in your heart, because he will know if you're lying to him.

DEREK: I know he's really intelligent.

NINA: Tell him that. Don't tell me.

DEREK: OK. I won't lie to you, because I know you're a very intelligent young man.

NINA: [Speaking as Dad.] And I want to tell you how it feels to see the damage I've done.

DEREK: And I want to tell you that I see how much damage I've caused and . . .

NINA: So tell Derek some of those things. Here's a moment to own up and make amends.

DEREK: I see my wrongs now. They're . . . well you turned out to be a good man. Got a wife, a lovely dedicated wife just like your mother is to me and . . .

NINA: [Speaking as Dad.] But you're a better man than I. If that's right, repeat, if not correct it.

DEREK: But you're a better man now than I was when I was your age. I'm just learning how, and if it wasn't for seeing you turning your life around, I wouldn't have changed mine.

NINA: [Speaking as Dad.] So in some ways you were almost my father.

DEREK: So in some ways you were almost like my father.

NINA: Let's switch roles. And respond to Dad. In some ways, you were almost like my father.

DEREK: That's kinda crappy.

NINA: Yeah, tell him. That stinks!

DEREK: I actually needed to see you be a father so I would know to take the right steps in life and instead I tried to find it elsewhere. I couldn't treat women the way you did, though. Even looking at girlie magazines made me sick. Even at twenty-one when you started talking to me about condoms. I was a virgin, and you didn't even know that.

NINA: [Doubling.] You failed me in a lot of ways, Dad.

DEREK: You failed me in a lot of ways and . . .

NINA: [Doubling.] And it's good to hear you're sorry, but I'm not ready to completely forgive you yet.

DEREK: It's good to hear you say that you're sorry and I'm working on for-giveness.

NINA: [Doubling.] Don't rush me.

DEREK: It's a slow process and I can't be rushed. I do, looking at you now, I do love you.

NINA: Reverse roles. [As Derek.] Looking at you now, I do love you. Respond to your boy.

DEREK: I love you, too, you know what I mean? You turned out right, and I knew it wasn't because of me.

NINA: I want to ask you something, Dad, as a special gift to your boy today. What can you say to him so that he when he gets stressed he doesn't have to have this dream to make him more stressed?

DEREK: Don't take life as seriously as I did. I put my trust and my hope into a lot of other things instead of my family, so just continue to be there with your family. Be honorable, the person I know that you are and take things easily. Do the opposite of me.

NINA: Reverse roles. Just concentrate on your family and be the honorable person that you are and take things easy. . . . What's the last thing you want to say to Dad now?

DEREK: [Laughing.] No more canned corn beef.

NINA: OK. And so you've given a voice to this little boy who was miserable. So what's the last thing you want to say to little Derek for now?

DEREK: Survive.

NINA: Do you know what I'm thinking? I'm going to ask you to reverse roles and see if there's a way you'd like to hear him a little bit better. Is that OK?

DEREK: Yeah.

NINA: Little Derek, is there something that you can say to big Derek that you'd like him to do so that he can take better care of you? He did one terrific thing—he gave you a voice.

DEREK: Take care of yourself now.

NINA: And will that help to take care of you? Can you think of one special thing you'd like him to do in everyday life that might help the both of you?

DEREK: Take time to listen to me.

NINA: OK. Reverse roles. Well, Derek, little Derek has asked you to take some time to listen to him.

DEREK: Yeah. I'll listen to you. I promise to listen to you. I promise to listen to you. Everyday.

NINA: Do you pray?

DEREK: Yes.

NINA: Would you be willing at some point in your prayer life to bring him in?

DEREK: Sure.

NINA: Could you tell him that, please.

DEREK: Hey little Derek, I promise to pray for you every day.

NINA: Does that feel complete for now?

DEREK: Yeah, I think when it's a prayer . . .

NINA: It's different, yeah. You brought him inside in a different way. OK let's just take a moment and bring that inside and say that again—about praying.

DEREK: Little Derek, I promise to say a prayer for you, to put you inside of my prayers every day.

NINA: And breathe.

DEREK: Feels better. Well, we made up for some sad moments, because the kid's had a tough time. But you helped him.

NINA: He needed some help. Thank you.

DEREK: Thank you.

NINA: What I'm going to ask you to do is move these scarves away so we can clear the scene. Just throw them over there so we have the whole scene removed. There we go. Like magic. Here we are today.

DEREK: I'm tired.

NINA: Yeah.

Reflections on the Session

In her reflections, Garcia (in Landy 2005) pointed out the significance of dream work in psychodrama and that Moreno's goal was to retrain the dream, that is, to discover a new ending. She noted that Derek's goal was to stop having the recurring dream, and she worked with him toward that aim. In asking Derek what was happening immediately prior to the dream, she connected the dream to his current life. In doing so, she discovered that Derek's father was a different man today, having embraced religion and family in a more positive way. With this information, Garcia was able to move Derek into a scene that offered, if not a retraining, at least a corrective to the dream as he addressed his more humble father, creating an opportunity for rapprochement in the real world.

The psychodrama session generated a great degree of affect for Derek. Garcia remarked: "The first moment that I noticed he had some feelings was when he spoke about his mother in relation to the dream, and I wanted to take a moment so that if he wanted to express those feelings he could." In speaking about her process in containing Derek's affect, she noted that she comforted him by touch, after asking his permission to place her hand on his shoulder. But when he was most upset, she held her hand several inches from his body, explaining:

I wanted to be able to feel from the heat of his body if he needed to have more time to [cry] so that I could be guided by what I needed to do as a double for him or to help him to express his feelings more deeply or to move back into a more cognitive space.

As in distancing theory, Garcia was gauging Derek's need for expression and containment.

As to her work with the roles of father, son, and the eight-year-old Derek, Garcia (in Landy 2005) offered this:

The reason for putting him into the father's role is so that they could have a dialogue . . . but also for him . . . to experience that his father is a different man today, and that there may be more openness for the kind of relationship he's always wanted to have with his father

And this:

And the reason that at the end I went back to the scene and asked him to connect with his eight-year-old self is that it's my belief that the integration of that eight-year-old self is absolutely essential to the healing. . . . The accepting, the love, and the expression of feeling on behalf of that child's self is what really will help with moving the healing forward. And at that moment when Derek made the promise to bring the child with him in his prayers, there was literally a change in his physiology, and that was about the internal shift that had taken place.

Garcia also reflected upon several basic psychodramatic techniques as powerful ways to move Derek toward expression and awareness. She made reference to moments of mirroring, as when speaking to Derek as the loving mother; doubling, as when expressing Derek's feelings of anger toward his father; and role reversal, as when she, as Derek, expressed love to the father.

Derek (in Landy 2005) also reflected upon his cathartic reaction to the psychodrama session, comparing his experience with that in role method:

I think it's because of the position I'm in currently that actually brought up a lot more emotion in me. Last week [in role method] the same thing was about to happen at one time when the therapist looked at me and that brought about a lot of affect, because obviously the male/male relationship that I have with the therapist stirred up a lot of emotion, but I was able to put up my wall and not do it.

He went on to say that the emotion was generated in the psychodrama session, because he was playing the role of his mother. In the previous session, working with the role of father, he experienced a greater degree of distance, as he worked within a story frame. Further, he spoke about experiencing a sense of being fully in the moment in the psychodrama session, which he attributed to his overabundance of emotional expression.

Staying with the emotional expression, Derek acknowledged the importance of Garcia's doubling at the time when he was most overwhelmed with feeling. He said: "I couldn't talk at the time. I needed someone to speak for me, just like I needed someone to speak for me when I was a kid."

Derek (in Landy 2005) also reflected upon Garcia's supportive touch: "I appreciated that because I don't want just anyone putting their hand on me.

I had that too much as a child so I'm conscious about touching people. I appreciated the fact that she asked me, because I was ready at that time for her to touch me gently."

And finally, reflecting upon the experience of addressing the eight-year-old child, Derek (in Landy 2005) said: "Now it felt like I was ready—he was ready to speak to the adult me, and he finally had a voice. He had a voice and someone who could actually listen to him. . . . It happened and I felt peace."

As he completed the second session, Derek experienced a catharsis of integration. The father and the son were more closely linked by means of the guidance of the mother. The young, abused child that was Derek discovered a voice that connected with the adult Derek. A spiritual moment tempered an emotional one, leading to a sense of peace.

THE POLARITIES

Emotion and Distance

We have already discussed the several forms of catharsis in psychodrama. Through catharsis of integration, clients experience a balance of emotion and insight, similar to that described as aesthetic distance in role method. In practice, catharsis of abreaction is much more common, although it does not preclude catharsis of integration, as we saw in the case of Derek. When Derek took on the role of mother, admitting to being physically abused in public by her husband, he experienced a deep well of feeling that needed release. When he released that feeling in action, he experienced a powerful catharsis of abreaction. Reflecting upon the moment one year later, Derek (2006) gave a very precise description of his catharsis:

> For years I had carried my mother's tears and my own sadness inside me, the emotions of the defenseless little boy. I could not shed my own tears as a little boy, because I was too busy using defense mechanisms to ward off constant attacks. When I was asked to reverse roles and speak as my mother about the abuse she endured, an overwhelming feeling of sadness and helplessness came over me. I felt trapped between what I felt for my mother and what I felt myself. As the therapist gave voice to my mother's feelings, especially knowing my mother never verbalized her emotions, I became very aware that her motivation was love for us. This coupled with the therapist's genuinely empathetic tone, which made me feel safe, I began to break down. In addition she didn't allow me to move on from that uncomfortable spot where my emotions were fighting to get out. She just waited and unable to escape, I started to cry.

But there was still more to come and Garcia stayed the course, encouraging Derek to take on the role of the young son and confront his father. He (Derek 2006) described this most intense phase as follows:

At that point a multitude of emotions came up and I had to cry them all out—anger, desperation, pain, hopelessness, resentment, hatred for what he did to me, and a tremendous relief came out of me when I proclaimed to my father that he fucked me up. It was really helpful to me when she spoke out what I was feeling, things that as an eight-year-old boy and even as a grown man today I was unable to express.

For Derek, the release of the powerful emotion was related to the safe distance created by Garcia through her choice of role reversal and doubling, through her comforting, empathetic, and, not incidentally, feminine presence, and finally through her choice to be respectful of his body. Derek (2006) remarked: "All I could remember about crying during this session was the support I felt from the therapist who did not touch me, which was a good choice, because I was feeling a mix of sorrow and anger."

It is usual in psychodrama for emotion to be reexperienced and then expressed. There are several reasons. The first is that clients play the role of themselves and are thus less distanced. The action occurs in first person and thus often feels real, as if a troubling past experience is occurring in the present. Derek's story in role method was a fiction about a father and son and pain and was therefore more distanced. In psychodrama, it was about Derek's father and Derek's pain as a boy and as a man. And it was about Derek's mother, a kind of guide figure, represented by the therapist. Psychodrama, in theatrical terms, is closer to Stanislavski's work with affective memory than to Brecht's alienation effect. Further, the techniques of psychodrama, such as the double, the mirror, and role reversal, help to deepen the affective experience of the protagonist. And finally, the director is trained to utilize these techniques to evoke catharsis on the part of the protagonist.

Moreno made it clear that catharsis centered foremost within the protagonist, and secondarily in the auxiliaries and the audience. Although protagonists worked in and through role, the work was not meant to be projective. The central role was that of self. When working in a group, the protagonist gave the projected roles to auxiliaries. In *psychodrama à deux* as demonstrated above, Derek played the projective roles of mother, father, and young self. But throughout, he returned to the central role of Derek in the present, telling the story of his life in the first person as authentically as he could remember. Even the figures in his dream had a reality and immediacy.

The distance that is created in psychodrama comes more from the presence of the therapist than from the approach. Garcia facilitated a catharsis of abreaction through her gentle but persistent guidance of Derek into a confrontation with an abused mother and an abusive father. And in the end, she facilitated a catharsis of integration by encouraging a moment of connection between the young boy and the grown man. In facilitating this

integration, she offered the needed distance to balance out Derek's overwhelming feelings of desperation.

Fiction and Reality

Like psychoanalysis and Gestalt therapy, psychodrama works with dreams,
as we saw in the case of Derek. And like role method, psychodrama works
with imaginative material such as myths and fictional stories and roles. Psychodrama also plays with dimensions of time as a protagonist moves in and
out of ego states in the past and future. However, psychodrama starts and
ends in reality, with a protagonist who has an actual difficulty with a significant other. To further enhance that reality, the protagonist plays out the difficulty with selected auxiliaries.

Roles played and stories told in psychodrama can certainly have an aspect
of surplus or heightened reality, but the reality-orientation of everyday life remains clear and present. In the previous psychodrama, Derek created the fictional role of little Derek and even recalled dream images of his mother and
father spitting at one another. He also created dramatic moments of confronting his father and comforting the hurt child that lives inside himself.
And yet throughout, Garcia reminded Derek that this was his story and that
she would help him revise it in such a way as to release some pain and restore
a sense of spontaneity. One could argue that such a journey is heroic and even
mythic. Although this may be the case, the journeyer remains on a well-worn
path, never too far from the sounds and smells and images of a recalled past.

Verbal and Nonverbal Expression

Like role method, psychodrama is an approach that harnesses verbal and
nonverbal expression. Oftentimes psychodrama directors will warm up an
individual or group through nonverbal activities in movement or guided
imagery, for example. In the case of Derek, Garcia very carefully warmed
Derek up to his drama through a verbal exchange of information concerning his present state of being and his willingness to work on a recurring
dream. At an early point in this exchange, Garcia noticed that Derek had
smiled when he referred to his mother. Garcia picked up on that nonverbal
cue and asked Derek to amplify it verbally. In doing so, she prepared Derek
to work with the most significant nonverbal moment of his drama, his expression of deep feeling. Intuiting that Derek could only do so by working
through the role of mother, Garcia mirrored the role of the good enough
mother that guided Derek to eventually confront his father and make peace
with his younger self.

In setting the scene of the dream, Garcia encouraged Derek to work with
chairs and scarves nonverbally to re-create a sense of heightened reality. As

Derek set the scene, Garcia helped him specify his choices through pointed questions and comments. Particularly poignant was the moment when Derek chose a gold scarf to represent his father and Garcia gave words to his nonverbal action: "It's his gold tooth."

Throughout Derek's difficult moments of powerful expression, Garcia remained by his side. One of her most significant interventions was to ask Derek's permission to touch his shoulder. In Derek's memory, however, she did not touch him, and this was also true as Garcia gauged Derek's need for touch and containment by holding her hand inches from his body as he sobbed. The important point is that Garcia offered the optimal degree of physical as well as affective containment to facilitate Derek's catharsis.

Continuously, Garcia reminded Derek to pay attention to his body—to breathe and to recognize the feelings contained in the body. She also encouraged Derek to give language to his feelings, doubling for him when necessary. At one point she said: "What's the nodding your head saying? Make it speak. Give it a voice." And with those prompts, Derek was able to transform the sensations in his body into words, articulating the feeling that released the tension in his body.

Each role reversal marked a nonverbal transition to and from dialogue with the figures Derek most needed to address—his mother, father, and younger self. As transitional moments before and after speech, role reversals serve as nonverbal bridges integrating not only feeling and thought, but also one role and another, one person and another, all of whom so require connection.

In drama therapy, Landy (1994) has made a distinction between psychodramatic and projective techniques. The former concern more reality-based situations and tend to be more dependent upon verbal exchanges. As such, psychodramatic techniques are most suited to higher functioning clients who have a good grasp of language. Projective techniques, as utilized in role method, can be more easily applied to nonverbal clients as they engage with puppets, masks, and miniature objects, animating them through their movement, sound, and imaginative action.

Action and Reflection

Like role method, psychodrama involves both action and reflection. For Moreno, reflection often occurred within the action part of the session. This can be seen, for example, toward the end of Derek's session, when he integrated the young part of himself with the present mature man. This confluence of action and reflection is a hallmark of catharsis of integration.

Yet in psychodrama, there is a clear distinction between the action portion of the session and the closure. During the sharing part of the closure, the protagonist and auxiliaries de-role and retreat from the *locus nascendi*.

Out of role, they and the remainder of the audience consciously reflect upon the meaning of the dramatic enactment as it relates directly to their lives. In the case of Derek and others experiencing *psychodrama à deux*, there is also a moment of reflection following the action. Because there was little time to reflect in Derek's brief forty-minute session, Garcia ended by asking him to strike the set, that is, clear the scarves and chairs and leave the dramatic roles behind. She and Derek sat face-to-face and checked in with one another. Derek did not at that time reflect upon his drama, but rather upon his present feeling of fatigue. Perhaps summing up the deeply intense work he had done, his final words were: "I'm tired."

Directive and Nondirective
Action/Transference and Countertransference

Directors in psychodrama, certainly ones modeling J. L. Moreno, are rather directive. They help choose protagonists and then help the protagonists set up, enact, and reflect upon their drama. They tend to be highly active not only in the stage managing, performance, and feedback, but also in modulating the emotional tone as they encourage moments of catharsis.

When directors work with a single client, they tend to be even more active, because they are not supported by auxiliaries and audience members. Nina Garcia exemplified such a director. Her task was to dramatize Derek's dream in such a way that he fully experienced the psychodramatic process through a range of techniques. As director, she encouraged Derek to play his own auxiliary roles, and when necessary, she took on the same roles in order to deepen Derek's experience.

As a gentle, containing woman, Garcia stood in for Derek's mother. She was aware that she would receive the transference, and she dealt with it first by mirroring a good enough mother figure for Derek. She chose not to directly take on the role of the mother, but rather moved it onto Derek. In doing so, she redirected the transference back into the drama, the appropriate place for the action to occur. As director, she recognized that Derek needed to play out all his roles and attempt to move toward integration with her help as director, not as transferential mother.

Toward the end of the drama, Garcia played a more active dramatic role, doubling for the father and for Derek. At the same time she directed Derek toward several role reversals and then a final catharsis of integration. As such, she did not garner more transference from Derek, but remained the therapist in the here and now who reminded Derek at the end to de-role and return to the present.

Garcia did not discuss her countertransferential feelings directly. She did, however, reflect upon her empathetic connection to Derek. Like Derek, she experienced a positive and strong sense of tele, a connection that she used to move the therapeutic process forward. She not only witnessed Derek's pain, but also internalized it and mirrored it back to Derek, thus helping him to proceed on his path toward integration.

In psychodrama, the therapist is generally more directive than her counterpart in role method. As such, she tends to invoke less transference. What is common to both approaches, however, is that when the transference is present, therapists of both redirect it back to the drama and the group. In psychodrama, the relationship of client and therapist is more about tele than transference. And in role method, the telic relationship is also a powerful indicator of the degree of safety and thus willingness of the client to delve deeply into a dilemma. As the directors in both approaches sometimes engage in role with the client, some degree of countertransference is to be expected. And yet, as the directors move out of role and redirect the client's projections onto the group or into the drama, they provide a sense of distance for themselves.

6

Developmental Transformations in Drama Therapy

Derek's final session was in developmental transformations, an approach developed over some twenty-five years by David Read Johnson, a major pioneer in drama therapy. His early research centered in the application of drama therapy to the schizophrenic condition. Johnson is also known for his clinical practice and writing in the field of posttraumatic stress disorder, having worked for years with Vietnam War veterans and others experiencing posttraumatic stress disorder.

HISTORICAL OVERVIEW

Johnson (2000b) defines developmental transformations as "an embodied encounter in the playspace" (87). The three aspects of body, encounter, and playspace will be discussed in the section on concepts. Like the two previous approaches, developmental transformations employ role-playing as a vehicle to drive the action and strives for a sense of spontaneity. Unlike the others, this approach encourages the client to constantly transform from one role to another in order to detach from conventional ways of behaving and discover a deeper sense of self in relationship to the therapist.

Historically, Johnson traced his approach to four main disciplinary sources: theater, psychology, dance therapy, and philosophy. In theater, Johnson acknowledges his debt to Viola Spolin (1963), the innovator of theater games, improvisational techniques used not only in actor training, but also in education and recreation. As developmental transformations is an improvisational method that often begins with sound and movement exercises, it draws great sustenance from Spolin's classical book, *Improvisation for the Theatre* (1963).

Johnson turned to two other theatrical sources representing, in some ways, the comic and tragic masks of ancient Greece. The tragic mask is epitomized in the work of theater artist Jerzy Grotowski (1968). Grotowski's model, like that of an earlier one developed by Antonin Artaud (1958), viewed the process of acting as a combination of somatic, psychological, and spiritual elements. The work of Artaud and Grotowski reflects the underdistance of the trance state of the sorcerer and shaman as described by Sarbin (1962). To illustrate this extreme position, Artaud (1958) used the metaphor of the plague to characterize the work of the actor, as both the plague and the theatrical performance

> releases conflicts, disengages powers, liberates possibilities. . . . The action of the theatre, like that of the plague, is beneficial, for, impelling men to see themselves as they are, it causes the mask to fall, reveals the lie, the slackness, baseness and hypocrisy of our world (31).

Grotowski subjected his actors to intense physical, psychological, and spiritual exercises intended to penetrate the mask and the lie. Although rejecting the specific therapeutic benefits of his actor training, he did say this (Grotowski 1968):

> Theatre . . . provides an opportunity for what could be called integration, the discarding of masks, the revealing of the real substance: a totality of physical and mental reactions. . . . Here we can see the theatre's therapeutic function for people in our present day civilization (255–56).

In many ways, the ideas of these two original and uncompromising voices echo those of Carl Jung plumbing the depths of the unconscious, and of Wilhelm Reich searching for the essential biophysical force in the universe. In these voices are also echoes of the spiritual Moreno searching for ways to take on the role of God and become the holy actor. In fact Grotowski, like Artaud before him, envisioned performance as a holy act in a shamanic sense as actors purify and mortify their bodies, reach into the spirit world for inspiration, and return to inspire their audiences.

Johnson and his colleagues (Johnson et al. 1996) noted that Grotowski pared theater down to its essential elements of actor, audience, and the encounter between the two. Grotowski's theater, like Johnson's drama therapy to come, was simple and elemental, without sets, costumes, masks, lights, and often without text. Grotowski referred to his as a poor theater and Johnson to his as a poor drama therapy. Both sought to realize Artaud's (1958) vision of stripping away the mask for the purpose of "impelling men to see themselves as they are" (31). For Grotowski and later for Johnson, the way to reach that transformation was through the body.

Developmental transformations, however, also wears the comic mask and as such projects a playful side, linking it to low comedy and farce, in the tradition of commedia dell'arte or theater of the absurd. In their article on poor drama therapy, Johnson and his colleagues (1996) write:

> Whereas Grotowski might be accused of a tragic view of life, developmental transformations clearly embraces a comic view. Grotowski's asceticism sets the boundaries of a moral imperative, whereas developmental transformations adopts a more forgiving attitude, accepting both the authentic and the superficial, truth and nonsense, sacrifice and gratification of desire, as playable human qualities (304).

Johnson's psychological sources begin in developmental psychology with the early work of Freud (1933), Werner (1948), Piaget (1962), Erikson (1963), Kübler-Ross (1969), and Levinson (1978). He also credits the influence of Freud (1933) and Kris (1982) in the development of the concept of free association. And finally he points to the influence of both object relations theorists like Klein (1975) and Jacobson (1964), and client-centered perspectives such as those of Rogers (1951) and Gendlin (1978).

In his early practice as a drama therapist, Johnson collaborated with dance therapist, Susan Sandel. Together they discovered many connections between therapeutic movement and drama. In fact, they developed a scale to rate psychiatric patients according to measures derived from drama and movement, such as stability of task, space, role structures, and complexity (see Johnson and Sandel 1977). Johnson attributes much of this early work in movement to Marian Chace, one of the pioneers of the profession of dance therapy. Johnson noted that Chace was influenced by Moreno and developed her approach to dance therapy while working with traumatized war veterans and psychiatric patients at St. Elizabeths Hospital in Washington, D.C., just after World War II. Shortly before her arrival, Moreno established one of his early psychodrama theaters at St. Elizabeths.

Johnson also refers to a dance therapy approach called authentic movement as a significant influence, especially the pioneering work of Mary Whitehouse (1979). Like developmental transformations, authentic movement is an improvisational form of bodily expression where one moves spontaneously with eyes closed, in response to an inner impulse. Authentic movement is usually practiced within a group, and all clients are witnessed and contained by a dance/movement therapist.

Finally, Johnson speaks of several philosophical influences. One is the existential perspective of Jean-Paul Sartre (1943), who spoke of the individual's struggle for freedom as he is held in the gaze of others. A second influence is the work of the postmodern philosophers, most notably Jacques Derrida (1978), whose ideas of deconstruction provide a way to understand the untangling of conventional role structures. In addition, Johnson speaks of the significance of Buddhism and its philosophy of nonattachment.

BASIC ASSUMPTIONS OF
DEVELOPMENTAL TRANSFORMATIONS

Johnson (2000b) has stated that his approach, although based in the many influences noted above, is primarily atheoretical. For Johnson, developmental transformations is more of a practice than a theory, predicated on the encounter between client and therapist. He writes (2000a): "Perhaps one function of theory in Developmental Transformations is to give the therapist support in letting go of the need for any framework or position, so as to be available to experience the encounter with the client" (88).

And yet, as we shall see, this approach has several key conceptual pieces as well as a philosophical point of view. This point of view is well articulated in Johnson's (in Landy 2005) introduction to his session in the film:

> The world is . . . impermanent . . . things are changing all the time. And this . . . instability that we all experience in the world is something that we all need to counter by holding onto things. In our work the therapist is going to be helping the client loosen his or her grip on these forms. The theory is that I fear if I'm going to give up the form that I'm holding . . . that I will fall into the void. We find that when we work with the clients they find that in fact rather than just falling into a void, another form is created. And in that way forms rise up, encrust, develop, solidify and then move on. We try to help the client feel less fearful of this process. . . . So the therapist . . . tries to encourage the client to move from a state of seriousness about themselves to a state of play. . . . Essentially the work comes down to this moment of trying to allow the person to take aspects of their world that they view as solid and to give it up for a moment and place those solid, serious things within the confines of the playspace and allow them to transform.

Rejecting role theory, with its postmodern view of a polymorphous self, and narrative therapy, with its constructivist view of the self, Johnson embraces a more spiritual, humanistic worldview, that of emanation theory. He (2000a) explains it as follows: "The world is understood to be emanating (i.e., flowing out) from a fundamental Source of existence that remains beyond comprehension" (88). For Johnson, "the world is naturally given, rather than willed" (88). Johnson also appears to embrace Grotowski's dualistic view of the self as comprised of an outer false self, developed in response to conventional demands, and an inner true self that is whole but that is reachable only through a deep and playful process of self-discovery. The road to the true self is through the body. And for Johnson, the body is the Source.

BASIC CONCEPTS OF
DEVELOPMENTAL TRANSFORMATIONS

Embodiment

Johnson (2000b) writes: "The Body is the source of thought and feeling, of physicality and energy" (89). In that he capitalizes "Body," it takes on an essential quality. He refers to states of disembodiment as loci of psychological distress. He notes that in the process of developmental transformations, the therapist aims to keep the Body in motion through sound, movement, gesture, and speech. In practice, the therapist gauges the flow emanating from the body and helps to modulate that flow.

Based in his clinical work, Johnson has identified four types of embodiment. Although not strictly developmental, each one suggests a higher level of relationship between the body of the client and that of the therapist or others in the group. The first is Body as Other. In this state, individuals perceive their bodies as objects for the other to behold. At this level, the person is identified by external factors such as race, ethnicity, appearance, and demeanor.

The second type is Body as Persona. At this level, individuals perceive their bodies as belonging to themselves, with all their individual characteristics intact. Furthermore, in the therapeutic encounter, they perceive the body of their therapist as linked to the full identity of the therapist, rather than to superficial characteristics.

At the third level, Body as Desire, one relates to the other in a more intimate, affective fashion. The Body becomes a source of fantasy, attraction, and repulsion. Johnson notes that in this phase one experiences both fear and support from the other.

The final type is that of Body as Presence, which Johnson also refers to as deep play. At this most basic state of being, one relates to the other as an autonomous entity. Both are aware of the presence of the other without any particular design or need to change the other. Both share the experience of being individuals who are in a relationship in the moment. Such a state of being implies intimacy without guilt. According to Johnson, these levels are often enacted chronologically in a therapeutic relationship, but in reverse order developmentally as mother and child move from intimacy to individuality.

Encounter

As in poor theater, developmental transformations removes all obstacles to the essential relationship between self and other, client and therapist. This relationship is called the encounter, a concept similar to that described by both Moreno and Perls. For Johnson, in the encounter the therapist becomes the client's play object while the client becomes the therapist's text. The therapist's task is to allow the essential issues of the client to emerge and to assume whatever roles the client requires. The therapist not only takes on the client's roles, but also plays them out in a manner that matches the client's needs. Johnson calls this process faithful rendering.

During the session, the therapist can also choose to revise the terms of the encounter, moving into the witnessing circle, a small circular carpet placed on the perimeter of the room, where the therapist sits and witnesses the play of the client.

Johnson distinguishes between the encounter in classical psychoanalysis and in developmental transformations. In the former, the therapist and client are separated, one reclining on a couch, the other sitting to one side, each involved in their personal inner experiences. In the latter, the therapist engages directly with the client, playing out levels of intimacy and separation. In developmental transformations, the encounter is the essential meeting of two players, one searching for intimacy and the other offering his presence as a means of helping the other arrive.

Playspace

The playspace is the psychological environment of the encounter, described by Johnson (in Landy 2005) as "a state of playfulness that exists between the client and the therapist." There are three main components of the playspace: restraint against harm, mutual agreement between the players, and "discrepant communication, which simply means that the boundary of reality and fantasy is represented simultaneously."

The playspace is similar to Moreno's notion of *locus nascendi,* the place of birth. Unlike Moreno, however, Johnson (2000b) believes that "verbal discussion or processing occurs within the playspace, not at the end of the session outside the state of play" (91). In both psychodrama and role method, work in the action phase of the drama is followed by a de-roling and then a verbal sharing or reflection upon the action.

Within the playspace, both players engage with one another improvisationally. As clients experience their thoughts and feelings, they are encouraged to express them physically through spontaneous and uncensored actions in sound and movement, in words and gestures. As the thoughts and feelings of clients change, so do their actions in the playspace.

Developmental transformations can be practiced individually and in groups. At the conclusion of the contracted time, the therapist says: "Take a minute." The session ends as both leave the playspace and resume their everyday lives.

THERAPEUTIC GOALS

Developmental transformations attempts to help clients detach from and deconstruct the "solid, serious things," and engage with conflictual aspects of their lives in a playful manner. Like Moreno, who believed that the survival of humankind lay in the ability to be spontaneous and creative in the face of the cultural conserve, Johnson believes that the ability to encounter another fully in the playspace through embodied action will lead to a greater sense of intimacy and offset a culture of alienation. Johnson views the therapeutic goal as a confluence of Source, Self, and Other. This is not too different from Moreno's triad of creativity, spontaneity, and cultural conserve. And it is even closer to that of Landy's guide, role, and counter-role.

ROLE OF THE THERAPIST

In an early article, Johnson (1992) specified three major roles played by drama therapists: that of transference figure, which he calls the psychological role; that of a character in the drama, which he calls the dramatic role; and that of therapist, which he calls the social role. Johnson, however, expands his understanding of role, opting instead for the broader concept of playspace to suggest that in the enactment both therapist and client play out "other states of imagination and drama that do not have the form and structure of typical roles" (112).

In the same article, Johnson speaks about many functions of the therapist in terms of a continuum that represents a spectrum of distance in relationship to the playspace. At the most distanced is the therapist as witness or mirror. Subsequent positions moving toward feeling are therapist as director, as side coach, as leader, as guide, and as shaman. In the guise of shaman, the therapist, having taken his own journey to the figurative spirit/imaginal world, enacts the healing drama for the client.

Johnson acknowledged that the good enough drama therapist is able to take on many of these functions as the situation demands. However, as stated in the film, Johnson (in Landy 2005) specified the function as follows:

> The therapist puts himself in the therapeutic playspace with the client and allows his body to be available for play with the client. In this sense the role of the therapist . . . is modeled a little bit more on the role of the actor. . . . As this process unfolds, the therapist is going to be applying various kinds of techniques to try to loosen the grip of the clients on various forms that they have attached themselves to.

Thus Johnson embraces the role method notion of therapist as guide and witness, as well as the psychodramatic notion of therapist as director, side coach, and leader. He even harkens back to the traditional healing function of the shaman. However, in developmental transformations the therapist takes on a new function, that of the client's playobject. While in this position within the drama the therapist cajoles, jokes, tricks, prods, provokes, supports, and provides feedback in action to clients on their bumpy journey toward transformation.

In both individual and group work, emergent issues of transference and countertransference are played out within the drama and allowed to transform. As the clients develop a greater capacity to play spontaneously, they are able to tolerate a greater sense of intimacy with the persona and the person of the therapist.

VIEW OF WELLNESS AND ILLNESS

From the viewpoint of developmental transformations, healthy individuals are ones who are in flow (see Csikszentmihalyi 1990), a term that is synonymous with Moreno's understanding of spontaneity and Landy's understanding of aesthetic distance. They are able to take on a variety of roles and enact them in a spontaneous fashion, without the need to hold onto old forms that are no longer useful. Johnson (in Landy 2005) encourages clients "to move from a state of seriousness about themselves to a state of play." Like Perls and Reich and the subsequent bioenergetic and movement therapists, developmental transformations offers an embodied, holistic image of health. The healthy state is one of *homo ludens*, human beings as playful.

As developmental transformations concerns an embodied encounter in the playspace, illness is marked by an inability to express oneself playfully and imaginatively through the body. Illness is also noted by an attachment to particular role forms that preclude the ability to transform into others. As the integrated person is able to transform from one state of being to another, the disintegrated person is stuck within a rigid personality structure.

ASSESSMENT AND EVALUATION

Johnson created two versions of an assessment instrument, the Diagnostic Role-Playing Test (DRPT), which has been used by many practitioners of developmental transformations. In the first version, DRPT-1, subjects are asked to enact five roles—grandparent, bum, politician, teacher, lover. Subjects are given various props through which to enact the roles. Several of these props are similar to those used by Moreno in his early spontaneity test.

In the DRPT-2, subjects are given the following directions:

> I am now going to ask you to do three scenes. After each one I will ask you some questions. Enact a scene between three beings in any way that you wish. Who or what these three beings are is up to you. Tell me when you are finished.

Following each scene, subjects are asked to respond to the following: "Tell me in as much detail as you can what happened in that scene. . . . Now, describe the three beings, one at a time" (Johnson 1988, 26).

In interpreting the results, Johnson looked at specific aspects of the role play, including:

1. spontaneity
2. ability to transcend reality
3. role repertoire
4. organization of scenes
5. patterns in the dramatic content of scenes
6. attitude toward enactment
7. style of role-playing

He also looked at such developmental concepts: the client's ability to structure space, tasks, and roles, the media of representation, the complexity of the characters and setting, the interactions among characters, and the degree of affect expressed.

Johnson's assessments are somewhat similar to Moreno's early sociometric tests and to those developed by Murray and his colleagues, as all use a role-playing approach to measure present levels of functioning. Both the DRPT-1 and DRPT-2 have been applied to work with a variety of client populations, most notably schizophrenics and traumatized war veterans (see Johnson and Quinlan 1993; James and Johnson 1997).

THE METHOD OF DEVELOPMENTAL
TRANSFORMATIONS

In individual therapy, treatment begins with one or more verbal sessions to provide a personal history of the client and to discuss both goals and ethical issues involved in working through touch and embodiment. The session takes place in a carpeted room with pillows and a small, round witnessing circle. The work begins with a physical warm-up that leads generally to a sound and movement improvisation. An image or scene often emerges from the movement, engaging both client and therapist in the play, and as the scene develops, it transforms into another and another, initiated by both players. The therapist begins by faithfully rendering the images of the client, but then works through a series of other techniques to facilitate both the play and its transformation. These include but are not limited to repetition and intensification, diverting or disrupting the play from a conventional story line, transforming the play to the here and now, and moving into the witnessing circle. At the conclusion of the agreed upon time, the therapist says: "Take a minute," and then exits the space. The client is left alone to reflect upon the session before leaving the space. The therapist generally discourages any form of verbal discussion, unless asked for by the client. Johnson (2000b), further clarifying the goal of developmental transformations, notes: "The purpose of not including a set-aside time for de-roling or verbal commentary is consistent with the overall goals of this therapy, which are to become present, rather than to gain insight" (93).

Developmental transformations is different from the three-part structure of warm-up, action, and closure that defines role method and psychodrama. It is more closely linked to the classical psychoanalytic structure of free association in that the therapist encourages and fosters the free flow of imagery on the part of the client. Distinguishing itself from the other clinical practices discussed above, developmental transformations does not require a verbal reflection and does not aim toward insight. It is also unique in that it embeds the therapist directly in the playspace with the client, altering in a significant way the dynamics of the relationship and the path toward reaching the therapeutic goal.

DEVELOPMENTAL TRANSFORMATIONS WITH DEREK

The transcript to follow features a developmental transformations session between Derek and David Johnson. The session will be followed by Johnson's reflections and then a discussion of the polarities.

DAVID: So just stretch out a little bit. Relax.

[David and Derek stretch.]

DEREK: Backstroke.

DAVID: Backstroke. Alright, so let me explain what we'll be doing. We'll begin a scene, which I'll start in a minute. As the scene proceeds, you're going to have thoughts and feelings that will come up inside of you. I want you to use those thoughts and feelings to transform the scene into another scene. If you transform the scene into a new scene, I will take a role in the new scene and follow along. If I transform a scene to another scene, you need to flow along with me. . . . Every once in a while during our work I'm going to go over here to the witnessing circle and I'll sit there and watch you, and you will continue to play out here alone. You can ignore me, you can look at me, you can make me into something, you can do whatever you want to, just don't come over and pull me into the play. And I will return and continue. At the end I will tell you to take a minute. I will de-role, and you take a moment to sit with your thoughts. OK? What's up for you in terms of what you're thinking about working on?

DEREK: Trying to think about issues I've been dealing with in the last couple of weeks. My father and I. Let's start with that.

DAVID: And the issue with your father and I is basically . . .

DEREK: Abuse.

DAVID: Abuse. Alright. I want you to put me in a position or a statue of some kind.

DEREK: Turn around. Hands up. Hands like claws. Bend over just a little bit. [Sculpts David as a statue.]

DAVID: Something like that?

DEREK: Yeah. You have to have a meaner . . .

DAVID: Meaner?

DEREK: Yeah. And turn around.

DAVID: Now I want you to place yourself in relationship to me with one part of your body touching one part of my body. We'll begin from here. Take your time developing the scene . . . [Derek puts one finger on David's chest, as if trying to stop an attack.]

[Derek and David begin pushing each other in an intimidating manner.]

DEREK: [Hissing.]

[Derek and David face off with their bodies. They attack each other. David raises his fist and Derek gets on all fours on the floor.]

DAVID: Where's my victim? I had a victim here and now my victim's gone.

DEREK: Your victim is gone.

DAVID: I can't abuse without a victim. I need a victim.

DEREK: Tough. Tough noogies.

DAVID: Where'd he go?

DEREK: Grrrr.

DAVID: There he is.

DEREK: Grrr.

DAVID: You know what I like best? Kicking the dog. Kicking the dog. I come in, I'm working hard. I work hard all day, I swing open that door, and I say: "What the fuck are you doing?!" [David mimes kicking Derek, who tumbles over.]

DEREK: Grrr. Dogs can fight back.

DAVID: Oh yeah? Oh yeah? The dogs I know hid in the corner. That's the dogs I know. Dogs run in the corner. That's what the dogs do. You know what I'm talking about? Dogs in the background. Dogs don't cause any real trouble. Because you know what happens when the trouble starts?

DEREK: Grrr.

DAVID: But you don't have any control this time.

DEREK: Grrr.

DAVID: Am I being mean enough? I'm probably not being mean enough. What are you laughing about? I have to be meaner. I don't feel mean enough. You know what I mean? I'm just a pushover. That's the thing. You know what? I'm not going to be able to match up to your dad. I'm not going to be able to be as abusive as he was. You know why? I'm a nice guy. I'm a nice white man. I'm a nice white mentor man, a nice white father figure. You know what I'm talking about?

DEREK: I don't need a father figure.

[Derek is lying on the floor on his stomach. David sits beside him, leaning on him with his arm.]

DAVID: About nice white men. You know what I mean, Derek?

DEREK: [Laughing.]

DAVID: They're really nice people. Soft, nice. Nice white men. Father figure mentors.

DEREK: I was told that in high school. Lots of nice white men in high school.

DAVID: Oh yeah?

DEREK: Yeah.

DAVID: We have a problem here.

DEREK: Yeah, we do have a problem.

DAVID: A big problem.

DEREK: Because you're a nice white man. [Bowing to David, and taking on the stereotype of a slave.] Massah. What you need, Massah? What you need me to do?

DAVID: I need you to get my bedclothes and my mattress. And I want you to set everything up for me.

DEREK: That's what my daddy did.

DAVID: Your daddy told you to do that?

DEREK: Alright, Massah. I'll clean up the shit. Let me get the toilet bowl. Whatever the Massah told him to do, he did.

DAVID: It's a long tradition, a long tradition.

DEREK: There's a whole lot of white massahs.

DAVID: I could use you, you know. My wife, you know, she's on me all the time about an equal relationship. I need someone who could really be a servant. I think you would be fine.

DEREK: Oh, Massah, whatever you say. There's one thing though, Massah.

DAVID: What's that?

DEREK: Don't let me get near your white wife. You know what they say about that.

DAVID: I'm not worried about that, because we have ways to deal with that, very quickly.

DEREK: Oh yeah. I won't get out of order. I promise you, Massah. My dad didn't get out of order.

DAVID: You're pretty comfortable with this issue, this race thing.

DEREK: Oh, my daddy used to come home and call me a nigger many times.

DAVID: Nigger? The N word.

DEREK: You can't say that word!

DAVID: I can't say that word?

DEREK: No.

DAVID: But this is developmental transformations. I can say whatever I want to. This is just play, it's not real, so I can say nigger.

DEREK: Yeah, right, Cracker! Honky.

DAVID: I can say nigger and you can call me honky.

DEREK: That's not the same.

DAVID: But here in the playspace, it's not really nigger.

DEREK: Oh, it's something else?

DAVID: It's play. Right?

DEREK: Right.

DAVID: It's play . . . Nigger.

DEREK: [Whipping David.] You wanna say it again?

DAVID: Yeah. Nigger. [Derek mimes kicking David repeatedly.] You fucking asshole. You fucking black, fucking weak, scared. . . . Ow. Ow. Ow. You're not letting me get up. Let me get up so I can fall more. You really need to give it to me. [David gets up but is beaten down again.] AHH.

DAVID: Now that's much better. Isn't that better?

DEREK: Alright, backhand. [Derek backhands David.]

DAVID: AHHH.

DEREK: That hurt. Wait, right there, right there. [Derek hits David again.]

DAVID: Ahh.

DEREK: [Derek kicks David.]

DAVID: We're enjoying this too much. . . . Were you stepping on me?

DEREK: [David is lying on floor while Derek puts one foot on his back, standing over him.] I am king of the niggers. Thank you, thank you. And look who is down on the ground. The good ole White man. [Laughs.]

DAVID: Oh, great Nigger King. Oh, great Nigger King. I need to, I need to, I need to honor you. I need to look up to you.

DEREK: Please do so.

DAVID: My whole life I've been wanting to be a Nigger King. I want to be black.

DEREK: Yes, please.

DAVID: I want to be black.

DEREK: From now on you won't call me black. You'll call me . . .

DAVID: I want to be black. I want to be from a family of modest means.

DEREK: Of who?

DAVID: Modest means. Poor.

DEREK: You want to be poor?

DAVID: I want to be poor. I want to be a poor black man.

DEREK: You want to eat spam every night? Canned corned beef?

DAVID: I want my daddy to waste all my money.

DEREK: Yeah we can do that. Please. Bread money? We don't need bread money. Here you go. . . . Where's my dinner? I need some dinner.

DAVID: OK, I'll bring you dinner. Alright, Daddy. Here you go. [David serves dinner to Derek.]

DEREK: Canned corned beef. Why don't we have any steak?

DAVID: We don't have any steak.

DEREK: Get me some Kool-aid.

DAVID: We only got the lemon-lime that you don't like.

DEREK: Shit, I can't even eat this. Lemon-lime? I want tropical punch.

DAVID: We don't have any tropical punch.

DEREK: Get the fucking tropical punch!

DAVID: Billy drank the rest of the tropical punch.

DEREK: Billy?

DAVID: If you have a problem with it, beat him. Not me. I don't drink the tropical punch, because I know what will happen if I drink the tropical punch.

DEREK: You think you're trying to be smart?

DAVID: Yeah.

DEREK: You're really trying to be smart. [Derek begins pulling his belt off.]

DAVID: No! Daddy! Daddy! Billy! Billy did it.

DEREK: Get the fuck out of this house and go to the army. You're a white ass nigger, huh?

DAVID: I'm a scared nigger! AHH. [Sits in the witnessing circle.]

DEREK: What's gonna happen with this motherfucker? I don't want no more damn spam. Fucking canned corn beef. One hard-boiled egg. And all the Wonder Bread I could eat. You gotta have the welfare cheese. The welfare cheese takes about five hours to melt. [Laughing and sitting on floor.]

DAVID: [Coming out of witnessing circle.] Ding dong. Ding dong. Hello? Your Wonder Bread order is here. We got Wonder Bread.

DEREK: That's not real Wonder Bread.

DAVID: We got real Wonder Bread. Contributions from a nice white man who's taking pity on you.

DEREK: I don't need no damn pity.

DAVID: No, you need food. And we've got food. We got Wonder Bread and we got cheese.

DEREK: Where's the powdered milk?

DAVID: It takes a while to melt, but it's cheese nonetheless. There's a very guilty white man who wants to help you out.

DEREK: [Lying on floor, laughing.] You touched me.

DAVID: Here comes the cheese. It's a bleeding heart. You're not going to meet him for about twenty years.

DEREK: I don't want no damn shit from the government. I don't want the government to give me shit.

DAVID: It's the bleeding liberal white government giving Wonder bread and cardboard cheese to this black citizen.

DEREK: [Laughing.]

DAVID: You see the label?

DEREK: Government cheese.

DAVID: Yeah, see. It says here, the label in the small print. Gee, we're sorry for the 350 years of slavery. We're sorry. Have some Wonder Bread on us. . . . Isn't that brilliantly wonderful. Doesn't that warm your heart?

DEREK: Oh yeah. It warms my heart. [Lying on floor.]

DAVID: Where is your heart? [Leaning on Derek, placing his hand on Derek's heart.]

DEREK: I have none.

DAVID: I don't feel anything.

DEREK: Not for a very long time. There is no beating.

DAVID: There's no beating of your heart.

DEREK: I'm like a dead man.

DAVID: Well, I took a CPR course once so . . . [Begins pressing on heart.]

DEREK: Don't break my ribs. You can break them now because they've been broken before.

DAVID: I like breaking ribs.

DEREK: Go ahead.

DAVID: I'm not really going to break them. I wouldn't. I mean, maybe.

DEREK: Go ahead then. Go ahead.

DAVID: Gonna break your fucking ribs.

DEREK: Go ahead.

DAVID: Oh shut up, you punk.

DEREK: You're calling me a punk? [Derek tries to sit up, but David pushes him back down.]

DAVID: Yeah. You're no son of mine. You're a piece of shit. You're a piece of shit.

DEREK: Get the fuck away from me. I'm a piece of shit? You're a piece of shit.

DAVID: Oh, you should've told me then.

DEREK: Yeah? Like I could.

DAVID: But you couldn't. You were a coward. So what you were six or eight or whatever age you were and he was what? Thirty-five? Forty?

DEREK: Nice old hands. A lot of veins going through that hand.

DAVID: Pow, yeah. Well, you were a coward for not speaking up and explaining to him about perpetrators and victims. How come you couldn't do that?

DEREK: Cause I was a retard.

DAVID: Cause you were a retard.

DEREK: Cause I was a retard.

DAVID: Yeah. You probably still are.

DEREK: You better shut up.

DAVID: Yeah.

DEREK: I'm a retard.

DAVID: Hey, white people are trying to help you out, but at bottom . . . retard.

DEREK: [Laughing.] Oooh . . . Those are fighting words. [David goes into witnessing circle.]

DAVID: See the witnessing circle? You can't get me in the witnessing circle. So I'm safe. Derek, you notice the color of the witnessing circle?

DEREK: Yeah. [On all fours, back turned to David.] PLLL. That's what I think of you and your witnessing circles.

DAVID: Derek, do you think we make black witnessing circles? No. The answer is no.

DEREK: We should make a black witnessing circle. Why isn't it black? They're always holding me down, my papa always told me. [David exits the witnessing circle.] Always holding me down. Not that powdered crappy milk. Not that hard to melt cheese. Not the slapping. Not the cussing. Not the putdown. Not the little nigger. Little nigger. Little nigger. You got a bad attitude, nigger. That was the nice word. Nigger. Nigger. Nigger. Nigger. Nigger. Nigger. Nigger.

DAVID: Nigger.

DEREK: Nigger. Nigger. Nigger.

DAVID: Nigger. Nigger . . . [David and Derek speak in gibberish.]

DEREK: [Laughing.] You're bigger by an afro. [David and Derek face off.]

DAVID: How come I'm not really scared of you?

DEREK: Do you think you could be afraid of me?

DAVID: I could work on it, but it hasn't really . . .

[Both begin bumping stomachs.]

DEREK: Are you afraid now? [Moves arms out.]

DAVID: No. In fact, that was a very nice move you made. [David allows his arms to flow up, like a dance, mirroring Derek.]

DEREK: That was kind of fun. [They create dancelike movements together.]

DAVID: Let's do it again.

DEREK: You make me afraid of you.

DAVID: I'm not afraid of you.

DEREK: I'm from a tough neighborhood. I was raised with stuff.

DAVID: But I'm not afraid of you. I'm not afraid of black people. I'm not afraid of you.

DEREK: What if I pulled down my pants. What up, dog? How you living? Are you afraid of me? Are you fucking afraid of me?

DAVID: No, I'm not afraid of you.

DEREK: You're not afraid of me?

DAVID: That's right. I'm just a nice white guy. And you're a nice black guy.

DEREK: Oh, I'm nice?

DAVID: Yeah.

DEREK: You're gonna see a black guy at ten o'clock at night you're not going to go on the other side of the street.

DAVID: You wanna know what I actually think? [Putting arm around Derek.]

DEREK: Yeah. Don't put your hands on me. Keep it from a distance.

DAVID: I thought we worked this thing through already.

DEREK: Worked it through?

DAVID: Yeah, this abuse thing. I thought it was worked though. Well, maybe there are other parts that you don't like. You are sorta cute.

DEREK: Cute?

DAVID: Sorta cute. I mean I really like you.

DEREK: Don't touch me when you say that. [Laughs.]

DAVID: You are kind of cute. You have a little bit of the masculine part of you, the feminine part of you sort of integrated nicely. You're wounded in an attractive way. People must love you.

DEREK: I'm cute in a wounded kind of way. [Laughs.]

DAVID: For people you want to help, you must be irresistible. [Derek laughs. David enters witnessing circle.]

DEREK: I'm going to be cute in a wounded kind of way.

DAVID: You've already done it. [Derek acts this out.] Can I just sort of gaze at you from here?

DEREK: Please do. Here I am, Mr. Black Man, 2005. The cute but wounded Mr. Black Man. Oh thank you, thank you, thank for the applause. Ahhh, that's the wounded side of me. Wait, let me see what the cute part is. No, not the nose. No, not the lips.

DAVID: Can I interrupt this moment. Can we do like a love scene?

DEREK: A love scene?

DAVID: Yeah, a love scene.

DEREK: Who's going to be the aggressor?

DAVID: I'm gonna be the lover. [David waves his hands up and down.] And you're going to be the lover. Not love. No. Just love. Between one human being and another. Not black or white. Not dominant or submissive.

DEREK: I don't trust many people who love me.

DAVID: Why not? Love is a wonderful thing.

DEREK: Oh alright. OK. [David exits the witnessing circle.]

DAVID: Have you ever done a love scene?

DEREK: Uh uh, not that I know of.

DAVID: The way you stroke your hair. It's just incredible. You have such grace.

DEREK: Thank you.

DAVID: You do. You're very authentic, genuine. Your voice is a little rough.

DEREK: Yeah.

DAVID: But no one's perfect. And it has nothing to do with love. Love has to do with . . .

DEREK: The heart.

DAVID: Your heart.

DEREK: OK. Love me. It's time that somebody loved me.

DAVID: It's time that somebody loved you. You got a little tense. Can I touch? I'll do it very lightly. [David puts arm around Derek.]

DEREK: Thank you very much.

DAVID: We don't want to go over the top. Because love takes its time.

DEREK: Everything takes its time. So how are we gonna fall in love?

DAVID: I've fallen in love.

DEREK: You've fallen in love already?

DAVID: Yes. With you.

DEREK: With me?

DAVID: Yes.

DEREK: Some say that's easy to do. [Laughing uncomfortably.] Laugh along with me.

DAVID: I laugh at you for falling in love with me. I want you to fall in love with me. We only have about ten minutes. I gotta work hard at this. I have to see that I actually like you. I do, I actually like you.

DEREK: Uh huh.

DAVID: No, really.

DEREK: Really?

DAVID: Yeah.

DEREK: Go ahead. I'll keep my eyes closed. What are you falling in love with? Tell me. My ears are open.

DAVID: You have great skin. You have a certain sincerity. Kind of beatific face.

[David and Derek begin to dance. David leads.]

DEREK: A beatific face.

DAVID: I like how you took control of that.

DEREK: I can do that once in a while.

DAVID: You can do that once in a while.

DEREK: Go ahead. Keep the compliments coming.

DAVID: You're in touch with your wounded self. You understand your history. Maybe not your future, but your history is good.

DEREK: My history is intact.

DAVID: Yes, your history is intact, but the future is a little weak. That will come.

DEREK: The future will come. I'm not even worried about my future. Come back. I'm enjoying this love part. . . . Come on, keep the compliments coming.

DAVID: There's too much on the footwork.

DEREK: Yeah, that's what I do. I keep moving.

DAVID: Yes. The footwork.

[Both stop dancing and face each other, holding hands.]

DEREK: To be or not to be, that is the question.

DAVID: Just think of what you could've done with a caring white man.

DEREK: [Laughing.] How about a caring black man? Think about what I could do with that. I have to be on the white man's side all the time. [David and Derek begin pulling each other back and forth.] Come over here a little bit.

DAVID: Come over here, to my side.

DEREK: Come on over to my side. Ahh.

DAVID: Come here. [David grabs Derek's arm.]

DEREK: Where are we going? Where?

DAVID: Just follow me. Come on. Come on. Trust me, trust me.

DEREK: I'm tired of trusting.

DAVID: No. No, you have to learn to trust people.

DEREK: How about I go on my own. Let go of my arm. Let go of my arm.

DAVID: I should let go of your arm, but then I'd be letting go of your arm. I should let go of your arm? I should let go of your arm. Alright, I've let go of your arm. [David is still holding Derek's arm.] There you go. How's that feel?

DEREK: You're still holding my arm.

DAVID: Alright, I'll let go. [He does not.]

DEREK: Feels a little lighter.

DAVID: Just follow me.

DEREK: Why don't you follow me? Take my arm. Let me grab your arm. Come here. [Derek takes David's arm.] We don't need to say anything. We just need to walk.

DAVID: How about we talk?

DEREK: No, I talk a lot.

DAVID: I like to talk, too. We can express our feelings.

DEREK: We can go feed the squirrels.

DAVID: Yeah, squirrels are good.

DEREK: You want to feed them? Let's give them bread, from the local bodega.

DAVID: Enough of that. That was a nice scene. I wonder what it would be like to grow old with you and walk in the park and feed the squirrels and the birds.

DEREK: A lot of pigeons, a lot of shit. Too many dogs. A couple of crack vials. You just ignore them, though. You just try to focus on the squirrels. They'll even take them from your hand, too.

DAVID: Oh yeah?

DEREK: I think I'm all walked out.

DAVID: Yeah.

DEREK: You're not half bad, you know that? Like the man with two brains.

DAVID: You're not half bad, yourself.

DEREK: Remember, I'm cute, too.

DAVID: Very cute. Remember when I first met you and we did that scene in Landy's class years ago and afterwards?

DEREK: I can't remember.

DAVID: That's when we first struck up the relationship.

DEREK: You ignored me.

DAVID: No, I didn't ignore you.

DEREK: You were totally into yourself.

DAVID: I was thinking I was totally focused on you, but I was focused on myself.

DEREK: Are we there yet?

DAVID: I don't know. Probably not.

DEREK: I'm going to sit down. I want to sit down.

DAVID: Let me help you. Sit down. [Derek sits on floor.] Are you comfortable?

DEREK: Yeah.

DAVID: Can I get you a pillow? A blanket over here? Would you like some Kool-Aid? We have some nice cold Kool-Aid. Tropical punch? And guess what? I have a steak for you. A steak sandwich. [David serves Derek.]

DEREK: Steak? No. No. I'm trying to get away from steak. How about a little couscous, a little feta cheese sprinkled over the top, some green scallions, a little bit of tomato. And um, can I get some bubble gum?

DAVID: Here you go. Somehow I just don't think that's going to be enough.

DEREK: That's enough. I had to survive on a hard-boiled egg. Let me alone with my couscous, please. [Derek puts head in hands.]

DAVID: Are you sure this will be enough? I really feel bad that I haven't been able to give you something you're going to use. So I'll leave you alone now. Bye. You sure there's nothing I can get you? . . . Take a minute.

[David walks to the witnessing circle. Derek remains seated on the floor, legs crossed, head down for several minutes. David exits and then Derek exits. They shake hands.]

Reflections on the Session

Immediately after the session, Johnson reflected upon the experience in a rather personal way. He focused upon the moment toward the end when he was walking around the space with Derek hand in hand. He mentioned that Derek would not allow him to fully hold his hand, only his thumb. For Johnson (in Landy 2005), that reluctance signaled Derek's resistance to the relationship. Very openly, Johnson expressed his sadness:

> There was a sadness that I started to feel at the end which I think for me related to . . . reach[ing] across some divide to be with him. There's a feeling that the divide is too wide. Not just between us, but even within. And I started to feel it within myself, too. So I think at the end I was filled up with the phrase: "I'm sorry." I started to feel: "I'm sorry," although I'm not sure what I'm sorry for. You know, it's not about race; it's about something more intimate than that.

This was the third of three sessions for Derek, and he had already played with moments of closeness and distance, testing out his comfort level with Landy and Garcia, both of whom took on the qualities of a reparative father and mother. He had battled tears in working with the distance of role method, which he later expressed in working through the cathartic method of psychodrama. But this approach was different. Johnson dared to take on the role of abusive father and then dared to play with other unplayable themes—race, sex, and intimacy. It could be that in the intensity of the play, Derek felt overwhelmed and needed to hold back his hand in order to protect himself from a flood of feelings.

What did Johnson mean when he said: "I started to feel: 'I'm sorry,' although I'm not sure what I'm sorry for." Was he sorry for being too provocative or for losing Derek in their walk toward intimacy? Did this experience trigger something within him of his own experience with his father, or of his white liberal guilt? Or was Johnson, as father, simply responding to Derek's need as son to receive an apology for years of abuse? Johnson was not aware of what had transpired in the first session where Derek wrote the words, "I'm Sorry," on the blackboard, fulfilling a wish that his father would ask his son for forgiveness. That early moment of hope, filled with so much pain, was focused upon Derek. At the end of the third session, the moment was transformed from client to therapist. And when Johnson, as therapist, experienced regret, he reminded us that in developmental transformations, as the therapist engages deeply in the play, his own issues can easily emerge.

It could be that at the end of the session both client and therapist were playing at the stage of Body as Presence, marked by viewing one another as objects of attraction and repulsion, experiencing both fear and support from the other. It could be that the regret is about having not reached the final level of Body as Presence, which Johnson (2000b) refers to as Deep Play, a moment where "client and therapist are intensely aware of each other and their bodies, and are freed up enough to work on their feelings of being bound or restrained by each other in play" (92). However, it is important to note that Johnson does not believe that this deeper level must be realized in developmental transformations, especially within a single session.

Johnson also reflected upon the importance of touch in developmental transformations, noting that it is a natural human activity, and that he always uses touch in response to a cue from the client. Referring to the beginning of the session, Johnson (in Landy 2005) said: "I requested that he touch one part of his body to me, but it was how he touched me that let me know something about his comfort with touch. And the way that he put his finger on my chest, I knew that he would respond to my pushing him." Referring to Derek's need for physical closeness and distance, Johnson added: "There were elements where he initiated and wanted some physical pushing or something. In general he did not. When he was kicking or hitting he was more comfortable in miming it and pretending to hit me."

Derek also reflected upon the issue of touch. He pointed out that in the love scene and the walking scene, he consciously held back both physically and emotionally. He stated (Derek in Landy 2005): "It stems from my own issues with men and not wanting any men that close to me. The love me scene wasn't necessarily in a sexual way; it was more emotional. I never had men come that close to me." He was, however, able to tolerate a certain level of ambiguity in both scenes because of "the deep need that I've always wanted for a man to love me, like a father." And he was able, finally, to transform from one who could not assert his boundaries in terms of touch to one who could say in the playspace: "Why don't you follow me? Take my arm."

A year later, Derek (2006) again spoke of the difficulty in playing out the love scene with Johnson, attributing the difficulty to his relationship with his abusive father. And yet, he was able to proclaim: "Our shared dance together in the playspace felt like a celebration of the beauty I never felt as a child."

Derek also reflected on playing out the dynamics of race through the roles of master and slave. He recalled that in growing up he had to be a "Yes, sir; no, sir" person in order to appease both his father and the white authority figures in his young life. In playing with the word "nigger" and in expressing his rage toward his father, "who reinforced the vile word," and those white people, who then as now perpetuate racist attitudes, he was able to release deep feelings. He said, "I felt like I took the word and redefined it according to my terms, and I was in control of the situation, for once."

In retrospect, Derek felt empowered by his session in developmental transformations. The child part of him was able to find a voice. And with the passage of time, he realized that at the end, when he rejected the foo. that Johnson was serving him, he did so out of guilt. One year later he (Derek 2006) was able to say: "I am able to receive and give gifts on my own free will. . . . That is one of the greatest steps to freedom for me as a man growing toward forgiveness towards an abusive father."

THE POLARITIES

Emotion and Distance

As in role theory, developmental transformations offers an understanding of emotional expression in terms of levels and degrees of distance. Certainly a great deal of emotion is generated when one is challenged, as Derek was, to confront a perpetrator. And because the approach is so much about playing with shameful material, such as abuse, race, and sex, the client is thrust into emotionally charged scenes. So how then does this approach grapple with emotion?

According to Freud, the reason why people repress painful memories is that they are too frightening to be brought to consciousness. Freud's method of solving the problem of accessing repressed material was to have clients approach their memories in an indirect way, speaking about whatever came to their minds freely and spontaneously. When a painful memory came to awareness, it was verbalized and then analyzed so that the client could understand its source and its manifestations in feeling and behavior. For Freud, catharsis was about recalling repressed feelings and giving language to these feelings, thus diminishing the affective power of the memory. The language, the analysis, and the insight distanced the potentially overpowering flood of emotions that might erupt when the repressed material is brought to consciousness.

In developmental transformations, the repressed material is expressed through the client's body in relationship to the body of the therapist which, in many ways, brings clients closer to their feelings, especially as they reenact past trauma. The reason clients like Derek can work with deeply charged emotional content is that they do so within the confines of a fictional playspace. When working with the potentially disturbing word "nigger" Johnson (in Landy 2005) reminds Derek: "I can say whatever I want to. This is just play, it's not real, so I can say nigger." The playspace distances the potential volatility associated with the demeaning word. It offers a clear restraint against harm (see Dintino and Johnson 1996) and provides an emotional safety net for the client.

In applying the distancing model of Scheff and Landy to developmental transformations, this approach suggests a move toward underdistance, that

onal reaction, in its use of touch and provocative action.
his approach creates distance by its theatricality and play-
run at the unbearable heaviness of being. Further distance
as the therapist helps clients transform from role to role and scene
to scene, discouraging them from attaching to any one role or theme. In addition, the artifice of the witnessing circle also tends to distance clients from
taking themselves too seriously. When witnessed, the client is a performer,
playing at his trauma rather than reliving it.

The distancing paradigm is also applicable to the therapist. He can retreat
to the witnessing circle, or he can initiate a transformation when the scene
feels too heated. However, because he remains the client's play object and
coactor within the drama, he has little opportunity to fully disengage and
direct the action from the outside. Thus there is the possibility of merging
with the roles played and, at times, unconsciously imposing his own drama
within the playspace. We get a glimpse of this when Johnson debriefs after
his session with Derek and openly addresses his feeling of incompletion,
saying, "I'm not sure what I'm sorry for."

Fiction and Reality

The concept of the playspace is clearly defined and exemplified by Johnson (2000b). It is a hallmark of developmental transformations and one that
resonates with a number of action approaches to healing including the liminal experience of the shaman, the transitional space of D. W. Winnicott, the
locus nascendi of psychodrama, and the aesthetic distance in role method.
The playspace is the figurative place of encounter where clients are able to
explore several levels of relationship as embodied by the therapist. These levels include the fictional as the therapist takes on projections from the client
and the actual as the client engages with the therapist in the here and now.
Most complex, the playspace is a transitional place existing between the fiction of the dramatic action and the everyday life of the actors.

Johnson has devised a number of techniques to help clients realize that the
playspace contains both fictional and reality elements. One, called bracketing,
concerns moving the scene into a fully fictional frame, such as a television
show, a movie, or a play. Through bracketing, the therapist reminds the client
that the work is a fiction. Another technique, called transforming to the here
and now, has the opposite effect, decreasing distance as it moves the action to
the present moment of reality. As mentioned above, when Johnson reminds
Derek that in the playspace he can use the word "nigger," he brings Derek
temporarily out of the fiction and into the reality of the moment.

As in role method and psychodrama, both aspects of fiction and reality
are present in the playspace, and the therapist's job is to move the client in
and out of both levels in order to fully explore the emerging issues.

Verbal and Nonverbal Expression

Of the three action approaches featured in the film, developmental transformations is the most nonverbal. Like all forms of action psychotherapy, there is a certain degree of verbal exchange as client and therapist set up boundaries and rules and engage in roles and narratives. Yet in this approach, the emphasis is upon embodied action. When Derek and Johnson play out scenes of abuser and victim, master and slave, lover and love object, the most powerful moments arise from the physical interactions. In the session, there are many moments of aggressive, ironic, and tender touch. At the beginning, Johnson plays a dog owner who kicks Derek as his dog. Later, Johnson as abusive master provokes Derek to whip him. And then, toward the end, Johnson moves the drama into a love scene that is both uncomfortable and tender, expressed physically through dance and through the struggle to hold one another as they walk through a symbolic park.

The nonverbal quality of developmental transformations places it firmly within its sources in dance and theater. As dance, the primary language of the client in that of movement. And as theater, modeled after the physicality of Grotowski, commedia dell'arte, and theater games, the body of the actor/client again becomes the primary focus of the action.

Action and Reflection

Developmental transformations is primarily about action and its flow. However, Johnson also writes about moments when the action stalls or even halts. He refers to this as the impasse and suggests a number of techniques to help move the client back into the flow of the drama. Johnson's approach is unique among other action approaches in that it is fully centered in the playspace, where the therapist and client work to maintain the flow from one role and one scene to another. There are rarely moments of verbal reflection following the play. Johnson does not, however, dismiss the concept of reflection, but rather sees it as emerging from the play. Reflective moments in the playspace occur as the therapist transforms the scene to the here and now and provides commentary within the play frame. We see this in the film when Johnson reminds Derek that it is acceptable to speak forbidden words in the playspace.

We have seen how Moreno also was able to express commentary in psychodramatic action. However, he made clear that following the action, all players were required to separate themselves from the *locus nascendi* and then engage with the audience through a process of sharing. At that point, the therapist might also offer a reflective commentary upon the psychodramatic action. During the psychodramatic sharing, the group experience is

d deepened as others, identified with the protagonist, are
' own hunger for enactment.

  .., two levels of reflection follow the de-roling of the actors
      ͜vement away from the fiction of the drama. The first concerns a
  ͜ʌection upon the fictional roles, and the second, a connection between
the fictional roles and the everyday lives of the role-players.

Directive and Nondirective
Action/Transference and Countertransference

In theory, developmental transformations is a nondirective approach,
certainly much more so than role method and psychodrama. In fact, Johnson (1991) refers to Carl Rogers as a significant source of inspiration.
Rogers was long associated with innovating nondirective, person-centered
psychotherapy, a radical shift from the reigning psychoanalytic perspective
of the analyst as more knowledgeable and powerful than the patient. For
Rogers, the focus of the therapy was on the patients who were prized by
their therapist and encouraged to direct their own healing.

In shifting the role of the therapist from that of director to that of actor,
Johnson allows the nondirective process to unfold in a spontaneous fashion. In practice, however, the therapist is also guiding the action from
within. The therapist as actor is trained to read the clients' actions and to
guide the clients in such a fashion that they reveal and transform their
dilemmas. We see this clearly in Johnson's work with Derek as the therapist
in role moves the client from scenes of aggression and humiliation to those
of intimacy and love. It is certainly true that Derek initiates many actions,
especially in the sequence involving master and slave. But it is equally true
that Derek's actions are directed or at least transformed in the drama by actions on the part of the therapist, most notably when Johnson suggests a
love scene from the vantage point of the witnessing circle.

In that Johnson interacted directly in role-play with Derek, he invited a
deep level of engagement and thus of potential transference from Derek.
Their work seemed to challenge the idea that the distanced therapist invokes the most transference. Playing out many aspects of the abusive father,
Johnson certainly provoked the father transference. And yet, in that he kept
transforming from role to role, not only of abuser, but also of lover, he did
not allow Derek to hold on to the kind of transference that was more clearly
evoked by Landy as father and Garcia as mother. As the roles shifted, the
possibilities of entering into and resolving the transference also shifted. At
the end, Derek did not fully perceive Johnson as any of the roles he had
played. He was not the abusive father or even the potentially loving father,
attempting to feed his hungry son. He was, in fact, a person with many potential personae, an actor, after all. As such, at the end, Derek moved closer

toward the level of Body as Presence. Although he could not accept the touch or the food offered by Johnson as loving father, he could, at least in retrospect, accept the attempts of David Johnson, the person, to reach out and touch him on a deep level.

At the end of the session, when Johnson mentions that he is sorry, it is unclear as to the source of his regret. From his own point of view (Institute for Developmental Transformations 2006), the moment was not one of countertransference, but one that emerged within the fictional dynamic of father and son. But it might also be true that the moment was about an unresolved personal issue. Because he and others who practice developmental transformations sometimes play at the borders of aggression and intimacy, it can be difficult to let go of the induced feelings. This issue is well known to actors who play highly emotionally charged roles, especially those trained in intense psychophysical techniques developed by Artaud and Grotowski. Without a period of closure and reflection, such roles often linger.

Because of the intensity of developmental transformations, even as it moves from one role and one scene to another, expressed through exaggerated and comedic action, strong feelings of transference and countertransference may be invoked, in ways different from other approaches, such as role method, psychodrama, and even the early somatic experimentation of Wilhelm Reich. In the latter approaches, the therapist remains separate from the client, directing the action from the outside and thus potentially providing an extra measure of distance. While engaging in action from inside the drama, it is easier to lose, however temporarily, the guiding qualities of the director.

Like many innovative thinkers throughout the history of action psychotherapy, Johnson has been unafraid to challenge traditional dictates of the therapeutic process. In doing so, however, his approach raises many important questions about the effects of the practice on both the client and the therapist in terms of touch and interpersonal boundaries, provocation and containment, concerns certainly raised at least since the earliest days of psychoanalysis. Among the three approaches, developmental transformations seem to be the least distanced as the themes are "unplayable" and as the body of the therapist is the object of play. Yet, like role method, developmental transformations is highly theatrical, as clients play forbidden games with a wink and a smile. And, according to the Institute for Developmental Transformations (2006), developmental transformations is containing because of the embodied presence of the therapist and the awareness on the part of the client that within the playspace, the therapist is fearless.

7

A Comparison of the Action Psychotherapies: Toward a Model of Theory and Practice

The idea of a formal method for healing the psyche reaches back into time and cuts across ancient and contemporary cultures. Traditional healing most always was characterized by expressive, action approaches. With the advent of Western medicine, such methods were rejected, only to be slowly rediscovered. Several of the early psychoanalysts returned to action as a means of redressing imbalances in the wounded psyche. Although we have not surveyed many post-Freudian developments in psychoanalysis, quite a few contemporary approaches readily embrace such dramatic concepts as enactment (see Johan 1992; Field 2006) and encounter (see Greenberg 1996), play and transitional space (see Winnicott 1971). Of the various forms of action psychotherapy practiced today, we have focused upon three: role theory/method of drama therapy, psychodrama, and developmental transformations, and have looked at their historical analogues in the work of such practitioners as Jung, Rank, Ferenczi, Reich, Murray, Kelly, Moreno, Perls, and others.

In drawing the line from the early days of psychoanalysis to more contemporary forms of action psychotherapy, we can see many connections. Johnson (1991) cites Freud's fundamental rule of free association as central to his understanding of developmental transformations as a spontaneous, uncensored flow of action. Freud challenged patients to suspend self-judgment and linear thought processes. For Freud, patients required the freedom to engage with forbidden areas of the psyche in order to bring unconscious material into the light of day. For Johnson, clients also require a method of free association to unlock repressed experience. The difference is that Johnson's vehicle is somatic rather than verbal, and his goal is transformation rather than insight.

195

Johnson also connects his work to Jung's method of active imagination in that Jung moved from the Freudian task of invoking thoughts to the more expressive one of invoking images. Jung (1947), foreshadowing the work of creative arts therapists, described his innovation in free association as follows:

> I took up a dream image or an association of the patient's and with this as a point of departure, set him the task of elaborating . . . his theme by giving free rein to his fantasy. This . . . could be done in any number of ways, dramatic, dialectic, visual, acoustic, or in the form of dancing, painting, drawing, or modeling (202).

Landy, as we have seen, connects his work not only to Jung, but also to Rank and Ferenczi, Erikson, and Murray. His most significant influence among the early psychotherapists, however, is that of Moreno. Although purporting to have developed a fully original conception of psychotherapy, opposed to what he called Freud's science fiction (Z. T. Moreno 2006b), Moreno was certainly aware of Freud's ideas of unconscious dynamics, catharsis, and free association. As modernist ideas that influenced a great deal of Western art and culture in the early part of the twentieth century, they shaped as well as were shaped by the particular genius of Freud. Further, Moreno recapitulated, perhaps unwittingly, many of the experiments in psychotherapy through the body, imagination, and spirit of his contemporaries, Jung, Rank, Ferenczi, and Reich.

In the previous chapters, we have explored in some detail three approaches to action psychotherapy and contrasted them in terms of several polarities of emotion and distance, fiction and reality, verbal and nonverbal expression, action and reflection, directive and nondirective action. Now let us compare these approaches with each other and with their predecessors in psychoanalysis and related disciplines to develop an integrated model of theory and practice in the action psychotherapies.

THEORY

Shared Assumptions in the Action Psychotherapies

The action psychotherapies share several common assumptions about the nature of the psyche and of healing. For one, action psychotherapists present a holistic point of view. The human being is a totality of somatic, affective, cognitive, social, spiritual, and aesthetic dimensions. This perspective has developed gradually from Freud's initial understanding of mind as comprised of id, the primitive, affect-based aspects of the unconscious; ego, the rational processes of everyday reality; and superego, the self-regulating processes based in the demands of the social world. Jung and later Rank added the spiritual dimension, which harkens back to traditional forms of healing, best exemplified in shamanism. Ferenczi added an interpersonal dimension, and Reich added a somatic and later cosmic dimension. The full holistic spectrum came into being with Moreno's notion of healing the psyche and the world through psychodrama, sociodrama, and axiodrama, incorporating the personal, the social, and the cosmic elements of human life. Perls recapitulated this holistic vision in his focus upon completing the Gestalt of psyche and soma. The vision of treating the full human being is well exemplified in most all forms of drama therapy.

A second commonality shared by the action psychotherapists is that of recognizing dramatic action as an essential means of healing. These therapists draw their understanding from the natural impulse of the child at play, an unconscious means of reflecting, rehearsing, and revising everyday experience. Action psychotherapists apply the unconscious impulse of the child at play to the conscious process of treating the adult, as well as child, in need of healing. Action demands a holistic response to the existential question, Who am I?, moving the patient from the couch to the playspace, from the exclusivity of cognition to expression through the body and the emotions.

Although Freud developed psychoanalysis based on an understanding of psychosexual experiences of children, his clear focus was upon the adult who accessed the child through memories recalled in treatment. As Freud saw play in the adult as childish and as a form of acting out, his was a verbal cure that demanded a mature ability to articulate and to reflect upon the meaning of past experience. Jung worked to understand the profound significance of the adult at play. His discovery came at a time of personal crisis, following his break with Freud. During this period, he recalled the pleasurable play activities of his childhood and began to play with stones and found objects, reconstructing a solid inner foundation upon which to build his mature ideas concerning the images of the collective unconscious. Later, Ferenczi developed an active technique of treatment, engaging more directly with the patient, returning to ideas rejected by Freud, especially those involving catharsis. When Ferenczi developed an analytical process that proceeded according to the principles of child analysis, he more fully embraced a playful, active approach.

But Jung, Ferenczi, and his collaborator, Rank, still remained, for the most part, within the orthodox setting of the consulting room. It was Wilhelm Reich, the most radical of the early analysts, who truly moved his patients off the couch, engaging not only with their words, but also with their bodies. Moreno took these experiments with action to the next logical step, creating an active therapy that was fully dramatic. He was the first to speak of therapy as an encounter between client and therapist. He was the first to demonstrate the wisdom and power of reworking the past through direct dramatic action, and he was the first to fully transform the clinical consulting room into a therapeutic stage.

Shared Concepts in the Action Psychotherapies

Although each of the action psychotherapies offers different conceptual pieces, there are several commonalities. Most all are dramatic in that they proceed through role and enactment in role. The central premise of the three featured approaches is that clients take on one or more roles and engage in some form of therapeutic enactment with the therapist and/or auxiliaries. The idea of role and enactment stems from shamanism, where the healer was more of a priest and performer than a physician, and the healer's knowledge was more spiritual and theatrical than biological.

Once physicians became healers and named their profession psychiatry, they rejected the theatrical and spiritual accoutrements of traditional healing. Freud and his associates did all they could to distance themselves from faith healers, spiritualists, and charlatans with no scientific training whatsoever. This might be one reason why Freud was quick to dismiss hypnosis and catharsis as valid means to uncover the content of the unconscious. Over the years, psychoanalysts were surprised to learn that some referred to them as shrinks, a term associated pejoratively with headshrinkers, traditional healers, and cannibals.

Some of the early analysts understood the significance of engaging in role reversal with their clients. We find this well expressed by Ferenczi and Rank (1925/1986) when speaking of the transference relationship:

> The analyst plays all possible roles for the unconscious of the patient. . . . Particularly important is the role of the two parental images—father and mother—in which the analyst constantly alternates (41).

We also find references in Ferenczi's work to observing the client spontaneously taking on a role to release feelings associated with a traumatic memory, as in the case of a patient with chronic asthma who regressed to the role of a child unable to breathe while under the influence of chloroform (see chapter 1). Ferenczi worked extensively with role-reversal toward the end of his career in his experiments with mutual analysis. As we have seen, Reich, too, engaged in role-play with his clients, attempting to crystallize a peak moment through the dramatic enactment.

Later Murray, Erikson, and other colleagues worked through role and dramatic enactment in their research at the Harvard Psychological Clinic and in screening military personnel for the OSS. George Kelly later developed fixed-role therapy, an approach to treating people recovering from the disasters of the Depression and the dust bowl. Moreno built his understanding of sociometry, psychodrama, and sociodrama around the role concept, and Perls understood the significance of role and counterrole in creating the dynamics of topdog and underdog in Gestalt therapy

The meaning of role and enactment varies from the early psychoanalysts who viewed these processes primarily in terms of the transference neurosis and the containing of impulsive moments of acting out, to contemporary drama therapists who view them as essential to exploring aspects of the self in relation to others. Interestingly, in the work of many contemporary psychoanalysts influenced by relational theories (see, for example, Mitchell 1988; Greenberg 1996), we find a more interactive and dramatic understanding of these terms. There is a continuity of the concepts of role and enactment over time, not only during the last century, but also further back into the history of traditional healing. As hard as some psychoanalysts have tried to quantify and analyze the unconscious, it is inevitable that moments of self-disclosure will be highly charged, leading to a range of dramatic actions as clients express themselves in all their ego states, from wounded child to angry adult. Given contemporary relational models of psychoanalysis, it becomes clear that the analyst is not a passive observer, but a cocreator of the healing drama.

One other concept shared by the action psychotherapists is that of the playspace. This notion is more shamanic than psychoanalytical in that the shaman journeys to a spiritual space, the *illud tempus* (see Eliade 1961), from which to receive the healing power of the gods to bring back to the natural world. And yet Winnicott was the first psychoanalyst to explain the relationship between mother and child, therapist and client in terms of the figurative space between them. Of this transitional playspace, Winnicott (1953) wrote: "It is the space between inner and outer world, which is also the space between people—the transitional space—that intimate relationships and creativity occur" (89). Johnson's notion of Body as Presence and of playspace echoes those of Winnicott. And in thinking about the illud tempus, literally, time now and always, as a time of origins, we come back to Moreno's notion of *status nascendi*. For contemporary action psychotherapists, the playspace is the psychological location of the drama. It is the stage that is like the world where persons reveal themselves through their personae.

Shared Therapeutic Goals in the Action Psychotherapies

As to therapeutic goals, the three featured action psychotherapists conceive of the following: balance and integration in role theory, spontaneity and creativity in psychodrama, and transformation and flow in developmental transformations. It appears that the differences among these approaches are more of degree than kind as all are about some internal shift as clients discover an expanded capacity to enact roles and tell stories freely through expressive means.

These goals are different, in general, from the cognitive ones of classical psychoanalysis, which are more about insight and understanding. Yet, throughout the history given in chapter 1, we see a shift in goals from the early work of Freud concerning the discovery of internal psychosexual dynamics to the more expressive goal of Jung in uncovering the archetypes of the unconscious and then to the most radical goal of Reich in deciphering the biophysical energy underlying the human organism. As these thinkers questioned the primacy of insight as the *sine qua non* of objectives, they led the way to later action psychotherapists. Landy adapted Jung's understanding of archetypes and polarities into his theory of role types and his goal of integration among role, counterrole, and guide. Moreno altered Ferenczi's notion of role reversal and mutuality and Reich's notion of mirroring and encounter, innovating his own goal of spontaneity training. Johnson adapted Freud's ideas of psychosexual development and free association, Reich's and Lowen's notion of flow and bioenergetics, and Winnicott's notion of transitional phenomena into his goals of development, flow, and transformation.

The Role of the Therapist in the Action Psychotherapies

In relation to the role of the therapist, the three featured action approaches are somewhat divergent. Moreno and Landy view the therapist more as a director, while Johnson views the therapist more as an actor, cocreating the drama. And yet, even in the formulations of Moreno and Landy, the director's role is not at all fixed. The director has the option of taking on a role in the client's drama as an auxiliary or double, when needed.

The therapist in role is antithetical to the classical psychoanalytic position of the distanced analyst. The reason for this separation was to foster transference on the part of the patient, a process that was intensified by the neutrality of the therapist. In later forms of psychoanalysis, initiated by Rank, Ferenczi, and Reich, the therapist engaged more directly with the patient, at times obscuring the boundaries as when Ferenczi began mutual analysis and Reich began to experiment with therapeutic touch and body manipulation. In the contemporary practice of psychoanalysis, influenced by ideas derived from object relations, ego psychology, self-psychology, relational and feminist theories, the role of the therapist becomes one of entering into relationship with the client in order to explore their intersubjectivity. With this innovation, the mutual relationship becomes much more important than the power dynamics of the expert treating the patient.

One important consideration in the dynamics of the relationship between client and therapist is that of boundaries. Applying the continuum of distance, when the boundaries are too rigid, then one will have more power over the other and provoke various projections from the other. Conversely, when the boundaries are too fluid, as in the example of Ferenczi's mutual analysis and Reich's experiments with touch and physical manipulation, neither will feel safe enough to develop a strong therapeutic alliance.

In comparing the three drama therapy approaches, it appears that role theory is the most distanced, as the therapist remains most often in the role of director, taking on auxiliary roles as needed, and as the client works through fictional roles and stories. And yet, while working this way, many clients enter deeply into their unconscious, affective worlds beneath the archetypal imagery, requiring cathartic release.

In psychodrama, the therapist also takes on the role of director, but as such moves the client toward a direct cathartic experience. As the least theatrical of the three, psychodrama works with reality-based roles and stories, thus moving clients deeply into their feelings. In doing so, it appears to be the least distanced. And yet, psychodrama can also be used to create distance through role reversal, moving a client out of an overwhelming role, and through catharsis of integration, linking emotion to reflection.

Developmental transformations is the most difficult to categorize within the spectrum of distance. On the one hand, it is closer to role theory in its theatricality and use of fictional scenarios, creating distance on the part of clients who are reminded that they are playing roles within the playspace. On the other hand, with the therapist as play object and with the emphasis upon touch and play with "unplayable" themes, it often reactivates strong feelings from the past in need of release, moving it closer to the cathartic function of psychodrama.

In all these forms, however, the therapists are mindful of working throughout the spectrum of distance and the options and implications of moving in and out of role. Most significantly, unlike some of their predecessors in psychoanalysis, drama therapists make use of the play and drama aspects of their work, reminding their clients of the distinction between the fictional playspace and the reality of the present moment. Because they work through representational play and drama, whether in the role of director or actor, action psychotherapists utilize a structure with clear boundaries, and thus create safe spaces for clients whose boundaries can easily become too rigid or too fluid.

Application of Models of Wellness and Positive Psychology

Drama therapists tend to favor models of wellness and positive psychology. In the former, the emphasis is upon means to develop a balanced lifestyle based in a confluence of mind, body, and spirit. The relatively new field of positive psychology extends from the work of Carl Rogers (1951) and Abraham Maslow (1971) and concerns issues of resilience and drawing upon strength-based strategies to build a more meaningful existence (see, for example, Duckworth, Steen, and Seligman 2005). Illness is viewed as an imbalance among states of affect, imagination, and embodiment, and the patient is referred to as a consumer or client.

The dramatic therapies take this notion one step further as the client is viewed as an actor, a creative artist who has the ability to transform chaotic states of mind into contained forms of expression. This idea harkens back to early psychoanalytical work on the self-healing function of the creative process, represented in Rank's first book, *The Artist* (1907), an attempt to understand the connection between creativity and neurosis. We also saw this in Jung's personal and clinical struggle to depict the psyche through visual and somatic images of the collective unconscious.

The figure of the artist who has the necessary medicine within (see McNiff 1992) was most clearly drawn by Moreno, who believed that all human beings were potential artists in everyday life. Moreno placed clients on a stage and trusted that they would find a way to re-create their life experiences in creative ways. Moreno's client was called protagonist, suggesting a hero on a life's journey. His protagonist, like the classical hero, is wounded from life's struggles but always up to the task of taking the journey. In action psychotherapy, clients are not seen as ill, but wounded, imbalanced. By virtue of taking the journey toward awareness, they arrive more balanced and whole.

Assessment and Evaluation in the Action Psychotherapies

As for assessment and evaluation, the action psychotherapies, for the most part, present action-based means of measurement. Landy's Role Profiles and Tell-A-Story reflect some of the earlier pencil and paper projective tests based in the work of Freud, like the Rorschach Inkblot Test; Jung, like the Myers-Briggs Type Indicator; and Kelly, like the Role Construct Repertory Grid. However, the action qualities of Moreno's tests of spontaneity and sociometry and Johnson's tests of role-playing, suggest a unique means of assessment. These approaches are well within the traditions established by Murray and his colleagues at Harvard and the OSS. In all these examples, subjects created roles and stories through dramatic action. Although more than half a century has passed since Murray's 1938 action-based battery of tests at Harvard, contemporary drama therapists continue to work on new ways to assess and evaluate subjects through action.

The Polarities

Let us now turn to the polarities of emotion and distance, fiction and reality, verbal and nonverbal expression, action and reflection, directive and nondirective action, transference and countertransference, to see how they play out within a common model.

Emotion and Distance

With the theory of distance developed by Scheff and expanded by Landy, the action psychotherapists have a foundation upon which to build their understanding of emotion and distance. Although all three featured approaches have particular views of enhancing and containing emotion, they can be clearly viewed within this paradigm, which can also reveal the emotional dynamics in psychoanalysis and related approaches.

The model provides a continuum from underdistance, the flooding of emotion, to overdistance, the denial of emotion. At the midpoint is aesthetic distance, the optimal moment of balance between feeling and thought, experience and reflection. As we have seen, the removed analyst is characterized by the overdistanced state. At the other pole of underdistance, we find ecstatic and primal healers, with few clear boundaries. This is the position of shamans working through trance and of primal therapists removing all obstacles to full emotional expression. At their most extreme, both Ferenczi and Reich worked at the edge of underdistance.

Of the three featured dramatic therapies, all move within the full spectrum of distance, and all attempt to realize a balanced state through their particular conceptions of aesthetic distance in role theory, catharsis of integration in psychodrama, and the playspace in developmental transformations. As mentioned above, role theory tends to be the most distanced, with its emphasis upon fictional roles and stories. Psychodrama tends to be the least distanced, with its emphasis upon reality-based roles and catharsis. Developmental transformations tends to be somewhere in-between, with its fictional playspace juxtaposed with a provocative invitation to play the unplayable. Having said this, all three approaches commonly work through provoking, releasing, and containing emotion. As such, they are all about the search for balance and integration.

It is possible to categorize the relative positions of the featured therapists in this book in terms of emotion and distance. In doing so, however, it is also important to realize that many in their practice moved regularly through the full spectrum of distance and that some changed their positions later in their careers. This is most clearly seen as Jung, Rank, Ferenczi, and Reich modified their analytical theories and methods, sometimes, as in the case of Reich, in an extreme fashion. In broad strokes, the therapists who played out their own roles with a degree of overdistance include Freud, early Rank, Kelly, and Wolpe. Those moving toward the center include Jung, Ferenczi, Moreno, Murray, Erikson, Lazarus, Johnson, Landy, Pitzele, and Fox. Those whose work elicited a great degree of affect include shamanic healers, Reich, Lowen, and Perls.

Fiction and Reality

Central to the dramatic therapies is the understanding of the metaphor of world as stage. Two parallel universes are in play—that of the life of the imagination and that of everyday reality. There is more of a confluence than a conflict between fiction and reality. Traditional healers were well aware of this confluence as they understood the intimate relationship between the spiritual and the natural worlds, one being the other's double. Every material object was imbued with a spiritual essence. When Freud first uncovered the dynamics of the unconscious, he was mindful of the convergence of conscious and unconscious experience, even though he focused most directly upon transforming unconscious experience to consciousness. Over time, he came to view the more overtly dramatic aspects of human experience as compensations for people's inability to be fully aware of reality. By using such terms as "transference neurosis" and "acting out," Freud viewed such dramatic action within the consulting room as a form of resistance.

In Rank's (1941) theoretical writing, we find a return to the wisdom of the shaman in his discussion of the double nature of reality. Jung moved this understanding into practice as he sought to make the connection between archetypal imagery and everyday reality. In doing so, Jung played freely in the fictional realms of dreams, fantasies, and myths, searching for a material counterpart to the primal images.

A more complete connection was made by Moreno whose understanding of the *theatricum mundi* metaphor led him to build a full theory and practice based upon dramatic action. At times he encouraged clients to enact fantasy characters and scenes, populated by gods and demons. And yet Moreno most often stayed within the scope of reality-based role-playing, as protagonists replayed unfinished moments in their lives. His contemporary Perls worked frequently with dream figures and inanimate objects, but he, too, quickly brought the work back to reality and the moment of relationship between client and therapist, as we saw in the cases of John and Gloria.

It is mostly in the work of the drama therapists that we see a more complete emersion in fictions as clients project aspects of their everyday lives upon fictional roles and stories. Derek's story of the father, son, and pain is a good example of the break from reality, as is his fluid role-play with archetypal figures in the developmental transformations session. In the case of role method, the fictional role-playing is soon after integrated with reality. Developmental transformations is different in that the fictional play is viewed as sufficient in itself to effect psychological healing. The assumption is that the players will return to reality on their own, without the overt urging of the therapist.

Although there are several ways that action psychotherapists conceptualize the relationship between fiction and reality, all point to the essential moment when clients move into the imaginal realm, whether it is called fiction, status nascendi, or playspace. While in that realm, clients explore actual dilemmas as if they were fictions. Not all agree on how and when to bring the clients back to reality. For some, there is a prescribed moment of de-roling and reflection. For others, the reflection occurs through action in the playspace. In spite of this difference, all seek to affirm the ancient wisdom that the fiction of the imagination coexists with the nonfiction of the natural world, one reflecting the other. In the universe of drama therapy and within the safety of the playspace, all roles are real and all actions are authentic expressions of the self. There is no shame in acting out or in acting toward a neutral object as if it were an intimate. In fact, within the playspace, all that is forbidden and resisted is to be celebrated through play in the hope that once it is brought back to reality, it will become transformed and acceptable. In early psychoanalysis, reality was privileged over fiction. In drama therapy, fiction is privileged over reality. Like effective theater, poised between the magic of theatrical illusion and the everyday life of the viewer, optimal therapy occurs in the mix of fiction and reality.

Verbal and Nonverbal Expression

Unlike dance/movement therapy, much work in the dramatic therapies is verbal as clients assume roles and tell stories in role. However, like other expressive therapies, drama therapy has a prominent nonverbal component. The nonverbal part is about action expressed through the body and the emotions. Drama therapy takes its cue from the art form of drama, which begins developmentally with the child at play and continues through the formal production of theatrical plays. In all forms of drama, the verbal text communicates the thoughts and feelings of the actors. Beneath the verbal text lies a subtext that suggests a deeper, implicit meaning, relating not only to overt action, but also to the underlying feelings and thoughts that motivate such action.

Freud certainly understood the notion of subtext in his formulation of the unconscious and of its defense mechanisms. However, Freud's method of accessing the psychic subtext was verbal. His attention was focused upon the spontaneous flow of the patient's story. Patients were, in fact, immobilized on a couch, talking heads describing rather than enacting their struggles. Freud's early experimentation with hypnosis was the one exception to his later talking cure, but he rejected it partially because it was too dramatic, too nonverbally expressive.

As Jung worked more with imagery, relating it not only to reality, but also to archetypal symbols, he began to explore nonverbal methods. He noticed, for example, that a visual image was often far more expressive of an unconscious state than verbal expression. In studying cultural myths and symbols,

Jung noted the repetition of various symbols. For example, the circle, represented in mandala drawings, was a symbol of wholeness, as was the alchemical four points of the quadrangle, representing the personality functions of intuition, sensation, feeling, and thinking. Throughout the development of his approach to active imagination, Jung added work in movement and drama as compliments to visual art expression.

Although Rank and Ferenczi remained wedded to a verbal means of analysis, they increasingly challenged the orthodoxy of the passive verbal cure. In describing their active therapy, they did not intend to abandon verbal analysis, but simply to allow moments of drama to occur spontaneously, without dismissing these moments as resistances to the real work at hand.

When discovering orgone energy, Reich became much more interested in nonverbal means of treatment. He recognized that in traumatized patients affect precedes memory, and thus he began to unlock affective responses through a direct manipulation of the body. In many ways, Reich was the first somatic therapist, leading to a number of bioenergetic and dance/movement therapists who fully embraced a nonverbal approach to treatment.

Like Reich, Perls focused upon the body, but was more verbally than somatically manipulative. His strength was in pointing out discrepancies between text and subtext, verbal description and body language. He was skilled at helping clients release emotions, especially that of shame, which he regularly evoked in his clients.

Moreno was also skilled in releasing the subtext held in the body and the emotions. He used language more as a warm-up to the action, eliciting certain details of time and place, of character and story. In the psychodramatic work, however, he applied the techniques of the mirror, the double, and the reversal of roles to penetrate the surface of the role and the story. In moving more directly into enactment, the subtext became highly visible in the somatic and emotional expressions of the protagonists.

The most obviously nonverbal approach to healing is that of shamanism. The shaman, as we have seen, is fully embodied and expressive through song, dance, and drama. Although a far cry from the spiritual trance-states of the shaman, the drama therapist makes use of a variety of nonverbal projective and expressive techniques, including puppetry and mask, sound and movement. In working through these approaches, clients are able to reveal the subtext expressively and then communicate its meaning verbally. The most nonverbal of the dramatic therapies, developmental transformations, does so with a minimum of verbal processing, relying instead on the moment-to-moment embodied expressions of the client.

Taken together, the action psychotherapies extend Freud's earliest intention of revealing the contents of the unconscious. Freud and his followers did it through an interpretation of the words of their patients. Those who fully embraced imagery and affect, movement and drama, did so through the many expressive channels that reveal not only text but also subtext. Though not yet fully aware of the dramatic therapies, many contemporary psychoanalysts, shifting from a classical Freudian one-person psychology to a two-person model, now recognize the significance of the nonverbal components of the relationship between client and therapist (see Mitchell 1997).

Action and Reflection

In shamanic healing, the experience is an active one. Both the healer and the clients are required to suspend their disbeliefs and accept the power of spiritual medicine. There is little or no cognitive reflection upon the action. Once in a shamanic ritual space, there are certainly nondramatic moments of mundane action and conversation, as in the preparation for rituals and in transitional moments from one activity to another. However, once the transpersonal ritual begins, there is little room for distance and reflection.

On the other side, the classical psychoanalytic experience is more about reflection than action. Previous to engaging in free association, patients reflect upon their dilemmas with their analyst who interviews and, if medically trained, diagnoses them. A process of reflection follows that of free association. It may be true that patients engaged in free association experience a form of imaginative action as they allow their thoughts to freely transform. And in contemporary forms of psychoanalysis centered in enactment, some actually refer to the action of words. For example, Mitchell (1997) writes: "All actions have interpretive implications, and all interpretations are actions" (182).

These later developments in psychoanalysis were foreshadowed by some of the earlier figures who attempted to move toward a greater balance of action and reflection, with Reich and the bioenergetic therapists ultimately tipping the scales in the direction of embodied action. It was again Moreno who noted that in the process of healing, action precedes and supersedes reflection, also noting at the same time the significance of reflection. Thus psychodramatists engage clients in a process of enactment that is followed by a closure marked by a reflection upon the experience of a particular client. Such reflection is not only cognitive, but also affective and social as group members identify and empathize with the dilemma of the protagonist.

In role method, there is a balance between the two, with action preceding reflection. Reflection has two components where clients reflect upon the fictional roles and stories and then their everyday counterparts. Developmental transformations, however, presents a different model, with reflection, when required, occurring fully within the playspace as the therapist transforms to the here and now. This approach raises the question as to whether a cognitive, verbal reflection is required at all in a playful, expressive form of psychotherapy. There are many examples of therapeutic actions that are effective without further reflection. One is in the natural, nonreflective play of children. There seems to be a therapeutic benefit in such play when, for example, children spontaneously yell at a doll after they have been yelled at by their mother, an action that often brings about a sense of calm. In various forms of nondirective play therapy and Jungian-based sandplay, especially with young children, moments of verbal reflection are minimal. And in many forms of therapeutic touch, exemplified earlier by Reich and Lowen and by many contemporary practitioners of somatic and dance/movement therapy, there is often little need for verbal reflection, as the healing occurs through the body.

Yet the action psychotherapies present a holistic model of healing. Even though action is privileged over reflection, the quieter cognitive moments of awareness are mirror images of the more dramatic moments of embodied action. Like the other polarities, this one, too, is most fully realized as a confluence. Current research in neuroscience (see Demasio 1994; Siegel 1999, 2001; Cozolino 2002) has demonstrated that cognition and affect are neurological relatives and that a therapeutic process requires some form of cognitive processing in order to repair neurological damage. Thus, somatic-based action psychotherapies must be mindful of incorporating a cognitive component, just as cognitive and depth psychotherapies need to be aware of the pitfalls of excluding affective and somatic processes. In the dramatic approaches of Moreno and Landy, we find an integration of action and reflection. Although Johnson's approach suggests that healing occurs fully through embodied play, there are still moments of reflection in action.

Directive and Nondirective Action/Transference and Countertransference

In the film, *Three Approaches to Psychotherapy*, there was a stark contrast between the nondirective, gentle approach of Carl Rogers and the directive, abrasive approach of Fritz Perls. His abrasive personality notwithstanding, Perls is more typical of other action psychotherapists in terms of his directive style. Many drama and action psychotherapists fashion themselves after theatrical directors who help actors discover the essence of their roles. The drama therapists direct by building a therapeutic scene through action with the building blocks of the body and the emotions of their clients.

The early analysts created an unequal power dynamic based upon their ability to interpret the mysteries of the unconscious. With the exception of Perls, many of the action psychotherapists at least shared power with their clients, viewing them as artists, capable of creating a healthier and more balanced reality. Some, influenced by feminist relational theories (see, for example, Gilligan 1982; Miller 1987; N. Chodorow 1991), viewed themselves less as directors and more as cocreators of a deeply intersubjective process.

Moreno, for one, recognized that all actors need directors to set the scene, develop, and resolve the action. Not only did he navigate these tasks, but he also moved his psychodramatic actors in and out of roles, sometimes at a dizzying pace as they engaged in doubling, mirroring, and role reversal.

Like Moreno, Landy generally directs the dramatic action. With Derek, he helped to invoke the story and its roles and to discover an integration among them. Johnson, however, takes a nondirective approach, at least on the surface, engaging with Derek as a playobject, an actor among actors. And yet, as we saw in his work with Derek, he moves the action forward by transforming the scenes and by manipulating the intensity of the scenes from within.

Like all but the most person-centered therapists, action psychotherapists are directors, and so they move the action in directions that will optimally help clients realize their goals. However, like most effective stage directors, once the clients are fully enrolled, the drama therapist will back off and let them engage in the delightful chaos of the creative process.

Because dramatic therapists actively direct the enactment, they provoke a certain degree of transference. Transference reactions will vary from the more distanced approach of role method, to the progressively less distanced ones of developmental transformations and psychodrama. We saw how, predictably, Derek transferred aspects of his father onto Landy and his mother onto Garcia. And we saw how the less distanced psychodramatic enactment invoked a greater degree of affect in the mother transference. However, with both approaches, the transference was moved by the therapist onto other objects, such as an empty chair, so that the client could take on the transferential figures himself and work them through. Derek as father and mother worked not only toward forgiveness and gratefulness, but also toward realizing his own power to parent himself.

Developmental transformations presents a further view of transference as the therapist does not linger in any one role. Further, when the therapist senses moments of transference, he will move them into a new form to see if they reemerge as more fixed thematic clusters. Again, given the goal of flow and transformation, the therapist aims to help the client detach from repeated transferential reactions.

Unlike the classical psychoanalytic conception of transference as a resistance to be resolved, dramatic therapists view it as an opportunity to explore another polarity of role and counterrole, another rigid form that requires fluidity. When transference is present in drama therapy, it is given a dramatic role form, sometimes more fixed and sometimes more fluid. That form may be held by the therapist or may be moved onto other people or objects in the space. When given a form, it becomes tangible in its very human manifestations—a father who never said I'm sorry and a mother who could not protect her son. Sometimes it takes on archetypal and exaggerated qualities—a man who beats his dog; a master who abuses his slave; a white male lover who wants to dance with a black man. Transference in the dramatic therapies is a moment to not only explore the relationship of client and therapist, but also the intrapsychic dynamics of a client, like Derek, who holds within him many divergent and confusing roles that require recognition and integration.

Drama therapists view moments of countertransference as opportunities to feed back certain feelings induced by the client within the fiction of the role-play. This is most clear in developmental transformations as the therapist engages directly in play with the client. As it is easy to be caught up in the stimulation of the moment and to indulge in one's own drama, developmental transformations therapists carefully monitor their countertransferential reactions so that the client does not unconsciously enact the therapist's drama. But such is true of so many dramatic therapists who elicit such compelling stories that they have a difficult time restraining themselves from jumping into the action.

In drama therapy, most therapists work from both directive and nondirective viewpoints, depending upon the needs of the client. All are trained to think and act like actors and directors. All are trained to recognize moments of transference and countertransference and to move them into the playspace where they will be embraced as solid reflections of self and other or transformed as fluid forms in search of a source.

PRACTICE

The practice of most forms of action psychotherapy can be traced to shamanism. The action of the shaman begins with a preparation, akin to an actor arriving at the theater to get into costume and makeup and to warm up body and voice before entering the rarefied world of the stage. The shaman also dons a costume, organizes props and music, and prepares emotionally for the mysterious journey to the spirit world. The shaman's performance, like that of the theatrical actor, is in the service of a community who seeks benefits from the performance, whether healing or entertainment. Following the performance, both shaman and actor remove their theatrical garb and return to their everyday lives.

The Structure of Action Psychotherapy

Most forms of action psychotherapy proceed in three steps. The beginning is a warm-up, wherein both therapist and clients prepare body, voice, and imagination to enter the playspace. The next phase is that of the action, where all players work within the playspace to explore a given dilemma through words, sound, and movement. A main characteristic of the action phase is that clients work imaginatively and expressively, breaking from an overdependence upon verbal expression and linear, rational thinking. And finally, nearing the end of a session, there is some form of closure, marked by de-roling and in many cases reflection upon the process though words and/or action.

This particular structure fully came into being with Moreno's development of psychodrama. Other psychotherapeutic models of psychoanalysis, cognitive behavioral therapy, and constructivism were less clearly structured. In these approaches, there was no distinction between the fiction of the playspace and the reality of the consulting room. There are, however, some exceptions, as in the use of the psychoanalytic couch as a kind of liminal space to induce a relaxing, open attitude toward accessing the unconscious. Other exceptions include Jung's work with images, Reich's work with the body, Murray and Erikson's work with role-playing and dramatic constructions, Kelley's work with fixed roles, and Perls's work with empty chair and role reversal. These experiments notwithstanding, much of early psychotherapeutic practice proceeded through an unstructured verbal conversation, in monologue and dialogue, between therapist and client.

Techniques of Conventional Psychotherapy in Relation to Action Psychotherapy

From these conventional approaches to psychotherapy, we find a plethora of techniques. The analysis of the transference, for example, is central to the verbal cure of psychoanalysis. According to Gill (1954):

> Psychoanalysis is that technique which, employed by a neutral analyst, results in the development of a regressive transference neurosis and the ultimate resolution of this neurosis by techniques of interpretation alone (775).

Analysis continued to be a main technique of various forms of psychoanalytic psychotherapy, including interpersonal and relational approaches, except that in the latter approaches, the patient got off the couch and into a chair in full view of the therapist so that both could engage more directly in a mutual relationship. As person-centered and existential-humanistic models came into play, the relationship became even more central. Such practitioners as Rogers became less interested in analysis as a technique and more in engagement, the development of an empathetic and authentic bond with the client. Perls built upon this tradition but developed more dramatic techniques, based partially on the influence of Moreno, to move the client into the body and into action.

Another range of techniques was developed in the practice of behavioral psychotherapy. These were practical, verified through empirical research. Techniques include exposure-based treatment, response prevention, operant conditioning, relaxation, and problem-solving training (see Gurman and Messer 2003). Relaxation techniques are most relevant to action approaches as they involve the body.

Techniques of cognitive therapy, focused upon modifying thoughts, often joined forces with those of behavioral therapy. They include developing options and alternatives to defeating thoughts, de-catastrophizing, and completing homework assignments. Cognitive approaches, as we have already seen, also involve more dramatic techniques including behavioral rehearsal and role-playing. In other popular models, including brief psychotherapy, marriage and family therapy, and group psychotherapy, many action techniques are regularly incorporated as part of treatment.

Techniques of Action Psychotherapy

The action psychotherapies involve a number of approaches developed throughout the twentieth century, including Gestalt therapy, primal therapy, and, to a lesser degree, transactional analysis and redecision therapy. However, the field is most fully represented by two basic disciplines— psychodrama and drama therapy. Psychodrama has remained essentially intact as a practice, although we have reviewed several innovations in, for example, Playback Theatre and bibliodrama. Drama therapy, on the other hand, is practiced in several forms such as role method and developmental transformations. Taking psychodrama and drama therapy together, we find a number of widely used techniques. One way to conceptualize the range of techniques is to view them according to their degree of distance. Certain techniques tend to elicit more or less intense emotional responses. In general, those techniques that are based in the reality of the present moment tend to be the most emotionally charged.

Psychodramatic Techniques

Among the dramatic techniques, the most reality-based are those used in psychodrama. The sense of reality comes from the fact that protagonists play themselves in the drama in relationship to significant others in their lives. Those others can be real people, like parents or siblings. They can also be fantasy figures, like God or the devil, but even so, the protagonist remains grounded in the here and now. The scenes dramatized, though not explicitly real, are reenactments of the past or previews of what might happen if the protagonists were to act in a given fashion. Although dramatic in its method, psychodrama is the least theatrical of the three featured approaches and most overtly cathartic. Even though protagonists are aware of acting a role in a drama, they easily become flooded with emotion as they confront a deep wound.

All role-playing involves the projection of self onto a fiction. In psychodrama, that projection is minimal, at least for protagonists, as they play aspects of themselves. In his psychodrama session, for example, Derek mostly played out the role of himself as man and boy. At times he also played auxiliary roles of mother and father, a process that involved a greater degree of projection. However, even those roles remained for the most part within the bounds of reality.

To create a greater sense of immediacy and thus emotional response, various psychodramatic techniques are applied including empty chair, role reversal, doubling, and mirroring. When Garcia felt the need to bring Derek closer to the expression of his feelings, she removed distance by employing the techniques of role reversal and doubling. When reversing into the role of mother, for example, Derek was able to access his feelings of pain and humiliation and release them through sobbing. When Derek was in the role of the grieving son, Garcia doubled for him as a means of helping him express his rage toward his abusive father.

Projective Techniques

Projective techniques in drama therapy provide a greater degree of distance as aspects of the self are projected onto fictional roles embodied in stories and in certain objects such as masks and puppets. In Derek's session in role method, he projected aspects of his abusive background onto the fictional characters of Father, Son, and Pain. In doing so, he was able to separate out from a direct reenactment of his past and thus experience a greater sense of safety. At the beginning of that session, while more in the here and now, Derek was concerned that he might look too dark in the film. When asked to take on the role of the camera, he projected some of his fears and hopes onto the inanimate object. At the conclusion of that interchange, he was able to reassure himself, as the camera, that he would be photographed in a good light. As a projective technique, such object work again provides a safe degree of distance, allowing the protagonist to experience a degree of balance.

In Erikson's Dramatic Productions Test, we saw how objects can take on the projections of the creator and how the forms created reveal a personal story. Much of play therapy, which is in many ways synonymous with drama therapy, depends upon the child's projection of internal feelings and thoughts onto play objects. In working with families, the therapist sometimes asks family members to choose puppets from a basket and to enact a puppet show. In doing so, they project aspects of themselves onto the puppet figures, enacting the actual family dynamics through the fiction. In that the puppet is an external object, separate from the clients, it embodies a safe degree of distance.

Many clients experience a greater degree of affect when projective objects move closer to their bodies. Mask work is generally less distanced than puppetry as the masks are placed on the client's face. Working with stage makeup is even more emotionally intense as it is actually applied to the face and difficult to remove. However, because work with masks and makeup tends to be playful and somewhat abstract, it provides a safe degree of distance. There are many exceptions. For some, masks are highly charged in their associations with horror, deception, and death, leading to a flood of feeling. For others, playing with such overtly theatrical techniques is infantilizing and thus causes too much distance.

As we have seen, psychodramatic techniques are readily used within such projective forms of drama therapy as role method. Landy asked Derek on several occasions to work with an empty chair and to engage in role reversal between father and son. So, too, are more projective drama therapy techniques used in psychodrama, as we saw when Garcia worked with scarves to symbolize certain settings in Derek's drama. Developmental transformations presents a more complex view of the efficacy of projective techniques. For one, the only projective object outside the body of the client is the therapist. In working with Johnson, Derek projected many of his issues of abuse onto the roles and scenes he co-created with Johnson. It seemed likely that Derek would experience intense emotional reactions in working directly with such provocative material as racial stereotypes. In some ways, Derek did have a strong emotional reaction through the play, but because he worked in an exaggerated fashion, the provocative content was distanced by the theatrical, sometimes farcical, style of presentation. Although very much an approach unto itself, demanding a great deal of skill from the therapist, developmental transformations' techniques of mutual play, improvisation, and transformation to the here and now are commonly used in other forms of drama therapy.

A Common Model of Practice

A common model of practice, then, offers a range of psychodramatic and projective techniques, useful for a range of clients. Projective techniques are best applied to those requiring a greater degree of safety and distance. This group includes people in crisis and those having experienced some form of trauma. By working through fiction, these people have the opportunity to approach their dilemmas indirectly in role and through story and then to reflect upon their dramatizations.

Given the three featured action approaches, role method may be most appropriate for those most traumatized. However, both psychodrama and developmental transformations have been used to treat trauma and PTSD. Moreno worked with traumatized veterans of World War II, and Johnson worked with traumatized veterans of the Vietnam War. In working with traumatized people, the therapist needs to be mindful of modulating levels of affect to minimize the possibility of retraumatization.

More stimulating, provocative, and cathartic methods are indicated for those requiring a greater degree of affect. This group includes depressed and alienated people who have distanced themselves from their feelings. In treatment, such people are encouraged to find ways to reenact unfinished business in an embodied manner. Doubles and auxiliaries are often used to help clients reach a deeper level of expression. In developmental transformations, the therapist employs humor, irony, exaggeration, and playful provocation to encourage the client to play the unplayable.

The full spectrum of psychodramatic and projective techniques is used in treating the mentally ill, from profoundly psychotic and autistic to those experiencing mood disorders. Despite the specific theoretical orientation of the drama therapist, all are trained to modulate levels of distance through their action techniques, helping clients find a way to enter the playspace with a readiness to engage in a dramatic exploration that is both challenging and containing.

Many action psychotherapists have been criticized for being overly stimulating, provocative, cathartic, and infantilizing while working with vulnerable populations. These criticisms have been repeatedly hurled at Moreno and Perls, as well as contemporary drama therapists, like Johnson. In a mental health system where the aim is mostly to quell symptoms, many are justifiably threatened by the use of nonmedical processes based in regressive forms of play and overt expressions of emotion. These kinds of criticisms stem from antiquity where Plato viewed drama as potentially dangerous to the state and into the Middle Ages where the church feared the primitive, immoral qualities of theater. Throughout history, many have viewed role-playing as a form of exhibitionism and prostitution.

Yet the practice of drama therapy, like that of theater, is about contained expression. Through drama therapy, the demons are released, but within the confines of the playspace. The delusions are expressed, but as characters in a drama with a story to tell. Disbelief and conventional rules are suspended for a time so that one can transgress and then return with a progressive point of view. Drama therapy and psychodrama are about leading people in need out of their ordinary circumstances and into an adventure extraordinary enough to provoke a shift that can be recognized on their return. When this work is most effective, the adventure concludes with a safe landing.

At the finale of his three sessions in role method, psychodrama, and developmental transformations, Derek (in Landy 2005) was asked which approach felt safest. At first he chose role method, "because it was more distanced from me." He also noted that psychodrama was safe in that, although highly cathartic, it was truthful. He said: "Safe is being who I am and not hiding it." Four weeks after he began filming, Derek rated the three approaches from most to least safe: psychodrama, role method, and developmental transformations.

With the passage of one year, Derek (2006) again reflected upon the comparative value of the three approaches. He modified his earlier statement, noting that he did not see the experience as competitive, but rather additive. He even said that the order of presentation helped him progress in his struggle with his father's abuse. These are his words:

> Role method was a great opener and warm-up to getting me started. It was a great use of distancing the issues by creating the roles. It helped me better understand and classify the roles that came up later in the other methods. Because of the role method session I was ripe and ready to get into psychodrama, allowing me to delve deeper into my psyche. I love the rawness of the method and the intensity of the reduction of emotional distance. After the intense psychodrama session, developmental transformations was a nice landing with its playfulness and the luxury of not analyzing or verbalizing in a cognitive fashion. Instead I was ready to play and flow with issues that did not come up in the previous sessions. I did not have to worry about specific goals or deviating from the process.

For Derek, the three approaches were highly interactive, cumulative, and complementary. In this single case, we see how a range of approaches converges. Each approach has a long history in both the shamanic and theatrical arts and the psychotherapeutic sciences. Despite their many differences in theory and practice, the dramatic psychotherapies present a common model of holistic healing through dramatic action. In a final interview with Derek (2006), one year after his experience as a client in the three approaches, he well articulates this commonality:

> Overall, each method individually contributed to healing the wounds in my personality and relationships, and together they functioned in a complimentary fashion, one preparing me for the next. In a perfect world, one would hopefully have access to multiple methods like I was fortunate to have in this experience. The different methods used are like unique musical instruments that sound exceptional by themselves but when put together work like a well-coordinated orchestra, capable of much more intricate and beautiful music.

8

Applications of
Action Psychotherapies to
Clinical Disorders

WHY DRAMATIC ACTION PERSISTS

A central premise of this book is that action approaches to healing have been in place for thousands of years in traditional healing practices and that even with the advent of scientifically based treatments in the late nineteenth century, dramatic action has continued to thrive. Derived from both shamanism and psychoanalysis, action approaches are present in depth psychotherapy and many other forms of clinical treatment, including cognitive-behavioral therapy, brief psychotherapy, marriage and family therapy, and group psychotherapy.

It is clear why shamanism has been rejected by Western clinicians, but it is less clear why dramatic action persists. One reason is that a growing number of physicians, psychiatrists, and psychotherapists embrace a holistic notion of healing that requires active engagement with the client's mind and body in order to effect optimal results. Some forms of alternative medicine also speak to the spiritual connection, offering evidence of the efficacy of prayer, martial arts, and herbal medication in healing (see Barnes et al. 2004).

The neurologist Demasio (1994) goes so far as to suggest that the seventeenth-century philosopher Descartes made an error in viewing human existence in terms of a split between mind and body, cognition and affect. For Demasio, Descartes's error, immortalized in the dictum, *cogito ergo sum,* profoundly influenced the practice of modern medicine. A more holistic approach views the patient with a physical illness as a cognitive as well as biological being and the patient with a mental illness as one requiring treatment through the body and emotions as well as the mind.

The early shamans and psychotherapists who practiced dramatic forms of healing certainly intuited its holistic benefits. However, there is now a growing body of scientific research in neuroscience that points to the holistic nature of the brain in its capacity to integrate cognitive, affective, and somatic signals. This research is well represented by Demasio (1994), who suggests that when the brain is damaged by physiological or psychological factors, it requires reparative therapies that speak not only to its cognitive function, but also its affective and somatic ones. Speaking from a holistic perspective, Demasio (1994) writes:

> Human reason depends upon several brain systems, working in concert across many levels of neuronal organization. . . . The lower levels in the neural edifice of reason are the same ones that regulate the processing of emotions and feelings, along with the body functions necessary for the organism's survival . . . thus placing the body directly within the chain of operations that generate the highest reaches of reasoning, decision making, and, by extension, social behavior and creativity. Emotion, feeling and biological regulation all play a role in human reason (xiii).

Demasio (1994) even goes further in his holistic speculations, linking mind not only to affect and body, but also to creative and spiritual processes. He offers this:

> Love and hate and anguish, the qualities of kindness and cruelty, the planned solution of a scientific problem or the creation of a new artifact are all based on neural events within a brain, provided that brain has been and now is interacting with its body. The soul breathes through the body, and suffering, whether it starts in the skin or in a mental image, happens in the flesh (xvii).

Like Einstein and other theoretical scientists who studied the physical universe at the subatomic level only to discover its underlying spirituality, Demasio recapitulates the incontrovertible wisdom of the shamans whose healing touch only worked because they knew that the soul breathes through the body. Let us now look at one application of action psychotherapy that is enriched by evidence and speculations from contemporary neuroscience.

NEUROSCIENCE AND TRAUMA

Neuroscience best informs the action therapies in its conceptualization of trauma. When traumatized, some people develop the symptoms of post-traumatic stress or PTSD, a condition noted by its persistence of symptoms in the absence of the original trauma. These symptoms include flashbacks, avoidance of memory of the trauma, hyperarousal and poor impulse control, disturbed body image, lack of attention and focus, and disturbances in sexual activity, eating, and sleeping. The symptoms are triggered when one is exposed to sensory experiences associated with the original trauma.

From a biological point of view, in trauma the natural homeostasis of the brain is disturbed. The normal balance between activities of the primitive subcortical areas of the right brain and the more developed cortical structures of the left brain is disrupted. In examining PET scans of the brain, Rauch et al. (1996) noticed that in reexperiencing earlier traumas, the Broca's region of the left brain, responsible for the ability to verbalize feelings, is deactivated, and the limbic system of the right brain, responsible for decoding danger and assuring survival, is hyperactivated, causing the individual to behave in an irrational manner. Because of this biological reality, people experiencing PTSD are unable to verbalize their feelings and tend to overreact, sometimes in an extreme fashion, to seemingly neutral stimuli. Furthermore, people with PTSD have impaired neurotransmitters whose functions are to control attention and arousal. Their ability to produce hormones that are normally activated when under stress is also impaired, leading to an inability to cope with the stress.

In addition, research has demonstrated (see Shore 2004) that trauma based in abusive relationships with caregivers blocks the healthy development, at least in right-handed people, of the right hemisphere of the brain which regulates the ability to modulate feelings, sensations, and perceptions. Thus trauma disturbs one's ability to engage in nurturing and nonabusive relationships. Because the brain of the young child is developing so rapidly, traumatic incidents have profound effects upon its growth. Perry and Pollard (1998) note that persistent traumatic episodes can severely impede the healthy growth of children not only in terms of social relationships, but also in terms of their ability to express and process thoughts and emotions.

Van der Kolk (2002b), an expert in conceptualizing and treating trauma, notes that long before scientific approaches to psychotherapy many cultures coped with communal traumas by means of ritual and theater. He makes reference to the ancient Greek tragedies with their themes of murder, war, and incest. In a more contemporary context, van der Kolk makes reference to films and plays about the traumas of the Vietnam War. Although war trauma has been recognized at least since the Second World War as a psychological problem, it really came to be fully acknowledged as a mental disorder in the aftermath of the Vietnam War, when it was first described as PTSD in the third edition of the *Diagnostic and Statistical Manual of Mental Disorders* (see APA 1980).

Van der Kolk is unique among researchers and psychiatrists in advocating for treatments that engage clients in action through the body. Well aware that experiences in trauma are held in the body, van der Kolk (1994) has applied his theory of the communal healing power of theater in work with traumatized children. Van der Kolk (2002b) explicitly states:

> Dramatic enactment is a way of dealing with, narrating and transforming their [traumatized inner-city children] traumatic experiences, by allowing the children both to share their personal experiences and to find action-oriented ways of coming to an alternative resolution to the once inevitable outcome of the original traumatic event. This work is predicated on the idea that, to overcome a traumatic experience, people require physical experiences that directly contradict the helplessness and the inevitability of defeat associated with the trauma (387).

Van der Kolk notes the ineffectiveness of traditional psychotherapies that have depended primarily upon verbal methods. Agreeing with Demasio, he, too, calls for holistic ways of understanding and treating human beings who have been abused. In building a case for implementing treatment techniques that are both holistic and creative, he cites Demasio (1999):

> Consciousness establishes a link between the world of automatic regulation and the world of imagination—the world in which images of different modalities (thoughts, feelings, and sensations) can be combined to produce novel images of situations that have not yet happened (258).

Van der Kolk has embraced a number of nontraditional approaches in treating trauma. One, Eye Movement Desensitization and Reprocessing (EMDR), mentioned earlier in connection to the work of Wolpe (see chapter 2), involves the client's recall of sensations related to a traumatic event while focusing upon the horizontal movement of the therapist's hand. The eye movement causes a bilateral stimulation of the brain that leads to a lessening of emotional intensity associated with memories of the original trauma (see van der Kolk 2002c).

ACTION APPROACHES TO TRAUMA

For our purposes, van der Kolk's work that is most action-oriented involves theater. He and his colleagues describe two theater-based programs in inner-city schools designed to ameliorate the effects of trauma and reduce incidences of violence. The first, Urban Improv, is a violence prevention program designed for fourth grade inner-city students in Boston, many of whom have directly experienced repeated trauma in their neighborhoods and families. The program combines aspects of behavioral rehearsal and Boal's Forum Theatre. A team of trained actor-teachers dramatizes a scene based upon a theme related to the lives of the fourth graders. At a high point of conflict, the director freezes the action and students are invited to step into the scene and redirect it, posing an alternative nonviolent solution. Following the action, students are divided up into small groups and asked to create their own scenes responding to the same problem. At closure, the full group reconvenes and discusses the implications of their choices.

The results of a quasi-experimental study (Kisiel et al. 2006) evaluating the effects of Urban Improv on 140 students showed that the theater-based work increased pro-social behaviors, prevented new onset aggression, and decreased hyperactivity and internalizing symptoms among those in the experimental group.

Trauma Drama, a second program based in the work of van der Kolk, was designed to prevent youth violence among an older population of young adolescents. Noting that this group as a whole had been exposed to traumatic experiences for longer periods of time, the directors included more clinical strategies in the treatment protocol. Although based in the Urban Improv model, the directors also include the goals of stress management and cooperative play, realized through action-oriented therapeutic techniques. A number of treatment protocols and research studies are underway, supported by grants from several agencies, including the Center for Disease Control. One pilot project has taken place in a specialized day school for adolescents with severe emotional and behavioral disabilities. The results have not yet been tabulated.

In collaboration with Streeck-Fischer, van der Kolk (Streeck-Fischer and van der Kolk 2000) specified six goals of trauma treatment. These include:

1. Safety
2. Stabilizing impulsive aggression against self and others
3. Affect regulation
4. Promoting mastery experiences
5. Compensating for specific developmental deficits
6. Judiciously processing both the traumatic memories and trauma-related expectations

what would your goals be

In his article on the creative arts therapies in trauma treatment, Crenshaw (2006) notes several more goals. The following two are based on van der Kolk's (2002a) work with traumatized children:

1. Developing an awareness of oneself and of the trauma
2. Learning to observe what is happening in the present time and to physically respond to current demands instead of re-creating the traumatic past behaviorally, emotionally, and biologically

Creating a story or someone would like their life to unfold

Two additional goals were added by Crenshaw (2006):

1. Teaching self-soothing to cope with hyperaroused physiological systems
2. Finding meaning, developing perspective, and a positive orientation to the future (24)

Role Method in Trauma Treatment

Let us look at ways that drama therapists have attempted to address these goals.

Reviewing the case of Derek, we see a young man who has endured a childhood of trauma in relationship to an abusive father. In role method, Landy began by addressing Derek's need for safety. The reality of the filming was that Derek exposed himself on camera to an actual audience of graduate students and to an unknown audience of professionals who would view the completed film at a later time. To provide a sense of safety, Landy used the camera as a projective object. By asking Derek to take on the role of the camera, Landy provided an opportunity for Derek to safely express his fear of being exposed in a negative light.

The projective use of the camera had a secondary effect in stabilizing Derek's impulse to denigrate himself. At the beginning of the sequence, Derek offers that he is nervous in front of the camera, admitting that the camera might reveal his dark skin. In the role of camera, Derek says that his function is to "shoot Derek." By staying within the safe boundaries of the fictional role, Derek is finally able to revise his aggressive impulse. The advice, "Be yourself," comes neither from the therapist nor directly from Derek, but from the camera. In accepting the advice for himself, Derek regains stability and is ready to move deeper into his therapeutic exploration.

Throughout the session, Landy, mindful of the figure of the guide, stood in as the reparative father, affirming Derek's actions even as he gently challenged him to take greater emotional risks within the safety of the relationship. He guided Derek into and out of the story and its enactment, and then the writing and dramatization of the letter of remorse. He stayed within close physical proximity to Derek, moving away on one occasion only to return at Derek's request. Landy's final reparative act was to take on the role of father and read the letter to Derek. In doing so, Landy attempted to guide Derek toward a positive orientation to a future controlled not by the father, but by the grown son who might just be able to forgive his father.

Role method regulates affect by distancing potentially overwhelming feelings. At a key moment in the session, Derek expresses a wish for an apology from his father. Mindful of the emotional weight of the trauma, Landy facilitated the expression of the wish through writing a letter, singing, and role-playing. Noticing that Derek was too removed from his feelings, Landy encouraged him to take on the role of father and read the apology to the son in increasingly more emotional ways. Then at the end, seeking an even greater level of affect, Landy moved Derek into the role of son, which he had initially resisted, and, in the role of father, read the letter to him. At that point, aware that he was full of feeling, Derek stepped back, noting: "You ain't getting me to cry here." Because he was given great leeway in exploring his emotions, Derek took control and modulated his own expression.

The telling and then dramatization of the story of Father, Son, and Pain was a projective way of helping Derek develop an awareness of himself as a traumatized little boy who inherited pain from his father's abuse. Within the story, he also found a way to sooth himself in sitting by the radiator and listening to its hiss. Although not fully able to master the fear of his traumatic past, he was able to contain it within a story frame and develop a new perspective as a grown man who will continue to climb the steep mountain of liberation from the legacy of pain. The projective play enabled Derek to work holistically, expressing pain through his body and emotions and giving language to a range of feelings, from sadness and disgust to remorse and self-affirmation.

The projective orientation of role method works best for traumatized people by providing distance from the original trauma, by regulating affect through the fiction of the roles and story, and by linking the fiction of the drama to the nonfiction of reality by building a cognitive bridge between the two. For people experiencing recurrent symptoms of PTSD, role method is especially useful in its attention to a guide figure who is first represented by the therapist, then created as a fictional character within the client's story, and finally internalized as an inner figure. The function of the guide as one who leads a hero on a treacherous journey to an unknown destination serves as apt metaphor for the hard journey from trauma to recovery. Further, as therapists play out the function of guide as witness, they provide an extra degree of comfort for clients who need unconditional validation.

Like van der Kolk and his colleagues, Landy h   ' through theater performance as a means of dealing with September 11th, Landy developed a theater-b fourth-grade children who had directly witnes World Trade Center from their classroom Christa Kirby, a drama therapy graduate st teaching artist from City Lights Youth Theat children master their experience in a safe v ters and fictional stories about a city in crisi sen by the children included heroes, villain

encouraged to enact moments of anger toward the terrorists, sadness toward the loss of lives, and pride at the efforts of first responders and other heroes to save lives and rebuild the city. In one story, for example, a girl created an interior monologue spoken by the Empire State Building who had been jealous of the grandeur of the World Trade Towers, only to feel a sense of guilt and then deep sorrow for their loss.

The children worked playfully and thoughtfully to create role types and then to examine their implicit humanity. They enacted, for example, a scene where the pregnant mother of the soon to be born Osama bin Laden speaks about her hopes for her new baby boy. In their creative process they discovered that villains are as human as victims and that heroes can be ordinary people, such as mothers. Toward the end of the process of exploration through drama, Landy created a play based on the children's roles and stories. The children performed the play to an audience of peers, teachers, parents, and friends. Following the performance, the actors engaged with the audience in dialogue. For some adults, it was their first opportunity to speak and to release feelings about their experience of the terrorist attacks.

This project, called Standing Tall, had several objectives, including:

1. To understand the human need to tell stories as a means of making sense of difficult, potentially traumatizing experience
2. To understand the therapeutic value of role-playing, storytelling, and story dramatization
3. To understand the concept of aesthetic distance in transforming potential trauma in real life into safely contained forms of enactment
4. To extract a sense of meaning from the events of September 11, 2001, for children and adults

Some of these objectives dovetail with those of van der Kolk and Crenshaw, especially that of finding meaning. Although there was no follow-up study on the effects of this work on forestalling posttraumatic symptoms, several months after the performance, parents provided feedback through written questionnaires. Landy interviewed the children and teacher six months after the play production, and a documentary film was made of the experience called Standing Tall, directed by Peggy Stern (2004), who spent time with the children and their teacher in the school and in their homes. These sources provide anecdotal evidence that the experience was highly effective in helping the children as well as the teacher regulate affect, develop awareness of the trauma, separate past from present, and develop a positive orientation to the future. In addition to the film, a study guide was created (2004) for teachers and therapists who wish to work within this therapeutic drama.

Psychodrama in Trauma Treatment

Psychodramatic work is generally more cathartic than that used in role method. With highly symptomatic clients, it is important to take great care in deciding when and if to directly reenact a traumatic moment. In fostering the goals of safety and affect regulation, the director carefully modulates the polarities of emotion and distance, fiction and reality, verbal and non-verbal expression, action and reflection. For the most symptomatic, psychodrama might be best used as a future projection, playing out scenes of what it might be like if a client could ask for support from his parents, for example. For many, trauma is triggered by nonverbal, sensory cues. Thus, psychodramatists might choose to initially work in a verbal fashion. In protecting clients from the possibility of retraumatization, they might also choose fiction over reality and reflection over action. On the other hand, it is important to remember that trauma experiences are stored in the body (see van der Kolk 1994; Rothschild 2000) and are often inaccessible to language. Many, including van der Kolk and Rothschild, strongly insist that traumatized people are well served through nonverbal, action methods of treatment.

The strength of psychodrama is that it contains as well as releases strong affect within the action and provides a range of techniques through which the director can guide the client. These techniques include auxiliary egos that represent positive or negative figures in the client's life, doubles, which help the client express or even repress difficult feelings, role reversals, that help move the client beyond emotional or verbal blocks, and sharing by audience members, who help create a supportive community.

In working with Derek through the range of psychodramatic techniques, Garcia realized several of the stated goals. She set up a safe atmosphere by talking with Derek and by asking him to describe his dream verbally. She provided comfort by assuring him that she would stay by his side, doubling for him when necessary. Garcia was well aware that Moreno envisioned the early, undifferentiated relationship between mother and child in terms of the double, the mother standing in to gratify the infant's needs.

In telling Derek that he would play all the roles in his drama, Garcia provided an opportunity for Derek to master his dilemma on his own. Further, during moments of regression, Garcia made use of role reversal, which Moreno recognized as a high-level developmental stage marked by an intersubjective relationship.

The most poignant moment in the psychodrama was the cathartic one. Garcia intended to help Derek safely release the pain of his trauma and thereby gain an awareness of its effects. This process began when Derek, in the role of mother, revealed a violent episode of being knocked out at the train station by her husband. When Derek was asked to reverse roles with the father, he was stuck in his identification with the mother's abuse. When Garcia asked how he felt in the here and now as Derek, he replied: "Desperate." And then he began to sob, expressing the desperation of the helpless mother and by association, the helpless eight-year-old boy, vulnerable to the rage of the abusive father.

During the sobbing, Garcia constantly checked in with Derek, urging him to be aware of his body and to keep breathing. To assure safe boundaries, she asked if she could double for him and if, as a means of comfort, she could touch him. She followed his lead, helping him both regulate his affect and take the reparative steps necessary to master the trauma.

In the end, having experienced desperation, rage, and forgiveness, and having released very powerful feelings, Derek arrived at a moment of integration. He was finally able to hold all the characters involved in the drama of abuse together—the mother, the father, the abused child, and the grown man struggling to live a life free from troubling dreams of abuse. To foster that integration, Garcia drew upon Moreno's spiritual roots, encouraging Derek to say a prayer for the young boy who was once abused by his father. In facilitating that moment, Garcia realized the final and critical goal of finding meaning and developing a positive orientation to the future.

Tian Dayton (2005) writes eloquently about psychodrama as a method of treating traumatized clients. In response to the current research in neuroscience, she notes that traumatic experience shuts down access to conscious reasoning in the cortex and is stored as unconscious sensory images in the subcortical parts of the brain that process survival reactions of fight, flight, and freeze. The multisensory approach of psychodrama allows the client to access the unconscious through the body within a supportive context.

Aware that trauma is stored and triggered in the body, Dayton focuses upon the body during treatment. When clients are unable to describe feeling states, she (Dayton 2005) asks them such questions as: "What's going on in your body? Where is it going on? Can you put your hand there? If that part of your body had a voice, what would it say?" (224). She also moves the client into action by asking: "What does your body want to do?" When the need to express a strong feeling is manifest, Dayton helps clients express that feeling safely, as Garcia demonstrated in working with Derek.

For Dayton (2005), psychodrama offers many benefits to the traumatized client including:

- Puts the locus of control inside the protagonist,
- Wakes up the body so the protagonist can begin to think and feel abut what she is experiencing physically,
- Allows the brain/body to do what it wants to do, such as stomp or shake, in order to release the residue of stored trauma,

- Helps the protagonist to get out of her head and get in touch with the split-off affect accompanying the real experience so it can be worked through, understood, and reintegrated,
- Allows the senses, which play such a pivotal role in how trauma is experienced and stored in the brain and body, to participate in healing,
- Restores spontaneity (223).

Dayton developed the technique of spiraling to work with trauma psychodramatically. In spiraling, the group is asked to share current conflicts. One person volunteers to work on a specific conflict. The director sets up the scene and begins to work on the conflict. When the protagonist clearly has transferred past feelings upon the current scene, the director asks: "When have you felt like this before? And with whom?" When the past characters are identified, the director freezes the scene and spirals back to the past, which Dayton refers to as the root scene or, in Moreno's terms, the *status nascendi*. The protagonist is then asked to choose people from the group as auxiliaries representing characters from the past. The past scene is then dramatized and brought to closure with an awareness of its meaning for the protagonist. Then the scene is spiraled forward to the present. The first scene is reenacted, with new insights gained from playing out the root scene. Following the psychodrama, the full group meets for sharing and closure.

As a method of working with trauma, spiraling helps clients keep intrusive memories from the past in the past and focus more fully and spontaneously in the present.

Developmental Transformations in Trauma Treatment

Developmental transformations has been used for many years in treating PTSD. Johnson and his colleagues worked extensively with Vietnam veterans and other traumatized populations in realizing the goals of finding meaning and a positive orientation to the future. This work included the development of a therapeutic theater program and ongoing research in collaboration with neuroscientists at the West Haven VA Medical Center from 1985 to 1997 (see Johnson 1987; James and Johnson 1996, 1997; Johnson et al. 1996; Johnson 2000a).

One example of treatment through developmental transformations involved work with an eight-year-old boy named Jamaar (see James et al. 2005). Jamaar was living with a foster mother next door to his biological family in whose home he had been repeatedly sexually abused by his adolescent uncle. Although the authorities were aware of the abuse, they did not prosecute the uncle or place Jamaar in a home further away. The uncle remained a threat, and Jamaar was in trouble, acting out aggressively and sexually at school, wetting his bed at home, and displaying a range of symptoms associated with PTSD, including hypervigilance and hyperarousal, denial, distrust, and dissociation. Although aware that he was sexually abused, even stating to his therapist that his uncle "put his dick in my butt," he refused to say anything more about the trauma.

Jamaar worked for two years with a developmental transformations therapist who worked toward realizing the goals of reembodiment, reduction of hyperarousal, dissociation, and shame. Treatment began with Jamaar utilizing art materials and puppets to give form to his trauma and its containment. His trauma was symbolized by drawings of various muscle-bound men with dangerous weapons. Containment was symbolized in a puppet figure who assured him that he was safe in his room at home. Soon he chose to move to a playroom that was empty except for a few pillows. When asked, "Where are the toys?" the therapist responded, "I am the toy."

In the playroom, Jamaar overpowered and humiliated the therapist in a number of games, teaching him how it felt to be abused. Throughout this early play, the therapist provided safety by reminding Jamaar that he was in the playspace and that all aggression against the therapist had no real-life consequences. At times the therapist modeled appropriate aggressive play and encouraged Jamaar's repeated need to kill him. At this point in the process, Jamaar was fully identified with the aggressor.

Although there was no reflection following the play sessions, the therapist helped process the aggressive moments within the play. As an example, Jamaar initiated pretend boxing matches with the therapist, winning every fight. Feeling quite helpless, the therapist said: "Now I understand why you don't have any friends. If you play this way with them all the time, always telling them what to do and never letting them win, they won't want to play with you anymore" (James et al. 2005, 77).

To provide further safety, the therapist created a beginning and ending ritual, taking down an imaginary magic box at the beginning to obtain the necessary tools to engage in the play and then safely, naming and packing up all the experiences they had shared during the session in a contained space.

Over time, as Jamaar allowed the therapist into his play as an ally, the therapist noticed that Jamaar became more embodied and less aroused, more relational and empathetic. And then Jamaar invented a game of tag that was played slowly and deliberately, first with the therapist's eyes closed, and then, with the lights out. The therapist became aware that Jamaar was symbolically re-creating the abuse he experienced from his uncle at night. To create another level of awareness, the therapist took on the role of an announcer with an imaginary microphone who provided a running commentary on the game. With this device, which at first created greater distance and safety, the therapist moved into a more direct naming of the trauma. At an opportune moment when Jamaar acknowledged the connection between the game and the past abuse, the therapist raised the imaginary microphone and boldly stated to an imaginary audience: "Boys and girls, Jamaar is here to play the game on behalf of all those children whose uncles put their 'dicks in their butts'; he is your champion" (80).

Energized by this playful, brash commentary, Jamaar increased his commitment to the game. As the game came to an end, the announcer interviewed Jamaar: "The boys and girls in the audience want to know how you deal with your sexual abuse" (80). And Jamaar responded: "You tell your foster mother and your therapist; you do good in school; don't fight; you just keep going" (80).

As the two years of treatment neared an end, Jamaar and the therapist repelled an imaginary attack from Jamaar's father, mother, and uncle. Jamaar was wounded but healed by the therapist in the role of wizard. To help Jamaar develop a further awareness of the scope of his trauma, the therapist as wizard sang a song to Jamaar, recounting the story of his trauma. Through sobbing, Jamaar released a great deal of affect, fully feeling his pain.

Jamaar's foster mother, as it turned out, adopted him. As a closing ritual, the therapist arranged for an adoption ceremony, inviting the new mother and several guests. All present celebrated Jamaar's new life. Jamaar's symptoms had markedly improved. For the first time he was able to experience his feelings and give them words.

In working with Derek, Johnson followed somewhat of a similar path as in the case of Jamaar. The difference is that Johnson was not aware of Derek's past history of trauma and only had one session to work with him. The session involved a great deal of physical contact. Aggression was portrayed throughout in such sequences as that of dog owner and dog, reminiscent of Perls's topdog and underdog, and of playing with the forbidden word "nigger." Johnson modeled and facilitated strong expression through language and gesture, helping Derek to master his fears of confronting an abusive parent.

In keeping Derek within the play frame, Johnson helped him make a distinction between his past as a traumatized child who, like Jamaar, wet his bed, and his current situation as an intact adult. It was more difficult for Derek to play out the love sequence, perhaps because of the sexual implications or more likely because of his difficulty with intimacy between men. And yet Johnson persisted in his symbolic walk in the park, attempting to explore a deeper sense of relationship with Derek in the here and now.

APPLICATIONS OF DRAMATIC THERAPY TO
OTHER FORMS OF PSYCHOTHERAPY

Each approach has limitations in trauma treatment. Role method can be too indirect and verbal. Psychodrama can be too cathartic and directive.

Developmental transformations can be too stimulating and provocative. And yet, when directed by sensitive and well-trained clinicians, all have the potential of realizing many of the goals specified by van der Kolk and Crenshaw. Given that all three approaches require many years of training and supervision, is it realistic to assume that a psychotherapist trained in other approaches can make use of them? On the one hand, it would be unwise, if not unethical, for a clinician to practice one or more of these approaches without proper training and supervision. On the other hand, taken together, these approaches offer a philosophy of treatment as well as a number of discrete techniques that can be learned by clinical psychologists, mental health counselors, and clinical social workers trained in any number of methods.

From a philosophical point of view, the dramatic therapies are holistic, proceeding through mind and body, affect and cognition, interpersonal and transpersonal relationships. It is possible to practice any one of the four primary orientations of psychotherapy—psychodynamic, cognitive-behavioral, humanistic/existential, and transpersonal—within a holistic framework, as we have already seen in the diverse work of Ferenczi and Erikson, representing the first orientation, Lazarus, Wolpe, and Kelly, representing the second, Perls and Moreno, representing the third, and Jung and the traditional healers, representing the fourth. Given the research in neuroscience pointing to the intricate interconnections between cortical and subcortical structures of left and right brain, there is now a more scientific rationale for engaging in a holistic treatment process, especially in treating trauma.

The dramatic therapies are not only holistic, but also creative forms of expression. Such a conception can aid psychotherapists in conceptualizing their clients as creative problem-solvers not only in thought, but also through dramatic action. Blatner (2005) calls for treatments that are more creative and spontaneous, interactive and playful, integrative and spiritual. In fact, he proposes a more user-friendly language for psychotherapy steeped in an understanding of role, noting: "For clients, simply talking about problems can easily drift into running around in circles, so shifting to a higher level of abstraction, using role language, helps them to identify patterns" (9).

In terms of techniques to be learned by non-drama therapists, Blatner (2000) states that psychodrama, as one approach, demands arduous training. Yet, in the spirit of encouraging an open exchange, he views several psychodramatic techniques as learnable and portable. At the top of his list is role reversal, a technique that is in many ways part of our daily lives. As an example, role reversal can be used in family therapy to better understand and resolve a conflict between a teenage daughter, who demands more freedom, and her mother, who demands more containment. By reversing roles and expressing themselves as the other, each can better appreciate the concerns and needs of the other. If the family therapist is not trained in psychodrama, she certainly would not proceed with a cathartic encounter between mother and daughter, but simply use the technique as a supplement to her customary approach.

ACTION APPROACHES IN ADDICTIONS

Psychodrama and drama therapy have been used regularly in the treatment of various forms of addiction (see, for example, Dayton 1994; Dokter 1998; Uhler and Parker 2002; Eliyahu 2003). Many recognize the intimate relationship between trauma and addiction as traumatized people often abuse alcohol and drugs and as chronic substance abusers have a tendency to create traumatic environments within their families (see Dayton 1994, 2000, 2005; Najavits, Weiss, and Shaw 1997). There are some overlapping symptoms for both groups including poor impulse control, dissociation and denial of reality, and lack of attention and focus. Addicts are also known to cope with painful feelings through either acting out or self-medicating with such substances as alcohol, drugs, and food.

Psychodrama in Addictions

Focusing specifically upon addictions, Dayton (2005) offers a number of psychodramatic exercises that are useful in psychotherapeutic and psychoeducational treatment. One example is Dayton's use of Moreno's locogram as a group warm-up to allow members an opportunity to identify their progress toward recovery. The locogram is a sociometric method of revealing connections among group members who respond to a question by placing themselves in a specific location within the room. One example is: Where do you feel you are in your recovery process? Dayton designates four locations within the room representing (1) feeling very solid in my recovery, (2) feeling neutral, (3) feeling shaky, and finally, (4) one open location representing another feeling not yet specified. Group members are invited to stand in the location that best represents their state of mind and to speak briefly about why they made their choice. If someone expresses a need to move the feeling into action, that person might be chosen as a protagonist for a psychodrama.

A second example is Dayton's (2005) sobriety checklist/locogram. This technique works like the first, except that the given locations refer to positive choices in the recovery process such as: (1) going to meetings, (2) getting enough rest, (3) having sober relationships, (4) eating well, (5) exercising, and

(6) other. Both examples can be used as part of a more conventional group therapy process, one that does not necessarily lead into dramatic action.

Dayton has adapted several psychodramatic techniques to work within a family system's model. Working through roles, Dayton (2005) suggests a warm-up exercise whereby the names of family roles associated with addictions are written on pieces of paper. Roles include addict, enabler, hero, lost child, scapegoat, mascot, and other. The papers are scattered around the room, and the therapist asks family group members to stand near the role with which they are most identified. All members discuss their choices and then move to other roles. Next they are asked to stand near the role they are least identified with and to again discuss why they made that choice. When directed by a psychodramatist, this warm-up can then move into enactment. When directed by a family therapist, this work can move into verbal discussion of the family dynamics as revealed in the role choices.

There are many other examples of both psychodrama and drama therapy applied to the treatment of addicts. For example, Uhler and Parker (2002) report on a highly successful program in Portland, Oregon, CODA, for female drug addicts. CODA offers both residential and outpatient group counseling. Counselors come from eclectic backgrounds with training in several forms of psychotherapy and counseling. The goals of the program include developing a positive feminine identity, a sense of purpose in life, a sense of personal and social responsibility, and an ability to define and utilize strength-based competencies.

In reaching these goals, the program relies heavily upon psychodrama and drama therapy in treatment. Uhler and Parker (2002) report:

> In action therapy, patients adopt roles and act out situations or perform rituals related to their problems. Role-play and role reversal allow patients to portray their problems to themselves and others, see and experience the world from new perspectives, gain understanding and empathy, and practice new response patterns (32).

The authors note that by replaying a scene involving a relapse to drug use, for example, clients overcome a sense of shame and build an awareness that can forestall any further relapses. The work in CODA adds the element of role training, similar to behavior rehearsal, a method of enacting scenarios that enhance positive choices such as refusing drugs, coping with cravings, and managing high-risk circumstances. Uhler and Parker report that many of the stated goals are regularly realized, even though this work has not been subjected to clinical trials. Given strong anecdotal evidence they note that "women using action-therapy techniques engage more strongly with treatment, stay in treatment longer, complete treatment more often, and express more satisfaction with treatment" (32).

DRAMA THERAPY IN THE TREATMENT
OF ANOREXIA NERVOSA

Anorexia nervosa is a physical condition marked by a refusal to eat, resulting in an extreme loss of weight, and a disturbance in body image. As an emotional disorder, anorexia is characterized by an inability to cope with painful feelings. It is primarily experienced by adolescent women, although it does affect some men as well as older women. It can be accompanied by such comorbid symptoms as substance abuse, self-harm, and depression. Many anorexics are compulsive in their behaviors surrounding food and exercise. If left untreated, anorexia can lead to death. For many anorexics, the refusal to eat is a passive form of suicide, reminiscent of the character of the hunger artist featured in a short story by Kafka (1993). It is a prevalent condition, affecting some 1 percent of all American women.

Psychodrama and drama therapy have both been applied to the treatment of eating disorders (see Young 1986; Hornyak and Baker 1989; Wurr and Pope-Carter 1998). In her edited volume, *Arts Therapies and Clients with Eating Disorders: Fragile Board*, Dokter (1994) features eighteen applications of action and other creative arts therapies to the treatment of anorexia and bulimia.

In her lead chapter, Dokter describes drama therapy work in a six-month residential treatment program with a group of eating disordered individuals in their twenties and thirties. She notes that conventional treatments for anorexic clients involve first an attention to the biological needs to secure healthy nutrition, and second an attention to psychological factors to provide a corrective for distorted perceptions of self and others. Dokter combines a psychodynamic orientation with her training in drama therapy. For the latter, she applies projective techniques as they are the least threatening and provocative.

Dokter explained that direct embodiment was fearful for many, as it involved too much self-disclosure. She created distance by first presenting clients with a basket of shells, stones, and wooden objects and asking them to sculpt the relationship among the objects. Noting that the objects represented significant people in their lives, she asked the clients to sculpt pictures of their past, present, and future. In the future projection, Dokter asked whether clients could envision a small change in their relationship to others as represented by the objects.

As many anorexic clients are verbal, Dokter allowed plenty of time to reflect upon their sculpts and other dramatic activities. She knew that the projective objects represented many feelings that had been locked inside, defended by the need to control all access to nourishment offered by others. Dokter frequently made use of continuums to counteract the clients' tendency to split the world into good and bad objects and to often get stuck in negative views of self and other. As an example, Dokter often asked her clients to sculpt important social events of the week, noting a repeated pattern of caring for others at the detriment of oneself. She suggested that all think of their responses along a continuum where one pole represented caring for others, and the opposite represented caring for oneself. Clients placed themselves somewhere along the continuum in response to the question: Where on this continuum are you most afraid or most comfortable? Then she asked them to construct stories or poems in response to their placement. When they were ready, they shared their creative work with others and reflected on better ways to care for themselves.

Treating Anorexia through Role Method

In working with an anorexic woman named Sally (fictional name) intermittently over a ten-year span, Landy made frequent use of sculpts and especially metaphorical stories. Sally worked as a lawyer with disadvantaged youth and was the mother of a young daughter. She began work in Landy's drama therapy group, which included people with a variety of mood and personality disorders. Sally was twenty-five-years-old, five feet, eight inches tall, and weighed eighty-five pounds. Her eating disorder began just after she gave birth. She had put on fifty pounds during her pregnancy, and once she delivered her daughter she had a fleeting thought that became a great solution to the powerlessness and confusion about her new roles of mother and wife. The thought that became a way of life was: "I don't need to eat, because I don't need food anymore." Eliminating her appetite for food gave her great pleasure and strength.

For the first year of group, Sally did not refer to her eating disorder, even though she had previously been hospitalized by force and received treatment as an inpatient and outpatient for years. Her presenting problem was of an unsatisfactory marriage. She came to group immaculately dressed and groomed. She was a successful professional, highly verbal and empathetic with others in the group. She was hesitant to engage in any movement activity or emotionally charged action, fearing a lack of control.

Four years into the group process, Sally had a breakthrough. She was engaged in a painful divorce from her husband of twelve years. He was fighting for custody of their daughter, and Sally told the group that she had discovered that he kept meticulous notes documenting her inadequacies as a mother. One man in the group became agitated as she talked and asked how she felt. "I feel angry," she said with very little emotion.

Landy asked Sally to physicalize her anger. She shut down. He then asked her to choose two members of the group and to sculpt anger. Sally replied: "I can't do this." Landy modeled the process for her, taking on the role of a sculptor, inviting a group member into the center and demonstrating how to shape his arm into an angry gesture. With some gentle urging from the group, Sally got out of her seat and chose two group members, a man and a woman. Then, unexpectedly, she sculpted three tableaux, one at a time. In the first, she had the man punch the woman in the stomach with one hand while he held his other hand at her throat. In the second, she sculpted a scene where the man forces a gun into the stomach of the woman. In the third the man held a tangle of IV lines above the woman's head. Sally called the lines a life-support system.

After setting up each tableau, Landy asked Sally to speak to the image of anger that she had created. After some hesitation, she did so. As she addressed the life-support system, tears welled up in her eyes. Trying to maintain her composure, she reflected upon the scene, acknowledging that she often plays two contradictory roles in her life—that of lifesaver and that of dependent victim.

Sensing that she was ready to go further into her feelings, Landy said: "The woman in the tableaux has been mugged, choked, and poked with guns and needles. How does she react?"

Sally replied: "She is angry."

"Can you show us how?" urged Landy.

With great passion, Sally turned to the man holding up the life-support system and blurted out: "I wish you were dead. I want you to be run over by a train. I want you dead!" She then cried openly, allowing herself to fully experience her feelings. But in a flash, she stopped and retracted the death wish, confessing to the group that she had the power of magical thinking that can cause death and destruction simply by wishing it. Although not yet ready to fully process the power of the drama and her outburst, Sally engaged with the group in reflecting upon the meaning of the enactment. Sally said that she often felt dependent, hooked up to her husband and mother as life supports, fearful that a separation would mean death. On the other side, she also dreaded too much responsibility, afraid that she might become overwhelmed playing out the role of life support for others. In response, one man told Sally that in expressing her anger and fear she was really "hooked-up," his expression for being spontaneous and connected to her feelings. Although she could not fully accept this alternative definition of hooked-up, Sally spoke of her need to be less self-destructive and more independent. It was still unclear to her that her death wish was focused upon herself, the part that was full of feelings of anger and pain.

It took six more years for Sally to learn to tolerate her strongest passions, those she had wished dead and buried. Landy provided great space, allowing her to freely come and go as she needed, reassuring her that he would keep her safe. After working through many roles and counterroles, many images in dreams and stories, she learned to trust her therapist and one day asked if she could bring in a song and a Power Point slide show she had constructed on her laptop computer. The song, "What It Feels Like for a Girl," by Madonna, is about many images of femininity—hidden qualities of strength and pain and the right to openly express sexuality and aggression. In fact, when Madonna produced the music video of the song, it was banned from broadcast television, because it depicted a sexy woman acting out violent fantasies of mischief and mayhem.

Sally's slide show accompanied the song. It included images of Sally in her various roles of sexual woman, wife, mother, daughter, and baby. She revealed herself as both voluptuous and anorexic, both child and adult, in relationship to her father, husband, daughter, and dog. Landy sat by her side as she played out her personal drama on the laptop computer. When the music and slide show ended, both therapist and client sat in the silence, aware of the gravity of the moment. Then Sally cried, a clarifying cry from the heart.

Landy later reflected upon the pain of intimacy. He acknowledged his own feelings of not quite knowing what to do, and then shifting from himself to the relationship, in which he could validate Sally's creative act by becoming audience and witness, fully embracing all the roles expressed in the music, the lyrics, the images.

Soon after, Sally wrote Landy a letter not only reflecting upon the session, but also summing up her years of work in drama therapy:

> Recently, as I began sharing moments of being in the moment with you, I found myself mourning and grieving over what was and wasn't six years ago. . . . Who would have known that my passion to share a song with you would have opened up so many unexpected issues? Do you see what happens when passion lives inside of me? It moves me and propels me to take action. . . . Somewhere in that music "I" existed. I wanted you to feel, see and hear it. I was alive in the melody and words. Then, sharing my slide show with you was both personal and deeply revealing of how much is never finished. No tight neat bows on anything. Unpolished and raw, I revealed myself—imperfect. When would it ever feel safe enough? When would it be done? It doesn't matter. The moments of creating are what they are and they will lead me to unknown spaces that are no longer as threatening as they once were. These unknown spaces are just other words for "Intimacy" and "Passion." Yes, working with a therapist is intimate, a place to practice and rehearse in a safe place for things to come. I realize my willingness to share with you recently is truly an expression of coming to peace. No matter the outcome, without pretense, following the heart is a place I would much rather be. I have visited that other place. It is deadening.

Six years earlier, Sally had tried to symbolically kill her anger and pain. And six years before that, she refused food as a form of passive suicide. As the therapy ended, she had a dream of driving in a car with Landy to visit her family. Along the way, she saw a dead dog lying in the road, killed by a passing car. Landy asked her to take on the role of the dead dog and to speak out. As the dead dog, Sally said:

> I know that Sally was enjoying the idea of being the passenger and not being in control, and because I was reckless, I ruined that for her. Sally loves a good adventure, but when she saw me run over, I stopped that process for her. Sally's wish that day when she was driving in the car with Robert was to absorb all the images that are formed when you go by something really fast and then at the end of the trip to sit back and know that she was truly in the moment of life.

Reflecting upon her monologue, Sally summed up her therapeutic work:

> Maybe it helps to give voice to all the parts of me, because it means surviving and not having a part of me die when it gets hit head on. Is that what it always felt like when I didn't think I could tolerate the pain? Did getting hit head on or slowly diminished by the force of someone's expectations really feel like I died? What does it mean to give the pain and vulnerability a voice? Robert said I know that you will be okay, because the dog may have died in your dream, but it still can talk. The dog told its story and then it wasn't so bad anymore. I have to forgive myself for being vulnerable, naïve, reckless, and all of those things that allowed me to feel like my very essence died.

Upon terminating therapy, Sally told Landy that eating disorder reduces the whole person to that one role. Verbal therapy does not work because it centers so much upon an understanding of the eating disorder. For Sally, drama therapy worked because it allowed her to be seen and then to see herself as a multitude of roles, so much more than her eating disorder. Very much alive, with a normal weight and in a new relationship, Sally learned to better tolerate all her roles and feelings.

OTHER APPLICATIONS OF ACTION PSYCHOTHERAPY

James Sacks and colleagues (2005) have amassed a vast bibliography of more than 5,000 publications in psychodrama and drama therapy relating to the treatment of a wide variety of conditions including, but not limited to, disorders of personality, mood, anxiety, addiction, development, dissociation, and adjustment. Action therapists have worked with a wide variety of populations throughout the life cycle including abused and autistic children and adolescents, mentally ill and displaced adults, frail and disoriented elders. They have worked in such facilities as schools, hospitals, clinics, nursing facilities, prisons, playgrounds, street corners, refugee camps, theaters, businesses, and consulting rooms.

Given its holistic and creative nature, action psychotherapy does not stop with disabilities but also has great usefulness in the growing arena of wellness and positive psychology, as already mentioned in chapter 7.

A SUMMARY OF ASPECTS OF
THE DRAMATIC THERAPIES USEFUL FOR
MENTAL HEALTH PROFESSIONALS

Within the many populations and treatment facilities, action psychotherapies offer a wide range of assessment instruments, theories, concepts, and
techniques that are useful to many clinicians. Below is a summary of a
number of them that have been discussed throughout this book.

Action Assessments

The following assessment instruments can be adapted by mental health
professionals from the role method of drama therapy:

Tell-A-Story (see Landy 2001a)
Subjects make up a story on the spot and then are asked a series of ques-
tions intended to assess the subject's ability to identify qualities, functions,
and styles of each character, to specify the theme of the story and the con-
nection between the story and the everyday life of the storyteller.
Role Profiles (see Landy 2001b)
Subjects are given seventy role types, each one written upon an index card.
They group the cards into four categories: I Am This, I Am Not This, I Am
Not Sure If I Am This, and I Want to Be This. Then they are asked a number
of questions to ascertain their ability to reflect upon their role choices.
Role Checklist
Subjects are given fifty-six roles on a single page, with four columns that
read: Who I Am, Who I Want to Be, Who Is Blocking Me, and Who Can
Help Me. The subjects are asked to check the roles under each column that
best describe themselves in the moment.

The following assessment instruments can be adapted by mental health
professionals from psychodrama:

The Social Atom (see Moreno 1946/1994)
Subjects use circles, triangles, and arrows to diagram their relationships to
significant others within their life.
The Role Diagram (see Moreno 1946/1994)
Subjects depict the roles that they play in their everyday lives in the form of
a drawing.
Spectrogram (see Moreno 1946/1994)
Subjects in a group are asked to place themselves along a continuum in the
form of an imaginary line traversing the room, in response to a question,

such as: How comfortable are you disclosing details about your life? They then discuss their choices with others.

Locogram (see Moreno 1946/1994)
Subjects in a group are asked to place themselves in one location of a room, in response to a question intended to divide the whole group into smaller units. They then discuss their choices with others.

Spontaneity Test (see Moreno 1946/1994)
Subjects are given a prepared scenario and asked to improvise a given role in relationship to trained auxiliaries.

The following assessment instruments can be adapted by mental health professionals from developmental transformations:

The Diagnostic Role-Playing Test (DRPT-1) (see Johnson 1988)
Subjects are asked to enact five roles—grandparent, bum, politician, teacher, lover. Subjects are given various props through which to enact the roles. They then discuss their role choices.

The Diagnostic Role-Playing Test (DRPT-2) (see Johnson 1988)
Subjects are asked to improvise three scenes, each one of which involves three beings. After each one they are asked to describe what happened in the scenes.

Action Theory

As mentioned in chapter 7 and earlier in this chapter, there are several theoretical ideas common to all three action approaches. These ideas can be incorporated into other psychotherapeutic orientations in part or in totality. The most prominent are the holistic, dramatic, and creative natures of the action psychotherapies. For one, many clinicians treating a traumatized client find it useful to consider understanding the somatic as well as cognitive effects of trauma and might even work in part through the body. If that client refers to the soothing quality of spiritual beliefs, the clinician can incorporate an understanding of the spiritual domain.

As to dramatic action, although most clinicians are not trained in the direct use of drama, they still can apply the metaphors of world as stage and people as actors to guide clients in and out of their life narratives, creating the optimal distance to help them view painful experiences from a safe vantage point.

Finally, the process of psychotherapy could well be enhanced by clinicians attuned to the creative process. Whether envisioned as an art, science, or some combination, psychotherapy concerns, in part, the creation of feeling forms and symbolic, aesthetic forms that require more or less than interpretation.

When people tell their stories of struggle, they do not necessarily do so in a rational, linear fashion. Some speak in metaphors; some use words to obfuscate feelings; some have no words available at all. Reading the narratives of these people requires aesthetic skills—an understanding of role and story, an ear and eye attuned to nuance and expressive forms, a knowledge of the ways and means of kinesthetic expression.

Action Concepts

A number of concepts stemming from these theoretical ideas can be incorporated into the frameworks used by various mental health professions. Such concepts include:

- Act hunger—the biologically based need to seek expression through action
- Aesthetic Distance—a balanced state of thought and feeling
- Auxiliary Ego—a member of a group who stands in for a significant other in the life of the protagonist
- Catharsis—the release of intense feelings leading to a sense of relief or integration
- Counterrole—another side or aspect of a given role
- Dramatic Action—like play, the spontaneous expression of thoughts and feelings through role and story
- Embodiment—the expression of a role, feeling, or thought through the body
- Encounter—the essential relationship between self and other, client and therapist
- Guide—a figure that integrates role and counterrole and that both witnesses and leads the client on the therapeutic journey; an inner figure of acceptance and containment
- Playspace—the psychological location of the encounter; a state of playfulness that exists between client and therapist
- Protagonist—the primary ego or client within a therapeutic session
- Role—a persona or archetypal form encompassing several related character traits
- Sociometry—the study of group process useful for understanding interpersonal relationships within a group
- Spontaneity—an ability to respond with some degree of adequacy to a new situation or with some degree of novelty to an old situation
- Story—the narrative of the client's life experience
- Surplus Reality—a heightening of everyday reality through a form of dramatic action that can change the direction of clients' lives

Action Techniques

The following techniques derived from the dramatic therapies can be applied to the work of various mental health professionals:

- Closure—providing containment through sharing feelings and reflecting upon the meaning of the session
- Doubling—giving voice to an alter ego that represents the inner life of the protagonist
- Empty Chair—interacting with an imaginary figure who represents an other with whom the protagonist has unfinished business
- Enactment—moving the story into action through role-playing, sound and movement, or some other expressive process
- Future projection—enacting an imaginary moment in the future
- Mirroring—modeling actions for protagonists so that they can view themselves in a more accurate fashion or discover a new way to play out an old situation
- Play—spontaneous, improvised action within the imaginal realm
- Role Training—preparing an auxiliary for the demands of a given role
- Role-playing—taking on the traits and physicality of another and acting as if one were the other. The other can be fictional or real, external or internal.
- Role reversal—switching roles with another person in the group or another part of oneself
- Soliloquy—a moment when protagonists remove themselves from the flow of the action and verbalize internal thoughts and feelings
- Storytelling—creating a narrative, whether real or fictional, whether based in the past or referring to the future, concerning a particular theme or issue in one's life
- Transformations—interactive play where the players spontaneously shift roles and themes in the moment
- Warm-ups—exercises and experiences intended to prepare mind and body for engaging in therapeutic work

HOW MENTAL HEALTH PROFESSIONALS CAN LEARN THE ACTION APPROACHES

Many of the dramatic concepts and techniques, such as role and playspace, enactment and mirroring, are well known to contemporary depth psychotherapists and others who have defined them according to their own theoretical orientation. However, there are many ways to learn these approaches through the lens of the dramatic psychotherapies. The most direct way is to train in one of the academic programs in drama therapy. There are three drama therapy programs in North American universities leading to the master's degree. They are located at California Institute for Integral Studies in San Francisco, Concordia University in Montreal, Canada, and New York University in New York City. Hunter College and the New School in New York City and Kansas State University in Manhattan, Kansas, also offer courses in drama therapy but do not grant a degree in the field.

A number of private training institutes have also developed that offer training and education in one particular approach. Developmental transformations can be studied at the Institutes for the Arts in Psychotherapy in New York City (www.artstherapy.net), directed by David Read Johnson, as well as in San Francisco, Holland, and Israel. Role method can be studied at New York University as well at the Institute for Drama Therapy (www.institutefordramatherapy.com), also in New York City. Psychodrama is generally taught through private institutes, of which there are many throughout the United States and indeed, throughout the world. In New York City, the prominent center is the Psychodrama Training Institute (www.psychodramanyc.com). Nina Garcia and her colleague Dale Buchanan offer training through the Psychodrama Training Associates (www.psychodramatraining.com) in Princeton, New Jersey, and in Florida at locations in Miami, Tampa, and West Palm Beach.

The professional organization representing drama therapists in North America is the National Association for Drama Therapy (www.nadt.org). The primary one in the UK is the British Association of Drama Therapists (www.badth.org.uk). The organization that represents psychodrama in North America is called the American Society of Group Psychotherapy and Psychodrama (www.asgpp.org). Its sister organization in the UK is called the British Psychodrama Association (gparrott.gotadsl.co.uk). Psychodramatists are certified by the American Board of Examiners in Psychodrama, Sociometry, and Group Psychotherapy (www.asgpp.org/ABE).

In the UK, there are five postgraduate training programs located at the University of Derby, University of Plymouth (St. Loye's), Roehampton University, University of Manchester, and Central School of Speech and Drama (Sesame). Drama therapy is taught on the undergraduate level in the Netherlands and in several certificate programs in Israel and Greece. Aside from this array of formal academic and institute-based trainings, there is a wide variety of workshops offered privately and collectively at professional conferences.

As mentioned earlier, the learning of these theories and methods demands a great investment of time and energy, both in the academic study and in the clinical internship and supervision process. Each professional organization has a clear posting of its ethical and educational guidelines.

However, given a complete professional training and supervision in a related form of psychotherapy, and given a commitment to apply action methods to treatment, mental health professionals can make use of many of the available educational and training opportunities to further their ability to understand and implement action methods.

9

An Integration

Hamlet, the psychologically complex character created by Shakespeare at the beginning of the seventeenth century, had a keen knowledge of acting and actors. In attempting to discover whether his uncle was truly the murderer of his father, Hamlet enlisted a traveling troupe of actors, giving them advice on how to stage "The Murder of Gonzago," a play that symbolically recapitulated the actual murder. Hamlet intended to carefully observe his uncle's response to the psychodramatic elements of the play, marking his agitation as a sign of implicit guilt. In coaching the actors, Hamlet implored them to: "Suit the Action to the Word, the Word to the Action" (Shakespeare 1600/1963, III, ii, 17–18).

Even though Hamlet's aim of entrapment was less than noble, his dramatic method was fully justified. In the scope of the play, it worked, provoking a guilty reaction and then confession from Claudius. Most important for our purposes is that Shakespeare, by way of Hamlet, recognized that in order to reveal a truth and to communicate it to an audience, there must be a congruence of language and action.

Shakespeare knew a thing or two about polarities and created symmetrical characters, themes, conceits, and ideas. At the conclusion of *Hamlet*, for example, the stage is littered with bodies, the old regime is decimated, but before the curtain descends, Hamlet's foil, Fortinbras, enters to mourn the old and herald in the new order. Shakespeare, the composer of brilliant language, was also the creator of action scenarios that gave the language such vitality that it continues to be not only read on the page, but performed on the stage.

Shakespeare's plays have the potential of taking the audience on a full journey toward destruction and back to renewal. The endings are not necessarily happy, but they are restorative. The old order is demolished. The king is dead, but he and his public have acquired a deeper awareness along the way, and a new order will renovate the broken community. Both drama therapists and psychiatrists have applied Shakespeare's insights to the therapeutic process (see, for example, Cox 1992; Jennings 1992; Cox and Theilgaard 1994). Like Shakespeare and the great theater artists, the action psychotherapists are restorative, leading their clients into and out of forbidden and broken places in the psyche. They do so with an awareness of the dramatic nature of the quest, dramatic not only in the thematic content of the eternal narrative struggles, but also in the form. Drama integrates actions and words, fiction and reality, past and present, thought and feeling, states of over- and underdistance. The dramatic worldview is a dialectical one whose goal, in Hamlet's terms, is "to hold as 'twere the mirror up to nature" (Shakespeare 1600/1963, III, iii, 16–23).

Drama has proven to be so resilient as metaphor and technique throughout the history of psychological healing because of its restorative and integrative nature. We saw this earlier in the book in the description of a contemporary shamanic healing ceremony that aimed to restore hope within a community of fishermen. The traditional shamans understood the doubleness of existence and used this dramatic knowledge to recapitulate the ancient wisdom of the hero's journey into the spiritual realm.

We saw the dramatic technique of hypnosis applied by Freud and Breuer in the treatment of hysteria. Although Freud rejected hypnosis, perhaps because it was too theatrical, he did not abandon the dramatic metaphor as he later developed the concept of transference to explain how past experiences are played out in the present moments of encounter between patient and therapist. We see this dramatic idea further developed in the work of contemporary analysts who moved beyond Freud's one-person psychology to a relational approach steeped in the encounter between human beings. Mitchell (1988) uses dramatic language in describing the dynamics played out between patient and psychoanalyst:

> The analyst discovers himself a co-actor in a passionate drama involving love and hate, sexuality and murder, intrusion and abandonment, victims and executioners. Whichever path he chooses, he falls into one of the patient's predestined categories and is experienced by the patient in that way (295).

A few years later, the interpersonal psychoanalyst, Edgar Levenson (1991), referred to the patient/therapist relationship as a "playground for the reenactment and experiencing of cardinal issues" (208). Such language resonates with Johnson's understanding of the playspace.

Further, with the burgeoning field of neuroscience, there is new evidence of the dramatic nature of the brain. With the recent discovery of mirror neurons, brain cells that respond to actions observed in the same way as actions taken, researchers now hypothesize a neurological connection between acting and seeing, between the emotional experience of self and that of the other (see Stamenov and Gallese 2002; Rizzolatti and Craighero 2004; Gallese 2005). Mirror neurons explain how catharsis, a moment of weeping when identifying with the tragedy of a protagonist, links one person's feelings to those of another.

Drama has endured as a form of psychological healing not only because it is restorative, integrative, and, as we have seen, holistic, but also because it is ultimately about survival. When Moreno wrote his seminal book, *Who Shall Survive?*, in 1934, he prophesied that those individuals and societies stuck in entrenched roles, embracing old solutions to new problems, will not survive well into the future. Those best fit to survive, according to Moreno, are those who are creative and spontaneous. Through their actions, these brave souls are capable of paradoxically replaying a future, that is, returning to the past in order to correct an embedded dilemma that, once transformed, will positively impact the future.

Perhaps Freud and Moreno are not such strange bedfellows after all. Freud, himself, was a creative survivor, who drew upon his courage to challenge the cultural conserve of Vienna at the turn of the century. Freud engaged deeply in the intense dramas played out on the couch as others dared to take mysterious journeys into the unconscious. Likewise, Moreno made use of language to help people like Barbara, the Viennese actress, understand the meaning of her psychodramatic process as she integrated her stage roles and domestic ones.

Despite John's version of the Gospels, the word was not necessarily the first incarnation of the spirit. In the beginning could just as well have been the act, as Moreno suggests. Even from a developmental perspective, the question of which came first, the sound or the movement, is an open one that continues to engage scores of philosophers and creative arts therapists. What is critical for our purposes is that through drama, polarities have the potential of integration—to be *and* not to be, to make sense of experience through words *and* through action. Neurologically speaking, drama is the moment when the brain, through its mirror neurons, integrates actor and observer, action and empathy.

Throughout this book, various polarities have been set up. A meeting of shamans is juxtaposed with a meeting of psychoanalysts. Healing through spiritual means stands against psychoanalysis. Thinking and feeling stand against sensation and intuition. Projective techniques stand against psychodramatic ones. Left brain cortical structures responsible for language and rational thought stand against right brain neocortical structures responsible for intuition and arousal. Throughout we have explored the therapeutic interplay of emotion and distance, fiction and reality, verbal and nonverbal expression, action and reflection, directive and nondirective action, transference and countertransference. Moving beyond the polarities, there is an implicit departure and return as action psychotherapy grows out of psychoanalysis which, over time, rediscovers its dramatic roots that are as ancient as early shamanic healing. This circular process occurs in a space far beyond the clashing of polarities. That space has been conceptualized throughout this book in Latin as the *illud tempus* and the *status nascendi* and in English as playspace, transitional space, and aesthetic distance, all noted by an ability to hold together discrepant states of being.

In a moment of indulging in that space, I leave behind the formality of the third person to take on a more direct voice. I recall my first experience many years ago as a patient in psychoanalysis. I was lying on a couch and was asked by my therapist to verbalize all thoughts and feelings that came to mind. It was difficult to filter though all the noise in my head, and I felt lost. But in front of me was a flower arrangement in a large glass bowl. I contemplated it for a long time until I saw images forming among the flowers rising from the bowl. As I engaged in the drama, I relaxed and began to name the images and the feelings associated with them. The therapist helped me stay with my feelings without fully diverting my attention from the Rorschach-like forms among the flowers. I thought of her containing presence like the glass bowl that held the flowers.

Recently, on my way to work, I passed a rather nondescript building and noticed a metal sign on a post that read: "No Parking—Wedding." And then I noticed another sign just behind the first reading: "No Parking—Funeral." As I walked on, I suddenly stopped, caught in the dissonance. I needed to know what kind of institution juxtaposed these two signs in its driveway. I looked up and saw that it was a church whose clergy regularly perform the rituals surrounding marriage and death. I wondered who or what had the power to contain the most dramatic moments of life—the beginning of a new family, the ending of an old. If these were spiritual polarities, I thought, they could only be reconciled by faith in a religion or a spiritual being powerful enough to hold together that which the human mind cannot.

This is a book about dramatic action and about an understanding that it is possible to reenact past events in the present as a means of affecting the future. It is about significant figures who dared to explore the unconscious mind, the unwieldy and unexplored group, the unknowable cosmos in order to learn not only how they function, but also how to enhance their functioning. And it is about encouraging mental health professionals to harness the knowledge of dramatic action in the service of facilitating integration among discrepant parts of the self, the family, and the group. This book is an answer to Hamlet's question, "To be or not to be." Like the bowl that holds the flowers, the therapist that holds the images and words, the mirror neurons that hold action and empathy, the spiritual belief that holds the realities of life and death—it responds at aesthetic distance. It is possible to be me and not me at the same time, acting my life even as I reflect upon it, learning who I am by taking on the roles of others.

The bad news is that life is not always dramatic, and we all have a tendency to get stuck in repeated, destructive patterns. The good news is that if we are actors in our life's drama, we have the capacity to revise old scripts, take on new roles altogether, and create ourselves anew just by engaging our imaginations and heeding the signs we pass along the way. As mentioned earlier in the book: "All the world is not, of course, a stage, but . . . crucial ways in which it isn't are not easy to specify" (Goffman 1959, 72).

References

Alger, H. (1872). *Phil, the fiddler*. Boston: Loring.

American Psychiatric Association (APA). (1980). *Diagnostic and statistical manual of mental disorders*, 3rd ed. Washington, DC: American Psychiatric Association.

Artaud, A. (1958). *The theatre and its double*. New York: Grove Press.

Axline, V. (1947). *Play therapy: The inner dynamics of childhood*. Boston: Houghton Mifflin.

———. (1969). *Play therapy*. New York: Ballantine Books.

Bannister, A. (1997). *The healing drama: Psychodrama and dramatherapy with abused children*. London: Free Association Books.

Barbato, L. (1945). Drama therapy. *Sociometry* 8, 396–98.

Barnes, P., E. Powell-Griner, K. McFann, and R. Nahin (2004). Complementary and alternative medicine use among adults: United States, 2002. *Center for Disease Control Advance Data Report #343*. Washington, DC: National Center for Complementary and Alternative Medicine.

Berne, E. (1961). *Transactional analysis in psychotherapy*. New York: Grove Press.

———. (1964). *Games people play*. New York: Grove Press.

Blatner, A. (1996). *Acting-in: Practical applications of psychodramatic methods*, 3rd ed. New York: Springer.

———. (2000). *Foundations of psychodrama: History, theory and practice*, 4th ed. New York: Springer.

———. (2001). Psychodrama. In R. Corsini, ed. *Handbook of innovative therapies*, 2nd ed. Hoboken, NJ: John Wiley & Sons, 535–45.

———. (2005). Beyond psychodrama. *New Therapist* 36, 15–21.

Blatner, A., with D. Wiener, eds. (2007). *Interactive and improvisational drama: Varieties of applied theatre and performance*. Lincoln, NE: iUniverse.

Boal, A. (1979). *Theatre of the oppressed*. New York: Urizen Books.

———. (1995). *The rainbow of desire: The Boal method of theatre and therapy*. New York: Routledge.

Bolton, G. (1979). *Towards a theory of drama in education*. London: Longman.

Bonny, H. (1997). The state of the art of music therapy. *The Arts in Psychotherapy 24*, 65–73.

Casey, G. (1973). Behavior rehearsal: Principles and procedures. *Psychotherapy: Theory, Research and Practice 10*, 4, 331–33.

Casson, J. (1997). Dramatherapy history in headlines: Who did what, when, where? *Journal of the British Association for Dramatherapists 19*, 2, 10–13.

———. (2004). *Drama, psychotherapy and psychosis: Dramatherapy and psychodrama with people who hear voices*. New York: Brunner-Routledge.

Cattanach, A. (1993). *Playtherapy with abused children*. London: Jessica Kingsley.

———. (1994). *Playtherapy—Where the sky meets the underworld*. London: Jessica Kingsley.

———. (1997). *Children's stories in playtherapy*. London: Jessica Kingsley

———. (2003). *Introduction to play therapy*. New York: Brunner-Routledge.

Chase, A. (2003). *Harvard and the Unabomber: The education of an American terrorist*. New York: Norton.

Chodorow, J. (1997). *Jung on active imagination*. Princeton, NJ: Princeton University Press.

Chodorow, N. (1991). *Feminism and psychoanalytic theory*. New Haven, CT: Yale University Press.

Condon, L. (2007). Bibliodrama. In A. Blatner with D. Wiener, eds. *Interactive and improvisational drama: Varieties of applied theatre and performance*. Lincoln, NE: iUniverse.

Cooley, C. (1922). *Human nature and the social order*. New York: Scribner's.

Corey, G. (2001). *Theory and practice of counseling and psychotherapy*, 6th ed. Belmont, CA: Brooks/Cole.

Courtney, R. (1968). *Play, drama and thought*. New York: Drama Book Specialists.

Cox, M., ed. (1992). *Shakespeare comes to Broadmoor*. London: Jessica Kingsley.

Cox, M. and A. Theilgaard. (1994). *Shakespeare as prompter: The amending imagination and the therapeutic process*. London: Jessica Kingsley.

Cozolino, L. (2002). *The neuroscience of psychotherapy: Building and rebuilding the human brain*. New York: W. W. Norton.

Crenshaw, D. (2006). Neuroscience and trauma treatment—Implication for creative arts therapists. In L. Carey, ed., *Expressive and creative arts methods for trauma survivors*. London: Jessica Kingsley.

Csikszentmihalyi, M. (1990). *Flow: The psychology of optimal experience*. New York: Harper & Row.

Dayton, T. (1994). *The drama within: Psychodrama and experiential therapy*. Deerfield Beach, FL: Health Communications.

———. (2000). *Trauma and addiction: Ending the cycle of pain through emotional literacy*. Deerfield Beach, FL: Health Communications.

———. (2005). *The living stage: A step-by-step guide to psychodrama, sociometry and group psychotherapy*. Deerfield Beach, FL: Health Communications.

Demasio, A. (1994). *Descartes' error: Emotion, reason and the human brain*. New York: Putnam.

———. (1999). *The feeling of what happens: Body and emotion in the making of consciousness*. New York: Harcourt Brace & Co.

Derek (2006). Personal communication.

Derrida, J. (1978). *Writing and difference.* Chicago: University of Chicago Press.

Diener, G. and J. L. Moreno. (1972). *Goethe and psychodrama.* Psychodrama and Group Psychotherapy Monograph no. 48. Beacon, NY: Beacon House.

Dintino, C. and D. Johnson. (1996). Playing with the perpetrator: Gender dynamics in developmental drama therapy. In S. Jennings, ed., *Drama therapy: Theory and practice.* Vol. 3. London: Routledge.

Dokter, D., ed. (1994). *Arts therapies and clients with eating disorders: Fragile board.* London: Jessica Kingsley.

———., ed. (1998). *Arts therapists, refugees and migrants: Reaching across borders.* London: Jessica Kingsley.

Duckworth, L., T. Steen, and M. Seligman. (2005). Positive psychology in clinical practice. *Annual Review of Clinical Psychology* 1, 629–51.

Dunne, P. (1992). *The narrative therapist and the arts.* Los Angeles: Possibilities Press.

———. (2000). Narradrama: A narrative approach to drama therapy. In P. Lewis and D. Johnson, eds., *Current approaches in drama therapy.* Springfield, IL: Charles C Thomas.

Eigen, M. (1993). *The psychotic core.* Northvale, NJ: Jason Aronson.

Eliade, M. (1961). *The sacred and the profane.* New York: Harper & Row.

———. (1972). *Shamanism: Archaic techniques of ecstasy.* Princeton, NJ: Princeton University Press.

Eliaz, E. (1988). *Transference in drama therapy.* Unpublished Ph.D. dissertation. New York: New York University.

Eliyahu, A. (2003). Cognitive-behavioral approach in psychodrama: Discussion and example from addiction treatment. *The Arts in Psychotherapy* 30, 209–16.

Emunah, R. (1994). *Acting for real—Drama therapy process, technique, and performance.* New York: Brunner-Mazel.

———. (2000). The integrative five-phase model of drama therapy. In P. Lewis and D. Johnson, eds., *Current Approaches in Drama Therapy.* Springfield, IL: Charles C Thomas.

Erikson, E. (1963). *Childhood and society.* New York: Norton.

Evreinoff, N. (1927). *The theatre in life.* New York: Brentano's.

Feldhendler, D. (1994). Augusto Boal and Jacob L. Moreno. In M. Schutzman and J. Cohen-Cruz, eds., *Playing Boal—Theatre, therapy, activism.* New York: Routledge.

Ferenczi, S. (1919). On the technique of psycho-analysis. Repr. in *Further contributions to the theory and technique of psycho-analysis.* New York: Basic Books, 1952.

———. (1920). The further development of an active therapy in psycho-analysis. Repr. in *Further contributions to the theory and technique of psycho-analysis.* New York: Basic Books, 1952.

———. (1925). Contra-indications to the "active" psycho-analytical technique. Repr. in *Further contributions to the theory and technique of psycho-analysis.* New York: Basic Books, 1952.

———. (1930). The principal of relaxation and neocatharsis. Repr. in *Final contributions to the problems and methods of psychoanalysis.* New York: Basic Books, 1955.

———. (1931). Child analysis in the analysis of adults. Repr. in *The problems and methods of psychoanalysis.* New York: Basic Books, 1955.

———. (1933). The confusion of tongues between adults and the child. Repr. in *Final contributions to the problems and methods of psychoanalysis*. New York: Basic Books, 1955.

———. (1952). *Further contributions to the theory and technique of psychoanalysis*. New York: Basic Books.

———. (1955). *Final contributions to the problem and methods of psychoanalysis*. New York: Basic Books.

———. (1988). *The clinical diary of Sandor Ferenczi*. Judith Dupont, ed. Cambridge, MA: Harvard University Press.

Ferenczi, S. and O. Rank. (1925/1986). *The development of psycho-analysis*. Madison, CT: International Universities Press.

Field, G. (2006). *Aspects of interaction in the psychoanalytic situation: A focused study on analysts' identification and experiences of enactment*. Unpublished Ph.D. dissertation. New York: New York University.

Fonagy, P. (2001). *Attachment theory and psychoanalysis*. New York: Other Press.

Fox, J., ed. (1987). *The essential Moreno: Writings on psychodrama, group method, and spontaneity*. New York: Springer.

Freud, S. (1911). *The interpretation of dreams*. Translated and edited by J. Strachey. New York: Basic Books.

Freud, S. (1914). Remembering, repeating and working through. In *Standard Edition* 12, 145–56. London: Hogarth.

———. (1930). Civilization and its discontents. In *Standard Edition* 21. London: Hogarth.

———. (1933). New introductory lectures on psycho-analysis. In *Standard Edition* 22, 5–182. London: Hogarth.

Gallese, V. (2005). "Being like me": Self-other identity, mirror neurons and empathy. In S. Hurley and N. Chater, eds., *Perspectives on imitation: From cognitive neuroscience to social science*. Boston: MIT Press.

Galway, K., K. Hurd, and D. Johnson. (2003). Developmental transformations in group therapy with homeless people with mental illness. In D. Weiner and L. Oxford, eds., *Action therapy with families and groups*. Washington, DC: American Psychological Association, 135–62.

Garcia, N. and D. Buchanan. (2000). Psychodrama. In P. Lewis and D. R. Johnson, eds., *Current approaches in drama therapy*. Springfield, IL: Charles C Thomas.

Gay, P. (1988). *Freud: A life for our time*. New York: Norton.

Gendlin, E. (1978). *Focusing*. New York: Bantam Books.

Gershoni, J., ed. (2003). *Psychodrama in the 21st century*. New York: Springer.

Gersie, A. (1991). *Storymaking in bereavement*. London: Jessica Kingsley.

———. (1992). *Earth tales*. London: Green Press.

———. (1997). *Reflections on therapeutic storymaking*. London: Jessica Kingsley.

Gersie, A. and N. King. (1990). *Storymaking in education and therapy*. London: Jessica Kingsley.

Gill, M. (1954). Psychoanalysis and exploratory psychotherapy. *Journal of the American Psychoanalytical Association* 2, 771–97.

Gilligan, C. (1982). *In a different voice: Psychological theory and women's development*. Cambridge, MA: Harvard University Press.

Glaser, B. (2004). Ancient traditions within a new drama therapy method: Shamanism and developmental transformations. *The Arts in Psychotherapy* 31, 77–88.

Goffman, E. (1959). *The presentation of self in everyday life.* Garden City, NY: Doubleday.

Gong Shu. (2003). *Yi shu, the art of living with change: Integrating traditional Chinese medicine, psychodrama and the creative arts.* Taiwan: F. E. Robbins & Sons.

Goulding, R. and M. Goulding. (1978). *The power is in the patient.* San Francisco: TA Press.

Grainger, R. (1990). *Drama and healing: The roots of dramatherapy.* London: Jessica Kingsley.

———. (1995). *The glass of heaven—The faith of the dramatherapist.* London: Jessica Kingsley.

Greenberg, J. (1996). Psychoanalytic word and psychoanalytic acts. *Contemporary Psychoanalysis* 32, 195–213.

Grotowski, J. (1968). *Towards a poor theatre.* New York: Simon & Schuster.

Gurman. A. and S. Messer, eds. (2003). *Essential psychotherapies.* New York: Guilford.

Hare, A. P. and J. Hare (1996). *J.L. Moreno.* Thousand Oaks, CA: Sage.

Harms, E. (1957). Modern psychiatry—150 years ago. *Journal of Mental Science* 103, 804–9.

Hillman, J. (1983a). *Archetypal psychology.* Dallas, TX: Spring Publications.

———. (1983b). *Healing fiction.* Barrytown, NY: Station Hill Press.

Holmes, P., M. Karp, and M. Watson, eds. (1994). *Psychodrama since Moreno.* New York: Routledge.

Hornyak, L. and E. Baker. (1989). *Experiential therapies for eating disorders.* New York: Guilford Press.

Hoyt, M. (2003). Brief psychotherapies. In A. Gurman and S. Messer, eds., *Essential psychotherapies.* New York: Guilford.

Hudgins, K. (2002). *Experiential treatment for PTSD: The therapeutic spiral model.* New York: Springer.

Hutt, J. and B. Hosking. (2005). Playback theatre: A creative resource for reconciliation. Unpublished paper, Brandeis University. Available online at www.brandeis.edu/ethics/BIF_Papers/Hutt_Hosking.pdf.

Iljine, V. (1910). Patients play theatre: A way of healing body and mind. Originally published in Russian, cited in H. Petzold. (1973). *Gestalttherapie und psychodrama.* Kassel, Germany: Nicol.

Institute for Developmental Transformations (2006). *Developmental transformations: Papers, 1982–2006.* New York: Institute for Developmental Transformations.

Irwin, E. (1985). Puppets in therapy: An assessment procedure. *American Journal of Psychotherapy* 39, 389–400.

———. (2000a). The use of a puppet interview to understand children. In K. Gitlin-Weiner, A. Sandgrund, and C. Schaefer, eds., *Play diagnosis and assessment,* 2nd ed. Hoboken, NJ: John Wiley & Sons, 682–703.

———. (2000b). Psychoanalytic approach to drama therapy. In P. Lewis and D. Johnson, eds., *Current Approaches in Drama Therapy.* Springfield, IL: Charles C Thomas.

———. (2005). Facilitating play with non-players—A developmental perspective. In A. Weber and C. Haen, eds., *Clinical applications of drama therapy in child and adolescent treatment.* New York: Brunner-Routledge.

Jacobson, E. (1964). *The self and the object world*. New York: International Universities Press.

James, M. and D. Johnson. (1996). Drama therapy for the treatment of affective expression in post-traumatic stress disorder. In D. Nathanson, ed., *Affect theory and treatment*. New York: Norton.

———. (1997). Drama therapy in the treatment of combat-related post-traumatic stress disorder. *The Arts in Psychotherapy* 23, 5, 383–95.

James, M., A. Forrester, and K. Kim. (2005). Developmental transformations in the treatment of sexually abused children. In A. Weber and C. Haen, eds. *Clinical applications of drama therapy in child and adolescent treatment*. New York: Brunner-Routledge.

Janov, A. (1970). *The primal scream: Primal therapy: the cure for neurosis*. New York: Putnam.

Jennings, S. (1973). *Remedial drama*. London: Pitman.

———., ed. (1987). *Dramatherapy: Theory and practice for teachers and clinicians*. Vol. 1. London: Routledge.

———. (1992). Reason in madness: Therapeutic journeys through *King Lear*. In *Dramatherapy: Theory and practice*. Vol. 2. New York: Tavistock/Routledge.

———. (1995a). *Dramatherapy with children and adolescents*. London: Routledge.

———. (1995b). *Theatre, ritual and transformation: The Temiar experience*. London: Routledge.

Johan, M. (1992). Enactments in psychoanalysis. *Journal of the American Psychoanalytic Association* 40, 827–44.

Johnson, D. (1987). The role of the creative arts therapies in the diagnosis and treatment of psychological trauma. *The Arts in Psychotherapy* 14, 7–14.

———. (1988). The diagnostic role-playing test. *The Arts in Psychotherapy* 15, 1, 23–36.

———. (1991). The theory and technique of transformations in drama therapy. *The Arts in Psychotherapy* 18, 285–300.

———. (1992). The dramatherapist in role. In S. Jennings, ed., *Dramatherapy: Theory and practice*. Vol. 2. London: Routledge, 112–36.

———. (2000a). Creative arts therapies. In E. Foa, T. Keane, and M. Friedman, eds., *Effective treatments for posttraumatic stress disorder*. New York: Guilford, 356–58.

———. (2000b). Developmental transformations: Toward the body as presence. In P. Lewis and D. Johnson, eds., *Current approaches in drama therapy*. Springfield, IL: Charles C Thomas.

———. (2006). Personal communication.

Johnson, D. and D. Quinlan. (1993). Can the mental representations of paranoid schizophrenics be differentiated from those of normals? *Journal of Personality Assessment* 60, 588–601.

Johnson, D. and S. Sandel. (1977). Structural analysis of movement sessions: Preliminary research. *Journal of the American Dance Therapy Association* 1, 32–36.

Johnson, D., A. Forrester, C. Dintino, and M. James. (1996). Towards a poor drama therapy. *The Arts in Psychotherapy* 23, 293–306.

Johnson, D., R. Rosenheck, A. Fontana, H. Lubin, S. Southwick, and D. Charney. (1996). Outcome of intensive inpatient treatment of combat-related PTSD. *American Journal of Psychiatry* 153, 771–77.

Johnson, D., A. Smith, and M. James. (2003). Developmental transformations in group therapy with the elderly. In C. Schaefer, ed., *Play therapy with adults*. New York: John Wiley & Sons, 78–106.

Johnson, R. (1986). *Inner work: Using dreams and active imagination for personal growth*. San Francisco: Harper & Row.

Jones, E. (1959). *The life and work of Sigmund Freud*. New York: Basic Books.

Jones, P. (2007). *Drama as therapy: Theory, practice and research*. London: Routledge.

Jung, C. (1916/1958). The transcendent function. In *Collected works*. Vol. 8. Princeton, NJ: Princeton University Press, 1975, "Prefatory Note" and pars. 131–93.

———. (1921). *Psychological types*. Repr. in *Collected works*. Vol. 6. Princeton, NJ: Princeton University Press, 1971.

———. (1928). The technique of differentiation between the ego and the figures of the unconscious. Repr. in *Collected works*. Vol. 7. Princeton, NJ: Princeton University Press, 1953/1966; third printing, 1975, pars. 341–73.

———. (1928–1930). *Dream analysis—Notes of the seminar*. W. McGuire, ed. Princeton, NJ: Princeton University Press, 1984.

———. (1933/1950). A study in the process of individuation. Repr. in *Collected works*. Vol. 9.1. 2nd ed. Princeton, NJ: Princeton University Press, 1968, pars. 525–626.

———. (1947). On the nature of the psyche. Repr. in *Collected works*. Vol. 8. Princeton, NJ: Princeton University Press, 1975: 159–234.

———. (1950). Concerning mandala symbolism. Repr. in *Collected works*. Vol. 9.1 Princeton, NJ: Princeton University Press, 1959/1969; fourth printing, 1975.

———. (1955). Mysterium coniunctionis. Repr. in *Collected works*. Vol. 14. New York: Putnam, 1974.

———. (1963). *Memories, dreams and reflections*. New York: Vintage Books.

———. (1969). The archetypes and the collective unconscious. 2nd ed. R. F. C. Hull, trans. Bollingen Series XX. Princeton, NJ: Princeton University Press.

Kafka, F. (1993). *The metamorphosis and other stories*. New York: Charles Scribner's Sons.

Kalff, D. (1980). *Sandplay*. Santa Monica, CA: Sigo Press.

Karp, M., P. Holmes, and K. Bradshaw-Tauvon, eds. (1998). *Handbook of psychodrama*. New York: Routledge-Taylor & Francis.

Kellermann, P. (1998). Sociodrama. *Group Analysis* 31, 179–95.

———. (2007). *Sociodrama and collective trauma*. London: Jessica Kingsley.

Kelly, G. A. (1955). *The psychology of personal constructs*. Vols. 1 & 2. New York: Norton.

Kendall, P. C. (1984). Behavioral assessment and methodology. *The American Review of Behavioral Therapy: Theory and Practice* 10, 47–86.

Kipper, D. (1996). The emergence of role-playing as a form of psychotherapy. *Journal of Group Psychotherapy, Psychodrama & Sociodrama* 49, 3, 99–120.

Kisiel, C., M. Blaustein, J. Spinazzola, C. Schmidt, M. Zucker, M. van der Kolk, and B. van der Kolk. (2006). Evaluation of a theater-based youth violence prevention program for elementary school children, *Journal of School Violence* 5, 2, 19–36.

Klein, M. (1975). *Writings of Melanie Klein*. Vols. 1–3. London: Hogarth.

Kris, E. (1982). *Free association: Method and process*. New Haven, CT: Yale University Press.

Krondorfer, B. (1995). *Remembrance and reconciliation: Encounters between young Jews and Germans*. New Haven, CT: Yale University Press.

Kübler-Ross, E. (1969). *On death and dying*. New York: Macmillan.

Lahad, M. (1992). Storymaking: An assessment method of coping with stress. In S. Jennings, ed., *Dramatherapy, theory and practice*. Vol. 2. London: Routledge.

Landreth, G. (1991). *Play therapy: The art of relationship*. Muncie, IN: Accelerated Development.

Landy, R. (1993). *Persona and performance—The meaning of role in drama, therapy and everyday life*. New York: Guilford.

———. (1994). *Drama therapy—Concepts, theories and practices*. 2nd ed. Springfield, IL: Charles C Thomas.

———. (1996). *Essays in drama therapy: The double life*. London: Jessica Kingsley.

———. (2000). Role theory and the role method of drama therapy. In P. Lewis and D. R. Johnson, eds., *Current approaches in drama therapy*. Springfield, IL: Charles C Thomas.

———. (2001a). Tell-A-Story—A new assessment in drama therapy. In *New essays in drama therapy—Unfinished business*. Springfield, IL: Charles C Thomas.

———. (2001b). Role profiles—An assessment instrument. In *New essays in drama therapy—Unfinished business*. Springfield, IL: Charles C Thomas.

———. (2003). Drama therapy with adults. In C. Schaefer, ed., *Adult play therapy*. Hoboken, NJ: John Wiley & Sons, 15–33.

———. (2004). *Standing Tall*. Study guide. Boston: Fanlight Productions.

———. (2005). *Three approaches to drama therapy*. Video and DVD. New York: New York University.

Landy, R., B. Luck, E. Conner, and S. McMullian. (2003). Role profiles—A drama therapy assessment instrument. *The Arts in Psychotherapy* 30, 151–61.

Landy, R., L. McLellan, and S. McMullian. (2005). The education of the drama therapist: In search of a guide. *The Arts in Psychotherapy* 32, 275–92.

Langley, D. (1989). The relationship between psychodrama and dramatherapy. In P. Jones, ed., *Dramatherapy: State of the art*. St. Albans, UK: Hertforshire College of Art and Design.

Lazarus, A. and C. Lazarus. (1991). *Multimodal life history inventory*. Champaign, IL: Research Press.

Levenson, E. (1991). *The purloined self*. New York: Contemporary Psychoanalytic Books.

Levinson, D. (1978). *Seasons of a man's life*. New York: Basic Books.

Lewis, P. (1993). *Creative transformation: The healing power of the arts*. Wilmette, IL: Chiron Publications.

Lewis, P. and D. Johnson, eds. (2000). *Current approaches in drama therapy*. Springfield, IL: Charles C Thomas.

Lieberman, E. (1985). *Acts of will: The life and work of Otto Rank*. New York: Free Press.

Lindkvist, M. (1994). Religion and the spirit. In P. Holmes, M. Karp, and M. Watson, eds., *Psychodrama since Moreno*. New York: Routledge.

———. (1998). *Bring white beads when you call on the healer*. New Orleans, LA: Rivendell House.

Linton, R. (1936). *The study of man*. New York: Appleton-Century-Crofts.

Lowen, A. (1967). *The Betrayal of the body*. New York: Macmillan.

———. (1993). *Bioenergetics*. New York: Penguin.

Lowenfeld, M. (1979). *The world technique*. London: George Allen & Unwin.

Magai, C. and J. Haviland-Jones. (2002). *The hidden genius of emotion*. Cambridge, UK: Cambridge University Press.

Marineau, R. (1989). *Jacob Levy Moreno 1889–1974*. New York: Tavistock/Routledge.

Maslow, A. (1971). *The farther reaches of human nature*. New York: Viking Press.

McNiff, S. (1988). The shaman within. *The Arts in Psychotherapy* 15, 285–91.

——. (1992). *Art as medicine: Creating a therapy of the imagination*. Boston: Shambhala.

——. (1998). *Trust the process*. Boston: Shambhala.

McReynolds, P. and S. DeVoge. (1977). Use of improvisational techniques in assessment. In P. McReynolds, ed., *Advances in psychological assessment*. Vol. 4. San Francisco: Jossey-Bass, 222–77.

Mead, G. (1934). *Mind, self and society*. Chicago: University of Chicago Press.

Miller, J. (1987). *Toward a new psychology of women*. Boston: Beacon Press.

Mitchell, S., ed. (1996). *Dramatherapy—Clinical studies*. London: Jessica Kingsley.

Mitchell, S. A. (1988). *Relational concepts in psychoanalysis: An integration*. Cambridge, MA: Harvard University Press.

——. (1997). *Influence and autonomy in psychoanalysis*. Hillsdale, NJ: Analytic Press.

Mitchell, S. A. and J. Greenberg. (1983). *Object relations in psychoanalytic theory*. Cambridge, MA: Harvard University Press.

Moreno, J. L. (published as Levy, Jacob). (1915). *Einladung zu einer Begegnung. Heft 2 (Invitation to an encounter, Part 2)*. Vienna/Leipzig: Anzengruber/Verlaf Brüder Suschitzky.

——. (published anonymously). (1920). *Das testament des Vaters (The words of the father)*. In *Die Gefahrten* 3:1–33. Berlin/Potsdam: Kiepenheuer Verlag.

——. (1934/1978). *Who shall survive?* Beacon, NY: Beacon House.

——. (1941/1971). *The words of the Father*. New York: Beacon House.

——. (1943). The concept of sociodrama: A new approach to the problem of intercultural relations. *Sociometry*, 6 (4), 434–449.

——. (1946/1994). *Psychodrama*. Vol. 1. Beacon, NY: Beacon House.

——. (1985). *The Autobiography of JL Moreno M.D.* (Abridged). Jonathan Moreno, ed. Moreno Archives. Cambridge, MA: Harvard University Press.

Moreno, J. L. and Z. T. Moreno. (1969). *Psychodrama*. Vol. 3. Beacon, NY: Beacon House.

Moreno, Z. T. (1944). Role analysis and audience structure. In Z. T. Moreno (2006) *The quintessential Zerka: Writings by Zerka Toeman Moreno on psychodrama, sociometry, and group psychotherapy*. New York: Routledge.

Moreno, Z. T. (1965). Psychodramatic rules, techniques, and adjunctive methods. *Group Psychotherapy* 18, 73–86.

——. (2006a). *The quintessential Zerka: Writings by Zerka Toeman Moreno on psychodrama, sociometry, and group psychotherapy*. New York: Routledge.

——. (2006b). Personal communication.

Murray, H. (1938). *Explorations in personality: A clinical and experimental study of fifty men of college age*. New York: Oxford University Press.

——. (1943). *Analysis of the personality of Adolph Hitler*. Washington, DC: Office of Strategic Services.

Murray, H. (1940). What should psychologists do about psychoanalysis? *Journal of Abnormal and Social Psychology* 35, 150–75.

Najavits, L., R. Weiss, and W. Shaw. (1997). The link between substance abuse and posttraumatic stress disorder in women: A research review. *American Journal on Addictions* 6, 273–83.

Ormont, L. (1992). *The group therapy experience: From theory to practice*. New York: St. Martin's Press.

OSS Assessment Staff. (1948). *Assessment of men: Selection of personnel for the Office of Strategic Service*. New York: Rinehart.

Pendzik, S. (1988). Drama therapy as a form of modern shamanism. *Journal of Transpersonal Psychology* 20, 81–92.

Perls, F. (1947). *Ego, hunger and aggression*. London: Allen & Unwin.

Perls, F. (1969). *Gestalt therapy verbatim*. Lafayette, CA: Real People Press.

Perls, F., R. Hefferline, and P. Goodman. (1951). *Gestalt therapy: Excitement and growth in the human personality*. New York: Dell.

Perry, B. and R. Pollard. (1998). Homeostasis, stress, trauma, and adaptation: A neurodevelopmental view of childhood trauma. *Child and Adolescent Psychiatric Clinics of North America* 7, 33–51.

Petzold, H. (1973). *Gestalttherapie und psychodrama*. Kassel, Germany: Nicol.

Piaget, J. (1962). *Play, dreams and imitation in childhood*. New York: Norton.

Pitzele, P. (1995). *Our fathers' wells: Personal encounters with the myths of genesis*. San Francisco: Harper Collins.

———. (1998). *Scripture windows: Towards a practice of bibliodrama*. Los Angeles: Torah Aura.

Propp, V. (1968). *Morphology of the folktale*. Austin: University of Texas Press.

Rank, O. (1907). *The artist*. Vienna: H. Heller.

———. (1936/1978). *Will Therapy*. New York: Norton.

———. (1941). *Beyond psychology*. New York: Dover Publications.

———. (1996). *A psychology of difference*. Princeton, NJ: Princeton University Press.

Rauch, S., B. van der Kolk, R. Fisler, N. Alpert, S. Orr, C. Savage, et al. (1996). A symptom provocation study of posttraumatic stress disorder using positron emission tomography and script-driven imagery. *Archives of General Psychiatry* 53, 380–87.

Reich, W. (1949). *Character analysis*. 3rd ed. New York: Orgone Institute.

Rizzolatti, G. and L. Craighero. (2004). The mirror neuron system. *Annual Review of Neuroscience* 27, 169–92.

Rogers, C. (1951). *Client-centered therapy: Its current practice, implications, and theory*. Boston: Houghton Mifflin.

Rothschild, B. (2000). *The body remembers—The psychophysiology of trauma and trauma treatment*. New York: Norton.

Sacks, J., M. Bilaniuk, and J. Gendron. (2005). *Bibliography of psychodrama: Inception to date*. Available online at http://asgpp.org/02ref/index.htm.

Salas, J. (2000). Playback theatre: A frame for healing. In P. Lewis and D. Johnson, eds., *Current approaches in drama therapy*. Springfield, IL: Charles C Thomas.

Sarbin, T. (1962). Role enactment. In J. Dyal, ed., *Readings in psychology: Understanding human behavior*. New York: McGraw-Hill.

Sarbin, T. and V. Allen. (1968). Role theory. In G. Lindzey and E. Aronson, eds., *The handbook of social psychology*. 2nd ed. Reading, MA: Addison-Wesley.

Sartre, J-P. (1943). *Being and nothingness*. London: Methuen.

Schattner, G. (1981). Introduction. In G. Schatter and R. Courtney, eds., *Drama in therapy*. Vol. 1. New York: Drama Books.

Schechner, R. (1985). *Between theater & anthropology*. Philadelphia: University of Pennsylvania Press.

Scheff, T. (1979). *Catharsis in healing, ritual and drama*. Berkeley: University of California.

———. (1981). The distancing of emotion in psychotherapy. *Psychotherapy: Theory, research and practice* 18, 1, 46–53.

Scheiffele, E. (1995). *The theatre of truth*. Unpublished Ph.D. dissertation, University of California, Berkeley.

Schiller, F. (1875). *On the aesthetic education of man, in a series of letters*. Oxford, UK: Clarendon Press; Repr. New York: Oxford University Press, 1982.

Schnee, G. (1996). Drama therapy in the treatment of the homeless mentally ill. *The Arts in Psychotherapy* 23, 53–60.

Shakespeare, W. (1600/1963). *Hamlet*. In *Works: A new variorum edition of Shakespeare*. H. Furness, ed. New York: Dover.

Shore, A. (2004). Commentary. *South African Psychiatric Review* 7, 16–17.

Shostrom, E. (1965). *Three approaches to psychotherapy I*. Videorecording. Corona Del Mar, CA: Psychological Films Inc.

———. (1977). *Three approaches to psychotherapy II*. Videorecording. Corona Del Mar, CA: Psychological Films Inc.

Siegel, D. (1999). *The developing mind: Toward a neurobiology of interpersonal experience*. New York: Guilford Press.

———. (2001). Toward an interpersonal neurobiology of the developing mind: Attachment relationships, "mindsight," and neural integration. *Infant Mental Health Journal* 22, 67–94.

Slade, P. (1954). *Child drama*. London: University Press.

———. (1959). *Dramatherapy as an aid to becoming a person*. London: Guild of Pastoral Psychology.

Snow, S. (2000). Ritual/Theater/Therapy. In P. Lewis and D. Johnson, eds., *Current approaches in drama therapy*. Springfield, IL: Charles C Thomas.

Solomon, J. (1938). Active play therapy. *American Journal of Orthopsychiatry* 8, 3, 763–81.

Spencer, H. (1873). *The study of sociology*. London: Henry S. King.

Spolin, V. (1963). *Improvisation for the theatre*. Chicago: Northwestern University Press.

Spoto, A. (1995). *Jung's typology in perspective*. Wilmette, IL: Chiron Publications.

Stamenov, M. and V. Gallese, eds. (2002). *Mirror neurons and the evolution of brain and language*. Amsterdam: John Benjamins Publishing Company.

Stanislavski, C. (1936). *An actor prepares*. New York: Theatre Arts Books.

Stern, D. (2000). *The interpersonal world of the infant: A view from psychoanalysis and developmental psychology*. New York: Basic Books.

———. (2004). *The present moment in psychotherapy and everyday life*. New York: Norton.

Stern, P. (2004). Director. *Standing Tall*. 24 minute videotape. Boston: Fanlight Productions.

Sternberg, P. and A. Garcia. (2000a). Sociodrama. In P. Lewis and D. Johnson, eds., *Current approaches in drama therapy*. Springfield, IL: Charles C Thomas.

———. (2000b). *Sociodrama: Who's in your shoes?* 2nd ed. Westport, CT: Praeger.

Streeck-Fischer, A. and B. van der Kolk. (2000). Down will come baby, cradle and all: Diagnostic and therapeutic implications of chronic trauma on child development. *Australian and New Zealand Journal of Psychiatry* 34, 903–18.

Sullivan, H. S. (1954). *The psychiatric interview.* New York: Norton.

Tangorra, J. (1997). *The many masks of pedophilia: Drama therapeutic assessment of the pedophile.* Master's thesis. New York: New York University.

Turner, V. (1982). *From ritual to theatre: The human seriousness of play.* New York: Performing Arts Journal Publications.

Uhler, A and O. Parker. (2002). Treating women drug abusers: Action therapy and trauma treatment. *Science and Practice Perspectives,* 30–37.

van der Kolk, B. (1994). The body keeps the score: Memory and the emerging psychobiology of post traumatic stress. *Harvard Review of Psychiatry* 1, 253–65.

———. (2002a). The assessment and treatment of complex PTSD. In R. Yehuda, ed., *Treating trauma survivors with PTSD.* Washington, DC: American Psychiatric Press.

———. (2002b). Posttraumatic therapy in the age of neuroscience. *Psychoanalytic Dialogues* 12, 3, 381–92.

———. (2002c). Beyond the talking cure. In F. Shapiro, ed., *EMDR: Towards a paradigm shift.* Washington, DC: American Psychiatric Press.

Villa Vicencio, C. (2001). Reconciliation as metaphor. Available online at http://www.ijr.org.za/sa mon/recon d.html.

von Franz, M. (1980). *The psychological meaning of redemption motifs in fairy tales.* Toronto: Inner City Books.

Wagner, B. J. (1976). *Dorothy Heathcote: Drama as a learning medium.* Washington, DC: National Education Association.

Werner, H. (1948). *Comparative psychology of mental development.* New York: International Universities Press.

Wethered, A. (1973). *Drama and movement in therapy: The therapeutic use of movement, drama and music.* Boston: Plays Inc.

White, M. (1998). *Papers by Michael White.* Adelaide, Australia: Dulwich Centre Publications.

White, M. and D. Epson. (1990). *Narrative means to therapeutic ends.* New York: Norton.

Whitehouse, M. (1979). C. G. Jung and dance therapy. In P. Lewis, ed., *Eight theoretical approaches in dance/movement therapies.* Dubuque, MN: Kendall/Hunt.

Wilensky, S. (2005). Bibliodrama scholar invites congregants to "get into other people's shoes." *Jewish Ledger.* Available online at http/bibliodrama.com.

Willet, J. (1964). *Brecht on theatre.* New York: Hill & Wang.

Winnicott, D. W. (1953). Transitional objects and transitional phenomena. *International Journal of Psychoanalysis,* 34, 89–97.

———. (1971). *Playing and reality.* Routledge: London.

Winters, N. (2000). The psychospiritual in psychodrama: A fourth role category. *The International Journal of Action Methods: Psychodrama, Skill Training and Role Playing* 52, 163–71.

Wolpe, J. (1990). *The practice of behavior therapy,* 4th ed. New York: Pergamon Press.

Wolpe, J. and A. Lazarus. (1966). *Behavior therapy techniques: A guide to the treatment of neuroses,* 1st ed. New York: Pergamon Press.

Wurr, C. and J. Pope-Carter. (1998). The journey of a group: Dramatherapy for adolescents with eating disorders. *Clinical Child Psychology and Psychiatry* 3, 4, 621–27.

Yablonsky, L. (1998). Comments and reports on significant social and crime issues. *Psychodrama Network News*. Winter.

Yalom, I. (1980). *Existential psychotherapy*. New York: Basic Books.

Young, M. (1986). The use of dramatherapy methods for working with clients with eating problems. *Dramatherapy* 9, 3–11.

Subject Index

act hunger, xii, 136–37, 240

Acting for Real, 93, 253

acting out, xv, 33–35, 38, 41, 101, 132, 197, 199, 204–5, 227, 231, 236

action, v, ix–xii, xv–xx, 1–3, 11, 15, 18, 21, 23, 25–26, 29–34, 37–42, 50–57, 59–67, 69–77, 79, 89, 91, 97–98, 102–3, 113, 127–28, 130–31, 133–37, 139–40, 142–45, 148, 159, 161–62, 165–66, 170–72, 190–93, 195–97, 199–15, 217–21, 225–26, 232–33, 235–32-241, 243, 245–48; and reflection, 3, 98, 113, 128, 161–62, 191,196, 202, 207–8, 225, 247; and words, xv, 2, 127, 140, 191; concepts, 240; directive and nondirective, 3, 98, 113, 128, 162–63, 192, 196, 208, 210, 247; in psychotherapy, vii, xx, 2, 26, 30, 38–39, 45–47, 49, 51, 53–55, 57, 59, 61, 63–67, 69, 71–73, 75, 85, 100, 131–32, 191, 193, 195–96, 202, 210–12, 237, 248; techniques, 241; theory, 239–40

action assessment, 238 (*see also* assessment)

action psychotherapy, vii, xx, 2, 26, 30, 38–39, 45, 47, 49, 51, 53–55, 57, 59, 61, 63, 65, 67, 69, 71–73, 75, 85, 100, 131–32, 191, 193, 195–96, 202, 210–12, 218, 237, 248

active imagination, 15–16, 22–23, 37, 127, 196, 206

active therapy, 30, 33–35, 37–38, 99, 197, 206

actor training, 165–66

Aesthetic Appreciation Test, 56 (*see also* assessment)

aesthetic distance, 57, 72, 94, 101–2, 105, 108, 136, 158, 172, 190, 203, 224, 240, 248

affective memory, 30, 101, 159

alchemy, 18–19, 105

alienation effect, 102 (*see also* Brecht, B.)

All's Well That End's Well, 103

alternative medicine, 217

American Board of Examiners in Psychodrama, Sociometry, and Group Psychotherapy, 242

American Society of Group Psychotherapy and Psychodrama, 242

anagnorisis, xii (*see also* Greek drama)

anima, 19

animus, 19

anorexia, treatment through drama therapy, 233–37 (*see also* eating disorder)
applied theater, 76
archetypal psychology, 87
archetypes, 13–14, 27, 94, 105, 200; and personality types, 18–23
artist, xvii–xviii, 11, 14, 23, 26, 28, 30, 33, 43–44, 59, 76–77, 85–86, 88, 93-94, 99, 106–7, 126, 133–34, 166, 202, 208, 223, 233, 246
Artist, The 23, 28–29 (*see also* Rank, O.)
aside, 52, 144
assessment, 22, 54–55, 68, 79, 98, 202, 238–39; in developmental transformations, 172–73; in psychodrama, 137–38, 142–43; in role theory, 110–11; with puppets, 92
As You Like It, 59
attachment theory, 91
authentic movement, 167 (*see also* dance/movement therapy)
autonomous healing center, ix, xiii
auxiliary ego, xi, 50, 62, 68, 81, 136–37, 139, 142–43, 162, 201, 213, 225, 240
axiodrama, 81, 197

Beacon Hill Sanatorium, 53
behavior rehearsal, 67–70, 90,139, 212, 220
Beyond Psychology, 25
Bible, 81–82, 148–49, 153
bibliodrama, 80–82, 212
bioenergetic analysis, 2, 40, 44, 70–72, 172, 206-7
brain, xvii, 2, 60, 186, 218–20, 226–27, 230, 246–47; bilateral stimulation, 220; dramatic nature of, 246; limbic system, 219 (*see also* neuroscience)
brief psychotherapy, 3, 73–74, 212, 217
British Association of Dramatherapists, 88–90, 95, 242
Buddhism, xviii, 168
bulimia, 233 (*see also* eating disorder)

canon of creativity, 135, 141
catharsis, xi–xii, 30, 35–36, 40, 51, 77–78, 83–84, 87, 101, 125, 132, 136, 139–40, 143, 158–59, 161–62, 189, 196–98, 201, 203, 240, 247; of abreaction, xi, 136, 139, 58–59; of integration, xi–xii, 136, 158, 159, 161–62, 201, 203; mental catharsis, 30
Cell Block Theatre, 90
Center for Creative Alternatives, 94, 242
Character Analysis, 39–41, 99
character armor, 41–42
child analysis with adults, 37–38
child drama, 87, 93, 261
City Lights Youth Theatre, 223
client-centered psychotherapy, 31, 72, 167 (*see also* person-centered psychotherapy)
closure, 53, 83, 140, 145, 161, 174, 193, 203, 207, 211, 221, 227, 233, 241
cognitive-behavioral therapy, 3, 68–69, 90, 211, 217, 230
cognitive dissonance, 103
cognitive therapy, 112, 212 (*see also* cognitive-behavioral therapy)
collective unconscious, 15, 18–19, 23, 27, 31, 197, 202
constructivism, 3, 67–68, 70, 211
couch, xv, 33, 36–37, 71, 133, 197, 211, 247–48
counterrole, 12, 29, 32, 51, 64–65, 90, 100, 103–4, 106–10, 112, 123–24, 128, 135, 171, 199–200, 209, 235, 240 (*see also* role and guide)
countertransference, xv, 2–3, 31, 34, 38, 98, 113, 128–29, 162–63, 172, 192–93, 203, 208, 210, 248 (*see also* transference)
creative arts therapy, 23, 94, 126 (*see also* expressive therapy)
creative process, 11, 23, 30, 85, 202, 209, 224, 239 (*see also* creativity)
creativity, x, xi, xv, xvii, 14, 23–24, 75, 89, 92, 105, 132, 135, 141, 171,

199, 202, 218 (*see also* creative process)

cultural conserve, 48, 50, 54, 132, 135, 141, 171, 247

Current Approaches in Drama Therapy, 91, 93

dance/movement therapy, 2, 44, 90, 92, 165, 167, 205, 208

deconstruction, 167

defense mechanism, 158, 205

de-roling, 112, 128, 145, 161–62, 170, 174–75, 192, 205, 211

Descartes' Error, 17

Development of Psycho-Analysis, The, 26, 29–33

developmental transformations, 3, 43, 92, 95, 98, 113, 129, 165–93, 195, 199, 201, 203–4, 206–7, 209–10, 212, 214–18, 227–28, 230, 239, 242; in trauma treatment, 227–29; witnessing circle, 170, 173–75, 179, 181, 183, 186, 190, 192

diagnostic role-playing test, 172, 239 (*see also* assessment)

distancing theory, 84, 94, 101–2, 105, 127, 156, 189–90, 216, 222; overdistance, 101–2, 105, 203; underdistance, 101, 105, 136, 166, 199, 203, 246 (*see also* aesthetic distance)

double, 24, 26–29, 100, 103, 138–41, 144, 149, 152–54, 156, 157, 159, 161–62, 200, 204, 206, 209, 213, 215, 225–26, 241, 246

Double, The 28 (*see also* Dostoyevsky)

Drama in Therapy, 91

drama therapy, xv–xvi, xviii–xix, 2–3, 16, 23, 31, 37, 41, 43–45, 61, 64, 68, 70, 74–76, 85–95, 97–130, 143, 161, 165–66, 195, 197, 201, 205, 212–15, 223, 231–34, 236–38, 242

dramatic action, 2, 47, 73, 86, 97, 102–3, 107, 113, 128, 132, 136, 143, 190–91, 197–99, 202, 204, 209, 216–17, 230, 232, 239, 240, 248

Dramatic Productions Test, 56, 58, 100, 213 (*see also* assessment)

Dramatis personae, 105

dreams, xvii–xviii, 11–13, 15, 17–19, 23, 36, 41, 47, 62–63, 196, 204, 225–26, 235–37; in psychodrama, 145–51, 156, 159–60, 162; in work of Perls, 62–64; of Jung, 17–19

drive theory, xvii, 1, 79

eating disorder, xx, 3, 89, 233–34, 237 (*see also* anorexia and bulimia)

ego, xi, xv, 9, 16, 19, 24–27, 36, 39, 41, 58–61, 65, 73, 81, 102, 134–37, 139, 142–43, 160, 196, 199–200, 225, 240–41

Ego and the Id, The, 25

Ego, Hunger and Aggression, 60–61

ego psychology, 39, 59, 200

emanation theory, 168

embodiment, 88, 133, 202, 228, 233, 240; in developmental transformations, 169, 173

embodiment, projection, role, 88, 95 (*see also* Jennings, S.)

emotion and distance, 3, 98, 101, 104, 112–13, 196, 202–3, 225, 247; in developmental transformations, 189–90; in psychodrama, 158–60; in role method, 125–26 (*see also* polarities)

empty chair, 62–64, 73, 109, 144–45, 209, 211, 213, 214, 241

enactment, xi, 2, 14, 30, 32–33, 36–39, 45, 50, 55, 69, 74, 80–81, 83, 85, 93, 101, 105, 112–13, 119, 125, 127–29, 136, 143–45, 162, 171, 173, 192, 195, 198–99, 206–7, 209, 212–13, 220, 222, 224, 232, 235, 241, 246

encounter, xi, xiii, 35, 47, 49–50, 54, 61, 63, 66, 71, 106, 129, 140, 165–66, 168–72, 190, 195, 197, 200, 231, 240, 246

epic theater, 102 (*see also* Brecht, B.)

Esalen Institute, 61, 63

existential-humanistic psychotherapy, 26, 211, 230
existentialism, 25, 29, 61, 109, 167, 217
expressive therapy, 11, 32, 44, 205 (*see also* creative arts therapy)
Eye Movement Desensitization and Reprocessing, 69, 220

Faust, 28, 134
feminist theory, 200, 208
fertility rite, ix
fiction and reality, 3, 98, 113, 196, 202, 204–5, 225, 246–47; in developmental transformations, 190; in psychodrama, 160; in role method, 126 (*see also* polarities)
fixed-role therapy, 67–68, 90, 100, 198
flow, 20, 43, 72, 168–69, 172, 174, 191, 195, 19--200, 205, 209, 216, 241
fool, 46, 106
Forum Theatre, 86, 220
free association, 9, 12, 17, 32–33, 35, 37–38, 126, 132, 167, 174, 195–96, 200, 207
future projection, 144, 225, 233, 241

Gestalt psychology, 60
Gestalt therapy, xvii, 2, 25, 31, 54, 59–62, 66, 68, 94, 97, 144, 160, 199, 212
Gestalt Therapy Verbatim, 61
Greek drama, 30, 45, 219
group analysis, 79, 257
group psychotherapy, 47, 49, 52–53, 75, 132, 212, 217, 242, 252–53, 257, 259
Group Theatre, 94
guide, ix, xix, xx, 10, 19, 38, 105–6, 108–13, 123–30, 156, 159–60, 171–72, 192, 200, 222–25, 239–40
guided imagery, 38, 160
guided imagery in music, 57

hero, 11, 19, 23–24, 26, 28, 49, 58–59, 99, 104–6, 111–12, 123, 126, 202, 223–34, 232, 246

hero's journey, 11, 111, 246
Hidden Genius of Emotion, The, 98
holistic model, xvii, 2, 33, 39, 55–56, 60–61, 70, 86, 172, 196–97, 208, 216–18, 220, 223, 230, 237, 239, 247
humanistic psychology, 23, 26, 93
hypnosis, xv, 17, 30, 32, 35–36, 40, 46, 101, 198, 205, 246 (*see also* Breuer and Freud)

I and Thou, 140
illud tempus, 199, 248
improvisation, xi, 50, 55–56, 77, 86, 88, 165, 167, 170, 173, 214
Improvisation for the Theatre, 165
improvisational theater, 82, 92, 133
infantile sexuality, 14, 31, 71
Institutes for the Arts in Psychotherapy, 242
Interpretation of Dreams, The, 13, 23
Invitation to An Encounter, 49, 140

Lila, 45 (*see also* Goethe)
Living Newspaper, 50, 77
Locogram, 138, 231, 239
Locus nascendi, 133, 161, 170, 190–91

Mahabarata, 81
mandala, 11, 16, 18, 57, 206
marriage and family therapy, 212, 217
masks, xi, 12, 19, 23, 35, 45, 102–3, 161, 166–67, 206, 213–14
Memories, Dreams and Reflections, 13
metaphor, xii, 3, 23–24, 36, 42, 81, 100, 103, 127, 133, 136, 166, 204, 239–40, 246; in stories, 234
mirror, xvii, 28–29, 42, 51–52, 67, 130, 139, 140–41, 144, 157, 159–60, 162–63, 171, 182, 200, 206, 208–9, 213, 241, 246–48
mirror neurons, xvii, 246–48
mood disorder, 70, 215
Moscow Art Theater, 101
Multimodal Life History Inventory, 70 (*see also* assessment)
multimodal therapy, 68

Murder of Gonzago, The, 245 (*see also* Hamlet)

Musical Reverie Test, 56–57 (*see also* assessment)

mutual analysis, 11, 37–39, 48, 99, 108, 198, 200–1 (*see also* Ferenczi, S.)

Myers-Briggs Type Indicator, 22, 202 (*see also* assessment)

myth, 5, 11, 13–14, 18, 23–24, 28–30, 88, 105, 126, 160, 204–5

narradrama, 93

narrative therapy, 31, 93, 168

National Association for Drama Therapy, 90, 242

neuroscience, 2, 3, 17, 76, 88, 113, 208; and trauma, 218–20, 226, 230, 246

New Testament, v, 81

object relations, xvii, 73, 91–92, 167, 200

Office of Strategic Services, 55–56, 198, 202

Old Testament, 81

orgone therapy, 40, 43–44, 206

performance theory, 101–2

Peripeteia, xii (*see also* Greek drama)

Persecution and Assassination of Jean-Paul Marat as Performed by the Inmates of the Asylum of Charenton Under the Direction of the Marquis de Sade, The, 46

persona, 19, 33, 51, 65, 172, 240, 257

person-centered psychotherapy, 192, 209, 211 (*see also* client-centered psychotherapy)

Phil, the Fiddler, 57

physical actions, in acting training, 102

play, 2, 13–17, 19, 30–32, 34, 38, 43, 45, 72–73, 87, 90, 92–94, 100, 102–9, 113, 119, 126–29, 132, 138–39, 168–69, 170–75, 177, 187–93, 195, 197–98, 201–5, 208–16, 221, 223–24, 228–30, 240–41, 245–47

Play, Drama and Thought, 94

play therapy, 2, 14, 58, 72–73, 89, 92, 208, 213

playback theatre, 82–84, 90, 93, 212

playspace, 165, 168, 170–72, 174, 177, 188–91, 193, 197, 199, 201, 203, 205, 207, 210–11, 215, 228, 240–41, 246, 248

polarities, xvi, 2–3, 21, 23, 63–64, 66, 100, 104, 113, 123, 125, 135, 145, 158, 174, 196, 200, 202, 208–9, 225, 245, 247–48; in developmental transformations, 189–93; in psychodrama, 158–63; in role method, 125–30

positive psychology, 201

postmodernism, 31, 103, 167–68

posttraumatic stress disorder, 3, 75, 215, 218–19, 223, 227–28

Presentation of Self in Everyday Life, The, 103

primal scream, 101

primal therapy, 212

projective techniques, 161, 213–15, 233, 247

protagonist, xi–xii, 51, 77, 81, 103, 106, 136–41, 143–45, 159, 160–62, 192, 202, 204, 206–7, 212–13, 226–27, 231, 240–41, 247

psychoanalysis, xv–xvii, xix, 1–3, 9, 11, 14, 23–26, 29, 32–34, 36–38, 46–48, 51, 59–60, 72, 91–92, 94, 99, 101–2, 112, 126, 129, 131–32, 160, 170, 193, 195–97, 199–201, 203, 205, 207, 211, 217, 247–48

psychoanalysts, 29, 31, 44, 54, 58, 59, 61, 72, 75, 86, 129, 132, 137, 195, 198, 199, 207, 247; a gathering of, 9–11; shamans and, 5–44

psychodrama, x–xii, xvi, 13, 25, 29, 31, 45–55, 61–62, 64, 67–68, 70, 73–78, 81–82, 85–86, 89, 90–95, 98, 100, 102, 129, 131–63, 167, 170, 172, 174, 187, 190–93, 195, 197, 199, 201, 203, 206–7, 209, 211–16, 225–27, 229–33, 237–38, 242, 245, 247; *à deux*, 144, 159, 162

Psychodrama Training Associates, 242
Psychodrama Training Institute, 242
psychological attitudes, 22; introvert, 20–22; extrovert, 20–22
psychological functions, 21–22; of thinking and feeling, 21–22; of sensation and intuition, 21–22
psychological types, 20, 22–23
Psychology of Personal Constructs, The, 67
psychopomp, 19, 105
psychosexual stages, 59, 62
psychospiritual roles, 76–77
puppetry, xi, 6, 45, 92, 102, 110, 127, 161, 206, 213–14, 228

Quintessential Zerka, The, 54

rainbow of desire, 86 (*see also* Boal, A.)
redecision therapy, 73–74, 212
rehabilitation through the arts, 52
relaxation, 38, 212; and neocatharsis, 35–37
Remedial Drama Group, 88
repetition, 29–31, 36, 40, 174, 206; and remembering, 29; in trauma, 137
repetition compulsion, 137
ritual, ix, 2, 5–6, 9, 16, 18, 36, 38, 93, 101, 207, 219, 228–29, 232, 248
role, xv, xvii, 3, 11, 14, 25, 29, 30, 35, 37–42, 46–52, 58, 64–69, 73–74, 76–78, 80–82, 88, 90, 93–94, 98–131, 133–35, 138–45, 148–49, 152–53, 157–63, 165–68, 170–74, 187, 189–93, 198–204, 206, 209, 213–14, 218, 222–25, 227–30, 232, 234–35, 237–42; and counterrole, 29, 64, 100, 103–7, 124, 199, 209, 240; and story, 94, 107–8, 110, 125–26, 240; in cognitive-behavioral therapy, 68–70; in fixed-role therapy, 67–68; in Gestalt therapy, 62–67; in redecision therapy, 73–74; qualities, functions, and styles, 105, 111–12, 138
Role Checklist, xx, 111, 238 (*see also* assessment)

Role Construct Repertory Test, 68, 100, 202 (*see also* assessment)
role diagram, 138, 142, 238
role method, 3, 41, 64, 67–68, 90, 94–95, 97–99, 101, 103, 105, 107–9, 111–30, 140, 143, 145, 157–61, 163, 170, 172, 174, 187, 190, 192–93, 204, 207, 209, 212–16, 225, 229, 238, 242; in anorexia, 234–37; in trauma treatment, 222–24
role-playing, xv, xvi, 32, 37, 40, 46, 51, 53, 55, 57, 60, 68–70, 72–73, 81, 86, 88, 93, 99–101, 103, 108, 112, 128–29, 165, 172–73, 192, 198, 202, 204, 210–13, 215, 223–24, 232, 239, 241
Role Profiles, 68, 100, 111, 202, 238 (*see also* assessment)
role reversal, 38–39, 42, 49, 60–62, 64, 66, 99, 139, 144, 157, 159, 161–62, 200–1, 209, 211, 213–14, 225, 230, 232, 241
role system, 106–7, 110, 112
role theory, vii, 3, 76, 94–95, 97–111, 123, 134–35, 168, 189, 195, 199, 201, 203
role training, 143, 232, 241
Rorschach Inkblot Test, 57, 202, 248 (*see also* assessment)

sandplay, 14–16, 127, 208
schizophrenia, 39, 43, 165; treatment of, 42–43
sculpting, in drama therapy, x, 7, 175, 233–34
self, x, 19, 26–27, 67, 72, 77, 88, 92–93, 97, 101, 103, 107, 110, 126, 134–39, 157, 159–61, 165, 168–169, 171, 184, 196, 199, 205, 210, 213, 221–23, 233–234, 240–41, 247–48
self-psychology, xvii, 91, 200
sesame, 87, 89, 92, 95, 242
shadow, 19, 27–28, 107
Shamanism, ix, 1–2, 5–11, 13, 15, 17, 19, 21, 23, 25, 27, 29, 31–33, 35,

37, 39, 41, 43, 45–46, 50, 54, 93, 126, 146, 166, 171, 172, 190, 197–99, 203–4, 206–7, 210, 216–18, 246–48; a gathering of shamans, 5–8

Singer-Loomis Inventory of Personality, 22 (*see also* assessment)

Sing Sing prison, 52

social atom, 53, 138, 142, 238 (*see also* assessment)

sociodrama, 47, 50, 52, 75, 77–81, 83, 93, 102, 131, 197, 199

sociometry, xiii, 47–48, 52–53, 75, 78–79, 131, 137–38, 142, 199, 202, 240, 242

soliloquy, 144, 241

somatic psychotherapy, 2, 40, 60, 71–72, 193, 195, 197, 206, 208

spectrogram, 138, 238 (*see also* assessment)

spontaneity, x, 41, 50, 72, 75–76, 86, 93, 132, 135–36, 139, 140–42, 144, 160, 165, 171–73, 199–200, 202, 227, 239–40

spontaneity test, 142, 173, 239 (*see also* assessment)

St. Elizabeths Hospital, 53, 167

stage, xi, xvi, 24, 28, 30–31, 34, 50–53, 59, 62, 69, 72, 77, 86, 93, 101–4, 125–26, 133–34, 138–39, 162, 187, 199, 202, 209, 214, 225, 239, 245, 247

Standing Tall, 224

Stegreiftheater, 50

story, xix, 2, 6, 16, 24, 28, 30, 35, 40, 55–58, 70, 78, 81, 83–85, 88, 94–95, 107–8, 110–12, 116–18, 122–23, 125–29, 157, 159, 160, 174, 202, 204–6, 209, 213–15, 222–24, 229, 233, 237–38, 240–41

storymaking, 70, 88, 95, 128 (*see also* story)

storytelling, 2, 57, 110, 112, 127, 224, 241 (*see also* story)

Strange Case of Dr. Jekyll and Mr. Hyde, 28

surplus reality, 133, 240

talking cure, 1, 9, 205

Tavistock Lectures, 15

Taxonomy of Roles, 76, 101, 105–6, 135

Tele, 135, 140–43, 162–63, 190, 236

Tell-A-Story, 110–11, 202, 238 (*see also* assessment)

theater, x, xvi, 45–46, 48, 50–54, 76, 80, 85–94, 99–102, 104–5, 126, 132–34, 144, 165–67, 169, 191, 205, 210, 215, 219–21, 223, 227, 237, 246; as therapy, 45, 95–96, 134, 227

theater games, 90, 93,165, 191

Theatre of Spontaneity, The, 86

Theatre of the Oppressed, 86 (*see also* Boal, A.)

theatre reciproque, 50 (*see also* Moreno, J. L.)

Thematic Apperception Test, 54, 56–58 (*see also* assessment)

therapeutic storymaking, 88 (*see also* Gersie, A.)

therapeutic theater, 45, 85–86, 134, 227

Three Approaches to Drama Therapy, xix, 3, 64, 98

Three Approaches to Psychotherapy, 3, 64, 70, 97, 208

topdog and underdog, 64, 100, 199, 229 (*see also* Perls, F.)

touch, 40, 190–91; in psychodrama, 137,149, 156–59, 161, 226; in developmental transformations, 173, 175, 179, 182–84, 188, 193, 200–1, 208, 218, 226

transactional analysis, 54, 73, 212

transcendent function, 15, 17 (*see also* active imagination)

transference, xv, 2–3, 25, 30–32, 34–38, 41, 98–99, 109, 113, 128–29, 132, 135, 140–41, 162–63, 171–72, 192–93, 198–200, 203–4, 208–11, 246–47; and countertransference, xv, 3, 98, 113, 128–29, 162, 172, 192–93, 203, 208, 210; neurosis, 199, 211, 204 transitional object, 72–73 (*see also* Winnicott, D. W.)

transitional space, 72–73, 190, 195, 199, 248 (*see also* Winnicott, D. W.)

trauma, xi, xvii, 2–3, 11, 24–25, 32–33, 35–38, 58, 69, 72–73, 78, 80, 84, 87–90, 125, 137, 142, 165, 167, 173, 189–90, 198, 206, 214–15, 230–31, 239, 252, 255–57; action approaches to, 220–29; and neuroscience, 218–20

Trauma Drama, 221 (*see also* van der Kolk, B.)

trauma of birth, 24–25

typology, of character, 41–44; of Jung, 21–22, 104–5; of archetypes and personality, 18–23; in Taxonomy of Roles, 104–5

unconscious, xiii, 11–13, 15–23, 26–27, 30–32, 34, 36–37, 40, 46, 54, 57–58, 91, 94, 99, 102, 113, 125–26, 135, 146, 190, 195–202, 204–6, 208, 210–11, 226, 247–48

Urban Improv, 220–21 (*see also* van der Kolk, B.)

Verbal and nonverbal expression, xvii, 3, 98, 113, 196, 202, 205, 225, 247; indevelopmental transformations, 191; in psychodrama, 160–61; in role method, 126–27 (*see also* polarities)

Vienna Psychoanalytic Society, 9, 11, 39 (*see also* Wednesday Psychological Society)

Vietnam War, 92, 165, 215, 219

walk and talk, 143

warm-up, 65, 112, 143, 173–74, 206, 210, 216, 231–32, 241

Wednesday Psychological Society, 9, 46 (*see also* Vienna Psychoanalytic Society)

wellness, 44, 98, 109–10, 141, 172, 201, 237

Who Shall Survive?, 82, 131, 135, 137, 247

William Wilson, 28

Words of the Father, 80, 125, 131

world technique, 58, 127

Youth, The, 28 (*see also* Dostoyevsky)

Name Index

Adler, A., 9
Alger, H., 57
Andreas-Salome?, L., 9
Aristotle, xi, 51, 132, 136
Artaud, A., 92, 166, 193
Axline, V., 14, 72

Barbato, L., 89
Berne, E., 54, 73, 100
Blake, W., 18
Blatner, A., xix, 2, 75–76, 81, 91, 230
Boal, A., 80, 86–87, 220
Bolton, G., 88, 94
Bonny, H., 57
Bowlby, J., 91
Brecht, B., 52, 80, 86, 94, 102, 159
Breuer, J., 17, 32, 35–36, 101
Breuer, J. and Freud, S., 32, 35–36, 101, 246
Brown, G., 94
Buber, M., 140

Casson, J., 45–46, 75, 88
Cattanach, A., 89
Chace, M. 92, 167
Charcot, J., 17, 46
Chodorow, J., 15–16

Claudius, 245
Cooley, C., 100–1
Cordelia, 106
Courtney, R. 91, 94
Crenshaw, D., 221–22, 224, 230

Dante, 106
Darwin, C., 134
Dayton, T., 76, 137, 142, 226–27, 231–32
De Maupassant, G., 138
De Sade, M., 46
Demasio, A., 17, 113, 208, 217–18, 220
Dent-Brown, K., 89
Derrida, J., 167
Descartes, R., 17, 217
Dionysus, ix
Dokter, D., 89, 231, 233–34
Dostoyevsky, F., 28, 138
Dunne, P., 93

Einstein, A., 218
Eliade, M., 10, 93, 199
Eliaz, E., 109, 129
Ellis, A., 3, 97
Emunah, R., 91–95

Erikson, E., 3, 54, 55, 58–59, 66, 93, 100, 167, 196, 198, 203, 211, 213, 230
Evreinoff, N. 85–86

Fenichel, O., 60
Ferenczi, S., xv, 2, 9–12, 26, 29–40, 44, 47–48, 58, 61, 68, 73, 86, 99, 108–9, 132, 195–98, 200–1, 203, 206, 230
Fortinbras, 245
Fox, J. 82, 100, 133–34, 137–38, 140, 143, 203
Freud, A., 14
Freud, S., ix, xv, xvii, 1, 2, 9–18, 20, 23–27, 29–33, 35–38, 40–41, 44, 46–48, 51, 55, 59–62, 71–72, 77–79, 99,101–2, 109, 132–33, 167, 189, 195–98, 200, 202–7, 246–47; and Ferenczi, 36–38; and Jung, 15–17, 20; and Rank, 23–25; fainting spells, 12

Gallese, V., 247
Gandhi, M., 59
Garcia, N., xix, 77–78, 91, 93, 131, 136, 138–39, 141, 143–62, 187, 192, 209, 213–14, 225–26, 242
Garcia, N. and Buchanan, D., 136, 138–39, 141, 143–44
Gendlin, E., 167
Gersie, A., 88–89, 94–95
Gill, M., 211
Goethe, W., 28, 45
Goffman, E., 100–1, 103, 249
Goldstein, K., 60
Goodman, P., 25
Gordon, R., 90
Goulding, R. and M., 73–74
Grainger, R., 88–89
Grotowski, J., 89, 92, 166–68, 191, 193

Hamlet, v, 134, 245–46, 248
Heathcote, D., 88, 94
Hillman, J., 16, 19, 127
Hitler, A., 56, 59, 78–79

Homburger, E., 54, 58 (*see also* Erikson, E.)
Horney, K., 60
Hutt, J. and Hosking, B., 83–84

Iljine, V., 85–86
Irwin, E., 2, 90–92
Jacobson, E., 167
Janet, P., 46, 99
Janov, A., 44, 128
Jennings, S., 88–89, 91, 94–95, 246, 253; on embodiment, projection, role, 88
Johnson, D., xix, 2, 44, 90–92, 95, 165–74, 187–93, 195–96, 199–200, 202–3, 208–9, 214–15, 227, 229, 239, 242, 246
Johnson, R., 16
Jones, E., 9–10
Jones, P., 85–86, 88
Jung, C., 2, 9, 11–23, 26–27, 29, 31, 35, 37, 44, 47, 55, 59, 87, 93–94, 99, 103–7, 126–27, 132, 166, 195–97, 200, 202–6, 208, 211, 230; and analytic psychology, 12–23

Kafka, F., 233
Kalff, D., 14–16
Kellermann, P., 79–80
Kelly, G., 67–68, 70, 85–86, 89–90, 100, 195, 198, 202–3, 230
Kindler, R., 92
King Lear, 106
Kipper, D., 66, 69, 139
Klein, M., 14, 167
Koffka, K., 60
Kohler, W., 60
Kohut, H., 91
Kraemer, W., 87
Kris, E., 167
Kübler-Ross, E., 167

Laban, R., 87
Lahad, M., 70
Landreth, G, 72
Landy, R., ix–xi, xv–xviii, 2, 15, 29, 76–77, 91, 94–95, 98–101, 103,

105, 108–13, 123–25, 128–30,
135–36, 156–58, 161, 168, 170–72,
186–89, 192, 196, 200, 202–3,
208–9, 214–15, 222–24, 234–38
Langley, D., 89
Lazarus, A., 69–70, 90, 139, 203, 230
Levenson, E., 246
Levinson, D., 167
Lewis, P., 13, 46, 93
Lindkvist, M., 87–89
Lowen, A., 44, 70–72, 132, 200, 203,
208
Lowenfeld, M., 14–15, 58

Madonna, 236
Mahler, M., 91
Marx, K., 47, 133
Maslow, A., 93, 202
May, R., 25
McCaslin, N., 91
McNiff, S., 113, 202
Mead, G. H., 100–1
Mitchell, S., 89
Mitchell, S. A., 109, 199, 207, 246
Moreno, J. L., x–xiii, xvi, 1, 3, 29, 42,
44–56, 59, 61–62, 66, 68, 73,
75–82, 85–87, 89, 93–95, 99–102,
131–44, 156, 159, 161–62,
166–67, 169–73, 191, 195–200,
202–4, 206–9, 211, 215, 225–27,
230, 231, 238–39, 247; in America;
52–54; in Austria, 47–52; in
meeting Freud, 47
Moreno, Z., xx, 49, 52, 54, 73, 75–76,
78, 81–82, 86, 95, 135, 137–38,
140, 144, 196; Foreword, ix–xiii.
Murray, H., 3, 54–60, 66, 100, 173,
195–96, 198, 202–3, 21; at
Harvard Psychological Clinic, 55,
198; at the Office of Strategic
Services, 55–56
Nash, E., 94
Nietzsche, F., 48

Odysseus, 106
Ormont, L., 113
Osama bin Laden, 224

Pavlov, I., 102
Perls, F., 1, 3, 25, 29, 31, 53–54, 59–66,
68, 94, 97, 100, 103, 132, 144, 169,
172, 195, 197, 199, 203–4, 206,
208, 211, 215, 229–30
Perls, L., 59–60
Piaget, J., 92, 167
Pitzele, P., 81–82, 89, 203
Plato, 215
Poe, E. A., 28
Portner, E., 92
Propp, V., 105

Rank, O., xv, 2, 9–11, 23–32, 40,
43–44, 47, 60, 68–69, 73, 99, 109,
126, 132, 179, 195–98, 200, 202–4,
206; on the artist, 26, 28–29; on the
double, 26–27; on will, 26, 29–33
Reich, W., 2, 11, 39–44, 47, 60–61,
70–72, 99, 128, 132, 146, 172, 193,
195–98, 200–1, 203, 206–8, 211
Reil, J., 45–46
Robbins, A., xix, Foreword, xv–xviii
Rogers, C., 3, 25, 31, 93, 97, 130, 167,
192, 201, 208, 211
Rothschild, B., 225

Sacks, J., 94, 237
Salas, J., 82, 84–85, 93
Sandberg, B., 90
Sandel, S., 92, 167
Sarbin, T., 100–1, 166
Sartre, J.-P., 167
Schattner, G., 90–91
Schechner, R., 93
Scheff, T., 94, 100–2, 136, 189, 203
Schultz, W., 53
Shakespeare, W., v, xi, 3, 51–52, 59,
103, 245–46
Shostrom, E., 3, 64, 70, 97–98
Slade, P., 87–89, 91–92, 94
Snow, S., 11, 93
Solomon, J., 72
Spolin, V., 165
Stanislavski, C., 85–86, 94, 101–2, 159
Stern, D., 31, 91–92
Stern, P., 224

Sternberg, P. and Garcia, N., 77–78, 93, 131

Stevenson, R. L., 28

Sullivan, H., 73

van der Kolk, B., 2, 219–21, 223–25, 230

Virgil, 106

von Franz, M.-L., 16

Way, B., 91

Weiss, P., 46

Werner, H., 167

Wertheimer, M., 60

Wethered, A., 92

Whitehouse, M., 167

Whitmont, E. C., 94

Winnicott, D. W., 14, 72–73, 91–92, 190, 195, 199–200

Winters, N., 76-77, 89

Wiseman, G., 88

Wolpe, J., 69–70, 90, 139, 203, 220, 230

Yablonsky, L., 78–79, 94

Yalom, I., 109

About the Author

Robert J. Landy, Ph.D., RDT/BCT, LCAT, is professor of educational theatre and applied psychology at New York University, where he is the founder and director of the Drama Therapy Program. A pioneer in the profession of drama therapy, he lectures and trains professionals internationally. He served as editor-in-chief of the international journal, *The Arts in Psychotherapy*, and has published numerous scholarly articles. His books include *Persona and Performance—The Meaning of Role in Drama, Therapy and Everyday Life, Essays in Drama Therapy—The Double Life*, and *How We See God and Why It Matters*, a study of children's perception of God. His seminal text, *Drama Therapy—Concepts, Theories and Practices*, has been translated into several foreign languages.

As a theatre artist, Landy has acted with such groups as the Roundabout Theatre Company and Theatre for the New City in New York and at various regional theatres. He has directed plays in Los Angeles and New York where a number of his dramas and musical plays have been produced. Most recently, his musical play, *God Lives in Glass*, was produced at the Provincetown Playhouse in New York City and various regional and educational theatres. For television, Landy created the series, *Drama in Education*, broadcast nationally on CBS-TV.

As a drama therapist, Landy has more than 30 years of clinical experience, having treated children, adolescents, and adults with a wide range of psychiatric, cognitive, and adjustment problems. He has also worked in prisons, developing drama therapy programs at correctional facilities in New York State. His work in drama therapy with children who witnessed the 9/11 attacks on the World Trade Center is featured in the recent documentary film, "Standing Tall," made by Academy Award winning director, Peggy Stern.